Channels of Influence:
CBC Audience Research and the Canadian Public

Although public broadcasting institutions have increasingly come under attack in recent years, there have been few attempts to reconsider their basic purpose. Ross Eaman argues that the most important reason for public ownership in broadcasting is to enable the listening and viewing public to have input in the determination of programming priorities.

Audience research provides the only means for public input into programming that is regular, representative, equable, and meaningful. In *Channels of Influence*, Eaman looks at the origins, development, and role of CBC audience research from the 1930s to the present and compares it to audience research in the United States and Britain. In examining the reasons why the CBC set up its audience research department and how it evolved, Eaman considers the extent to which its methods fulfil the criteria necessary for genuine public input into programming.

Based largely on previously unexamined archival sources and business records, as well as personal interviews and in-house research reports, this account includes a history of audience measurement methods in Canada and a critique of ratings as an instrument of cultural democracy.

ROSS A. EAMAN is Associate Professor, School of Journalism and Communication, Carleton University. He is author of *The Media Society: Basic Issues and Controversies*.

ROSS A. EAMAN

Channels of Influence: CBC Audience Research and the Canadian Public

UNIVERSITY OF TORONTO PRESS
Toronto Buffalo London

© University of Toronto Press Incorporated 1994
Toronto Buffalo London
Printed in Canada

ISBN 0-8020-2811-X (cloth)
ISBN 0-8020-7688-2 (paper)

Printed on acid-free paper

Canadian Cataloguing in Publication Data

Eaman, Ross Allan, 1945–
    Channels of influence : CBC audience research and
    the Canadian public

    Includes bibliographical references and index.
    ISBN 0-8020-2811-X (bound)   ISBN 0-8020-7688-2 (pbk.)

    1. Canadian Broadcasting Corporation – Influence –
    Research. 2. Television viewers – Canada – Research.
    3. Radio audiences – Canada – Measurement – History.
    4. Television programs – Canada – Rating – History.
    5. Radio programs – Canada – Rating – History.
    I. Title.

HE8689.9.C3E3 1994   384.54′06′571   C94-930138-8

University of Toronto Press acknowledges the financial assistance to its
publishing program of the Canada Council and the Ontario Arts Council.

Contents

Preface

A wise man will not ignore public opinion in regard to particular matters, such as the distribution of offices and preferment; for here the populace, when left to itself, does not make mistakes, or if sometimes it does its mistakes are rare in comparison with those that would occur if the few had to make such a distribution.

Niccolò Machiavelli, *Discourses*

This work examines the relationship between the Canadian Broadcasting Corporation and the public. It began as a history of CBC audience research and that remains its primary focus. But in the course of my research, I became convinced that audience research plays – or should play – a special role within a public broadcasting organization such as the CBC. This role is to facilitate cultural democracy in broadcasting in the sense of enabling the public, rather than the market or the state, to determine the kind of radio and television services that public funds are used to provide. The purpose of audience research should be to make programming more responsive to public wants and needs as indicated by the public itself through its reactions to particular programs and types of programming, its general listening and viewing behaviour, and its underlying beliefs and values in relation to the broadcasting system.

The CBC has seldom been associated with the idea of cultural democracy. This is not only because cultural democracy was originally an American concept and has often been used as a defence against government regulation of the mass media. It is also because cultural democracy is usually identified with the principle of serving the lowest common denominator, which is thought to be alien to the ideal of public service broadcasting. This lack of association is unfortunate from the standpoint of both cultural democracy and public broadcasting. On the one hand, it makes it difficult to envisage how, in the field of broadcasting at least, cultural democracy could be pursued along lines that would also recognize the needs of minority audiences. And on the other hand, it closes our eyes to the possibility of a different conception of public broadcasting as embodied in the CBC, one which might provide a better justification of the role of public broadcasting than the traditional public service rationale.

Democracy exists to the extent that institutions and processes are characterized by accountability, equality of treatment, and participation. A political system, for example, is democratic to the degree that the government is accountable to the people, treats all members of society equally, and provides reasonable opportunities for public participation in decision-making. But other institutions, including broadcasting organizations, can also be assessed in terms of these attributes. The CBC is at least partly democratic in so far as it is accountable to Parliament. It is even more democratic in that it seeks to serve the needs of all Canadians more or less equally. But to be fully democratic it must also allow the public to have a say in its basic practices and priorities, especially with regard to the provision of programming, which is the main function of any broadcasting service.

Public participation in the shaping of CBC program services must, of course, be pursued within the context of the CBC's mandate as legislated by Parliament through the broadcasting act. If the public disagrees with this mandate, then it must seek to influence Parliament, not the CBC, to effect its change. At the same time, as Lord Bryce once suggested in *Modern Democracies*, public opinion can only deal with broad principles; it cannot address matters that are highly specific or technical. Thus public input into programming must necessarily be confined to aspects that are sufficiently general to give rise to public opinion, but not so fundamental as to have been decided by the terms of the broadcasting act. Within this limited sphere of potential public involvement, however, there are still numerous important questions to be decided. These pertain to such things as levels of Canadian content (assuming that minimum regulatory requirements are maintained); the relative emphasis on local, regional, and national programming; and the balance between different programming categories. The challenge for audience research within a public broadcasting organization is to develop adequate methods and tools for ascertaining in a sufficiently meaningful, precise, and accurate manner what the public thinks about such matters.

The belief that audience research has the capacity to empower the public to communicate its views to broadcasters entails a rejection of one conception of audiences in favour of another. Majid Tehranian has suggested that 'audience' was originally 'an Aristotelian, rhetorical concept in which the sender of a message attempts to influence, persuade, or manipulate a passive receiver.' A current version of this concept is the idea that audiences are essentially aggregates of inert consumers created by programming for deliverance to advertisers. But, for Tehranian, 'empowerment means the creation of communicators rather than audiences *cum* consumers or subjects; it demands full, active, communicative citizenship.'[1]

This approach also has its antecedents in antiquity. As Leo Bogart observed a number of years ago, 'in the classic tradition, drama exists only in relation to the audience. Murmurs, rustles, coughs, and laughs communicate reactions back to a cast long before the curtain provides the signal for applause.' From this standpoint, the audience is 'conscious of itself, of its presence and purpose in being where it is, and of its own reactions.'[2] Because radio and television programs are received over many different channels in relatively isolated settings, listeners and viewers could never comprise an audience in the sense associated with the theatre. They could never experience the social cohesion that arises out of the collective setting of theatrical drama. But it does not follow that they need be reduced to passive spectators without any influence over what is broadcast. If broadcasters wish to do so, they can transform silent, uncommunicating audiences into an active and influential public.

This book is not intended to be a comprehensive technical or descriptive study of the methods and practices of audience research, and I have deliberately steered as widely as possible around sampling theory. But in addition to tracing, for the first time, the development of audience research within the CBC and of audience measurement services in Canada, I have argued that program ratings are an inadequate means for ascertaining what the public wants and needs from radio and television broadcasters. As a result, it has been necessary to touch upon various technical matters along the way. And it is, in any event, virtually impossible to write about the history of audience research without considering the methodological problems that have plagued the field from its inception in the late 1920s to the introduction of people meters sixty years later.

I would like to thank the current director of CBC Research, Barry Kiefl, and his staff, especially Stan Staple, Philip Savage, Constance McFarlane, and Mary Blazecka, for their assistance with various aspects of this work. Mr Kiefl kindly agreed to be interviewed and provided feedback at all stages of manuscript preparation; Mr Staple also provided a useful interview; Mr Savage commented on several draft chapters; Ms McFarlane prepared a thorough and insightful critique of the entire manuscript; and Ms Blazecka helped with numerous administrative matters. This is not to imply that they endorse my arguments, and they are in no way responsible for whatever errors or misconceptions may remain. But I would like to express my appreciation for the way in which they gave freely of their time and knowledge.

My gratitude is also extended to Neil Morrison, Ken Purdye, and John Twomey for interviews about their careers at the CBC; to Arthur Laird for his comments on the chapter on the panels; to Carleton University, especially former dean of arts Janice Yalden, for supporting a special research leave in 1990–1, and current dean of arts G. Stuart Adam, for a grant to assist with the preparation of the index; to the staff of the National Archives of Canada, including those working in the Moving Images and Sound Archives division, for their assistance in finding various materials; to Leone Earls for similar help at the CBC Reference Library in Toronto; to George Brandak at the University of British Columbia (Special Collections) for facilitating use of the Plaunt Papers; to Owen Charlebois for allowing me to consult and make copies of records at the BBM Bureau of Measurement in Don Mills; to Christine Boyd and Karen Robertson, who worked as research assistants; to Sheryl Hamilton, who assisted with proofreading; to Paul Attallah and Vincent Mosco in the School of Journalism and Communication at Carleton for critiquing various chapters; to Ernest Dick, CBC corporate archivist, for his support and encouragement over many years; and to Virgil Duff, executive editor, and Lorraine Ourom, freelance editor, at the University of Toronto Press, for their many suggested improvements to the manuscript. Finally, I would like to thank my wife, Pat Bolla, for bringing her social science expertise to bear on my humanistic frame of mind.

A Note on Terms

Although this book is not a technical study of audience research methods, there are three terminological distinctions the reader will need to keep in mind. The first is the distinction between a rating and a share. A rating has traditionally been defined as the estimated percentage of all radio or television households in a given area (local, regional, or national) in which at least one person is tuned to a particular program. This could be based on an average minute, an average quarter-hour, or the duration of the program, depending on what system of measurement is used. However, audience measurement agencies such as the BBM Bureau of Measurement in Canada no longer define a rating in terms of households. For BBM a rating is simply 'the estimated audience expressed as a percentage of the *total population*,' while a share is 'the estimated audience expressed as a percentage of the *total listening* [or viewing] *audience.*'[1] A network television program might, for example, have a rating of 18 and a share of 33. However, audience researchers sometimes speak of a station's or network's share of listening or viewing over a period of time – for example, the CBC English television network's share of anglophone viewing in 1992–3.

The second distinction is between ratings in the strict sense just defined and ratings in the broad sense of the term. Broadly defined, ratings comprise *all* quantitative measurements of audience size, including shares, cumes (the number of different persons who listen or view for at least one quarter-hour within a time period), and a number of other measures. Which sense is intended will be clear in most cases from the context; otherwise, it will be specified. It should be pointed out that this is a long-standing distinction. In 1960, for example, a CBC report on ratings began by defining the term in its strict sense and then explained that 'in this report ... the word "rating" is used generally for all kinds of measurement of broadcast audiences, whether it be strict rating as a per cent of total radio and TV homes in the area, or the number of homes viewing or listening to a program, or the share of audience of a particular station, etc. In this loose sense a "rating" is just a quantitative measurement of the audience to a radio or TV broadcast.'[2]

The third distinction is between 'audience' and 'public.' Within the context of radio and television, the term 'audience' will simply be taken to refer to any aggregate of listeners or viewers specified in terms of a programming unit, a geographic area, and a time period. Thus one can speak of the audience for a certain program, or for part of a program (including a particular commercial), or for a type of programming, or even for the collective programming of a station or network. The audience can be related to a particular city, to one or more provinces or states, or to an entire country or set of countries; and the time period in question can range from that involved in a single broadcast to a week, a season, or longer.

The term 'public' is more problematic. Its use has sometimes been restricted to those who participate in public affairs, so that apathetic or powerless members of society are not part of the public. It has also been used very generally to refer to all members of a society, as in 'the general public.' In this work, it will be assumed that members of society comprise a public or publics by virtue of certain shared interests. The public for broadcasting in Canada (the so-called listening or viewing public) thus consists of all Canadians whose interests are affected by decisions made in the broadcasting sphere, regardless of whether they take an active interest in the decision-making process. It thus includes Canadian children, but not for the most part Canadians living outside the country, except in so far as they have an interest in things like Radio-Canada International.

CHANNELS OF INFLUENCE

1

From Public Service to Public Participation: The Role of Audience Research

The CBC should be in a position to regularly feel the entertainment pulse of its sponsors, or customers, the Canadian Radio Audience, and should be quick to detect, and act upon, those signals which indicate pleasure, displeasure, or perhaps actual antagonism.

E.C. Stewart, 1948[1]

A comprehensive history of the Canadian Broadcasting Corporation would have to examine its development from many angles, including its political relationship with the federal government, its efforts to promote an indigenous Canadian culture, and the role of its journalism in facilitating democracy. Some of these topics have been studied in more depth than have others, but they have all been recognized as integral to any assessment of the performance of the CBC. There is one angle from which the CBC has seldom been considered, however, and which is no less important for understanding its significance as a national institution. This is its relationship with the public, not in terms of public relations in the conventional sense of the term, but from the standpoint of public participation in the determination of its priorities, especially with respect to programming. This topic cuts across the more traditional ways of looking at the CBC and constitutes a basic theme in its overall history. It is for this reason that it has been chosen as the starting-point for what I hope will be a series of works on the history of the CBC.

PUTTING THE PUBLIC INTO PUBLIC BROADCASTING

In an address to the Vancouver Institute on 21 November 1959, Alan

Thomas, a professor in the College of Education at the University of British Columbia, complained that the means available for the public to communicate to broadcasters were 'crude and grossly ineffective.' The audience, he said, 'generally has had only one weapon, that of refusing to give its attention to the emission.' But in his view, it had the potential to play a much greater role in broadcasting. 'To date our basic assumptions regarding broadcasting have been limited to a conception of one-way transmission. Implicit in all of our deliberations has been the assumption that material chosen by a small group of technicians, with or without public advice and control, should be communicated in the most attractive way possible to the great audience.' For Thomas, however, it was 'quite possible to visualize the process as working the other way.' 'Having created an audience out of our population,' he declared, 'we must now find a way to make this audience responsible and articulate.'[2]

Although the public has never been asked if it would like to have a greater say in programming, there is some indirect evidence that it would. In 1972, for example, the CBC tried to determine the extent to which television 'provokes feelings of frustration in the viewer because of his lack of personal control over, or interaction with, the television available.' The survey it conducted made no distinction between CBC-TV and other television networks. Nor did it give any explanation of what was meant by 'control' or 'interaction.' But on the basis of the responses given to two specific questions, it was estimated that 53 per cent of anglophones 'often' found their lack of control over television to be frustrating, 40 per cent 'occasionally' had such feelings, and only 7 per cent were 'rarely' or 'never' troubled in this manner; while for francophones the percentages were 33, 46, and 20 respectively.[3] Though it would be unwarranted to draw any general conclusions from the results of one survey, the study did point to the possibility that Canadians would like more input into programming.

But where within the broadcasting system might Canadians reasonably expect to have a significant influence over programming? Though described in many government documents as a single, unified system, Canadian broadcasting is made up of two distinct components with different economic bases. The private broadcasting industry, while subject to government regulation, is necessarily governed by the dictates of the market-place. While it cannot alienate the public and still attract audiences of sufficient size and appropriate composition to satisfy advertisers, neither can it be expected to allow public opinion to determine its programming priorities. Public input is a more reasonable expectation in the case of the public broadcasting sector, where the CBC is the dominant, though not the only, player. But even here public participation in program decision-making is by no means guaranteed.

In the first place, the CBC does not receive all of its funds from the public purse. While the largest proportion of its overall funding is still provided by the federal government, it also obtains a substantial – and increasing – part of its revenues from advertising. The dual basis of its funding creates a situation in which the principles underlying public broadcasting could conceivably be compromised by commercial considerations. At the same time, the degree of control which the government exercises over CBC finances could also undermine the autonomy of the corporation in the provision of programming. The crucial consideration, however, is the CBC's own conception of public broadcasting. In the final analysis, the part that the public plays in public broadcasting will depend on how those in charge of the CBC view its role. The public cannot contribute in a meaningful way unless the CBC itself actively and genuinely facilitates its participation.

Public ownership of broadcasting facilities has usually been defended in terms of the supposed threat of American cultural imperialism, the alleged dangers of rampant commercialism, and the apparent economic incapacity of the private sector to produce an adequate amount of high-quality Canadian programming. These are valid reasons for state support of broadcasting in Canada. But they are not necessarily permanent problems or the only ones that can be dealt with best through publicly financed broadcasting. Justifying public broadcasting simply in terms of these kinds of problems runs the risk of leaving it defenceless should they – or interest in them – abate or even disappear.

A more permanent defence of public broadcasting is provided by linking it to the concept of public service. From this perspective, the purpose of channelling public funds into broadcasting is to provide the public with an organization that is primarily responsive to its broadcasting needs rather than those of the market-place or the state. This is the approach that has been adopted in Britain, but it still leaves open the question of who is to determine the public's needs. And the implication is usually that it is the responsibility of the cultural elite to establish programming priorities. In other words, the idea of public service broadcasting has seldom included the idea of public involvement in program planning.

In a recent attempt to redefine public broadcasting, Liora Salter notes that public broadcasters have a greater capacity than commercial broadcasters to reach special- as well as general-interest audiences. She criticizes efforts to equate public broadcasting with either minority-interest programming or public access to production facilities. And she argues that further privatization would mean shifting more responsibility for determining what is in the public interest on to a private corporation, whose primary responsibility is to its shareholders. I would agree with these points, but as far as I can see, she does not identify any new principles for a 'refashioned form of public service.' In particular, she does not broach the question of who is to decide which interests and needs – whether general or special – are to be served by publicly funded broadcasting facilities.[4]

Despite its outward attractiveness, it is the concept of public service itself that stands in the way of redefining public broadcasting in democratic terms. For it diverts our attention from the fact that public broadcasting should not exist merely to ensure that programming serves the public interest. Its aim should also be to enable the public itself to determine wherein its interest lies. In other words, the main justification of public ownership in broadcasting lies in the value of public participation. Public broadcasting is a worthy ideal in and of itself, not just a means to other desirable ends. It thus should not be relegated to a secondary position within the broadcasting system, even though it need not have a monopoly to fulfil its role.

For the public to have a genuine influence over radio and television programming, there are four criteria that would have to be satisfied. First, its input would have to be regular; it would not suffice that it be consulted every three or four years in the manner of elections. Second, since it would not be possible for all Canadians to be involved personally or directly, those who do participate would have to constitute a representative sample of Canadians. Third, participants would have to be treated more or less equally in the way that everyone's vote in an election counts the same. And finally, the input that is obtained would have to be meaningful in the sense of relating to matters of consequence rather than to trivial programming considerations.

PARLIAMENT, ADVISORY COUNCILS, ENQUIRIES, AND
AUDIENCE RESEARCH

It is not immediately obvious how these four criteria can be fulfilled.
Parliament, which has control over broadcasting, is supposed to speak
for all Canadians. But it is not well designed to represent the public as a
broadcasting audience. Its members are seldom chosen on the basis of
their views on broadcasting, certainly not on specific programming
matters; they rarely consult their constituents about broadcasting
issues; and they do not, in any event, constitute a representative cross-
section of the Canadian population. Moreover, Parliament is expected
to maintain an arm's-length relationship with the CBC to ensure that it
does not become an instrument of government propaganda.

It was for these reasons in part that a number of early supporters of
public broadcasting in Canada proposed the creation of advisory councils to represent the public on questions of programming. These were
first discussed during deliberations on the Aird commission report of
1929 and were provided for in the broadcasting acts of 1932 and 1936.
But the idea of advisory councils overlooks the fact that there are two
distinct ways in which one person or group can represent other people.
One form of representation occurs where someone speaks or acts on
behalf of others as a result of formal or tacit delegation of authority. In
such cases, the person doing the representing is not assumed to be like
those being represented. A different form of representation occurs
where someone is taken to reflect the attitudes, beliefs, or values of others by virtue of being like them. This is the kind of representation that is
attempted in surveys based on scientific sampling.

It is not only Parliament that cannot be expected to represent the
views of Canadians on radio and television programming, but also
bodies such as the CBC board of governors (later directors) and small
advisory councils. The membership of such bodies usually consists of
those who are judged to be 'leading citizens' in the community. The
Massey commission of 1949–51 was typical in assuming that the
national advisory councils on talks which it favoured would be made
up of 'leading Canadians in all fields of intellectual interest.'[5] But the
main problem with such bodies is that even if they were made up of
people from various walks of life, they could never be large enough to
do justice to the diversity of public opinion and could never be sufficiently balanced to form a representative sample of Canadians.

This shortcoming is partly overcome in the case of formal enquiries such as royal commissions and task forces on broadcasting, which have generally consulted widely before drawing up their recommendations. For example, the Aird commission listened to 164 verbal presentations at public sessions in 25 cities and received an additional 124 written statements; the Massey commission received 462 briefs and heard over 1,200 witnesses; and the Fowler commission of 1955–6 held public hearings across Canada and received 276 briefs. However, such enquiries are not continuous and even from the standpoint of representativeness are by no means adequate. The presentations which they elicit usually come from formally organized groups, many of them representing vested interests, such as station owners, radio and television dealers, advertisers, and educators. As the Massey commission admitted, 'most of the briefs and most of the interviews came to us from organized societies. We heard little from the citizen who represented no one but himself.'[6] The Fowler commission believed that it had 'heard the voice of Canada,' but of the 276 briefs it received, only 30 were from private citizens.[7]

In the light of these points, it is perhaps not surprising that Thomas should have concluded in his 1959 talk that the development of a 'responsible and articulate' audience had not made much headway in Canada. Nonetheless, this assessment overlooked a major development that had occurred a few years earlier within the CBC. This was the creation in 1954 of a Bureau of Audience Research with a mandate to engage in qualitative as well as quantitative audience studies. Understandably, when a copy of Thomas's paper made its way to the bureau's research library, someone scrawled on the last page: 'Hasn't this man ever heard of a thing called Audience Research!'[8] For it is only through audience research that the public can possibly have input into programming that meets the requirements of regularity, representativeness, equality, and meaningfulness. The establishment of its own research facility reduced the CBC's dependence on outside agencies for audience studies. It did not, however, guarantee a new relationship between the CBC and the public. For this to develop two things were necessary. First, the new research unit had to develop appropriate methods for determining the public's programming needs and desires. And second, the results of this research had to become an integral component of program planning. One objective of this book is to determine the extent to which these requirements for public participation have been fulfilled. It is, in short, to see whether the CBC has contributed – or is even in a position to contribute – to cultural democracy.

The basic principle of cultural democracy is that the public should decide priorities in those areas of cultural creation where its resources provide the economic means for production and distribution. This principle does not necessarily rule out cultural creativity without public input into priorities, provided that it is based on non-public resources. It also leaves open the matter of what constitutes the public and does not in itself provide an answer to the question of how it might be able to influence cultural priorities in a meaningful and effective way. But it assumes that the resources which make broadcasting possible are, in the final analysis, public resources.

Opponents of cultural democracy occupy a range of positions. At one end of the spectrum is the view expressed by two CBC audience research staff in 1960 that 'when the public is free to choose among various mass media products, the vast majority tend to choose the trivial as against the serious, the ordinary as against the unusual, the diverting as against the significant.'[9] Or as the American sociologist and editor of *Look* magazine Leo Rosten put it in remarkably similar terms a few years later, 'it chooses – again and again and again – the frivolous as against the serious, escape against reality, the lurid as against the tragic, the trivial as against the significant.'[10] Statements like these led Bernard Rosenberg to conclude that it was not simply 'tough executives' in the cultural industries who 'crudely and brutally assert the complete disdain they feel for their audiences.' Indeed, what Rosenberg found 'really distressing' was that 'so many philosophers, historians, psychologists, and other academics should also be irremediably contemptuous of the people at large.'[11]

A more moderate form of criticism can be found in the reports of some of the royal commissions that have dealt with culture and broadcasting in Canada. For example, the Massey commission criticized 'the indifference of the listeners [to the CBC] who enjoy or resent their fare in silence,'[12] while the Fowler commission assumed that 'the audience does not normally express considered judgments on its wants in entertainment, except in relation to what is familiar.'[13] These views were consistent with early research on mass communication, which emphasized the passivity as well as the powerlessness of audiences. As J.C.W.

Reith, the first head of the British Broadcasting Corporation, once remarked in response to criticism that listeners did not like BBC programs: 'It is occasionally indicated to us that we are apparently setting out to give the public what we think they need – and not what they want – but few know what they want and very few what they need.'[14] Or as Canadian journalist Peter Trueman has written recently, 'people don't know what they want until they see it. Most of us are not producers, after all, but consumers.'[15]

Less condescending is the view that the public is capable of improving its cultural tastes, but must be guided in its choices by a cultural elite. As Reith put it, it is 'not insistent autocracy but wisdom that suggests a policy of broadcasting carefully and persistently on the basis of giving people what one believes they should like *and will come to like*, granting, of course, discretion, understanding and resolution on the part of those who carry it out. The supply of good things will create the demand for more.'[16] This approach was shared by early advocates of public broadcasting in Canada, such as Carleton Stanley, president of Dalhousie University. 'Radio could be used to educate popular taste in music, as the development of the B.B.C. has shown, and in other serviceable ways,' he wrote in 1932. 'But this obviously must be under intelligent supervision.'[17]

Against these views, it might be argued that the public has an inherent right to decide for itself what it does and does not want from its broadcasting system. However, it does not follow that the public must actually be involved in the selection of programming. While retaining ultimate control over who makes decisions, the public could conceivably delegate authority to certain citizens to make programming choices on its behalf. This is what normally happens in political democracy and, critics of cultural democracy might argue, the same thing should occur in the cultural sphere. If, therefore, cultural democracy is to be justified, it must be by some means other than an appeal to public rights.

In the final analysis, the only justification of cultural democracy is that the public is somehow capable of making better judgments about its own welfare than is any group within it. This is the basic defence not only of cultural democracy but of democracy in general. As Richard McKeon once observed, 'democracy is based on a conviction that the people are better qualified than any limited or select group to make decisions concerning truth as it affects them, concerning the values presented for contemplation and guidance, concerning their individ-

ual destinies, and concerning their common good.'[18] Belief in the public' s inherent wisdom does not eliminate the need for leadership, but
it does entail that leaders in a democracy should function differently
than in an authoritarian state.

Ironically, apologists for cultural democracy have seldom defended
it on these grounds. At most, they have argued that it is the right of
people to shape their own culture, not the better part of wisdom to
have them do so. But usually they have not tried to justify cultural
democracy at all. Instead, they have used it to rationalize other practices, while leaving the doctrine itself undefended. It is simply taken to
be a good thing in itself. The question of whether audiences justify this
faith in their choices is virtually ignored.

In *Who Controls the Media?* (1974), for example, Martin Seiden
invoked cultural democracy to show that American corporate media
power is a myth. 'Do the owners, their employees, and those who buy
time and space in the media in fact possess the power over the audience which both they and their critics agree is inherent in mass communication?' Seiden asked. In his view, 'the evidence shows that the
reverse is the case. It is with the audience and not the media that the
power resides.' The reason, according to Seiden, lies in the economic
structure of American cultural industries. 'Our media system operates
on the premise that the audience is the customer and those who own
and use the system are salesmen. This relationship permeates the
mass media, affecting its financing, the nature of its content, and even
the character of political advocacy.'[19] The mechanism through which
the mass media respond to audiences varies from one area to another;
newspapers and magazines rely on circulation figures, the film industry uses box office receipts, and radio and television depend on audience polls or measurements based on sampling. But Seiden thought
that the basic principle is the same throughout. 'The audience is continually surveyed for its opinions and this information results in con-
tinual adjustment of media output. No other nation has a mass
communications system so finely tuned to the desires of the audience
it serves.'[20]

Opponents of cultural democracy would paint a bleak picture of
what would happen if the CBC designed its radio and television programming in strict accordance with the needs and desires of Canadians *as expressed by Canadians themselves.* The CBC would be
transformed into a mass-entertainment medium with little or no room
for arts, culture, and information. Levels of Canadian content would

plummet, especially on television, through massive imports of American programming. And services that exist largely for the benefit of minorities would have to be abandoned or at least be reconstituted in the interests of the majority.

The situation is not as simple as this, however. If audience measures designed to meet the needs of advertisers are taken as an accurate guide to the public mind, then the results for arts and culture might well be catastrophic. But if more sophisticated means are used to facilitate public input, there are strong indications that a very different scenario would materialize. Indeed, there is some evidence that Canadians overall would prefer even greater amounts of Canadian, cultural, and minority-interest programming. To the extent that CBC audience research has attempted to find out what the public wants in terms of broadcasting, the results provide no basis for fearing public opinion as a guide to programming policy.

CULTURAL DEMOCRACY AND NATIONAL IDENTITY

In so far as public input into the determination of radio and television services is an important aspect of participatory democracy in general, its desirability might be considered to be self-evident. Nonetheless, the implications of such participation for the debate about Canadian cultural identity are worth pointing out. It has long been maintained by cultural nationalists that high levels of Canadian content in the mass media are essential for the development of a distinctive national identity. But a number of writers have recently challenged this claim. Where, some have asked,[21] is the proof that Canadian content has actually produced a distinctive identity? And where, ask others,[22] is the evidence that Canadians do not have their own identity despite high levels of foreign content in media such as film and television?

Both questions pose major difficulties for traditional cultural nationalists. But they do so because the critics have construed the relationship between content and identity in essentially mechanistic terms. It is, in fact, virtually impossible to demonstrate a clear causal connection between Canadian content and something as elusive as national identity. Indeed, in periods such as the 1920s and 1960s, an increased concern about national identity was stimulated by increased foreign content in some of the Canadian media.

Cultural nationalists are themselves partly to blame for oversimplifying the relationship between media content and national identity. In their haste to justify various measures to increase Canadian content, they have failed to probe very deeply into the way in which national identities develop. A national identity comprises several layers of culture or shared patterns of thought and behaviour that have meaning or value for a society. These range from common customs, habits, and mundane beliefs (or culture in the broad, anthropological sense) to esoteric expressions of the purpose and order in life (what is usually described as high culture). For Canadian cultural nationalists, the processes by which culture is spread are essentially passive in nature; the masses imitate new forms of behaviour and consume the products of high (as well as popular) culture. There is little mention in their writings and speeches of the fact that culture is created by all members of society.

It is, however, only through the activity itself of producing a culture that identities emerge, whatever the level of culture. All cultural creation is a two-way street. It begins as a conception in the minds of certain individuals. But to become part of a society's culture, new ways of thinking or behaving must be selected and sanctioned by its members as helping them to understand or deal with their own experiences. In the case of both high culture and popular culture, this process is most likely to happen when the original act of creation has occurred in response to the expressed needs of society as a whole. A country can scarcely be expected to have a substantial and secure national identity if the mass of the people lack the means to influence its creative sources. In addition to adequate means of production and distribution, there must also be channels whereby the public can help shape what is produced. In the final analysis, the only meaningful measure of cultural identity is the degree to which all members of society are engaged in the joint process of cultural production.

To the extent that Canadians consume foreign cultural products, they are in effect re-creating other cultures. This activity is not necessarily negative in itself; it may help to make Canadians more cosmopolitan in their outlook. But when it reaches certain proportions, it becomes significant by virtue of what Canadians are *not* doing as well: namely, creating their own culture through their choice of, and influence on, Canadian radio and television programs. It is for this reason that audience research needs to play a democratic role.

2

Public Broadcasting in Name Only: The Origins of Programming Paternalism

In so far as ... the operation of a national radio company administered by a directorate of twelve leading citizens [is concerned] – this just makes one yawn. Can you imagine, Radio Fans, the kind of radio entertainment which would emerge from a directorate consisting of an official from a Trade Labor Union, a representative of the United Farmers, the Bishop of an Anglican Church, a University President, some one nominated by the Daughters of the Empire or Native Sons, the General Manager of a Canadian Bank, etc., etc.?

'Pro Radio Publico,' 3 February 1931[1]

In its 1986 report, the Caplan-Sauvageau Task Force on Broadcasting Policy observed that 'Canadians are not always given to philosophical discourse on the phenomena that surround them, and public broadcasting seems an indisputable example of this generalization.' Unfortunately, the task force itself did not do much to rectify the situation. Instead, it simply reiterated the rhetoric of promoting national unity and identity and drew from a current British report which justified public broadcasting on the grounds of public service. Public broadcasting, Caplan-Sauvageau affirmed, helps to ensure that all members of society are served 'regardless of social status, place of residence or aesthetic preference,' and that there is 'freedom from control by vested interests, whether political or financial.'[2] These are important considerations, but what is missing from Caplan-Sauvageau's discussion is any reflection on the democratic objectives which originally inspired the British idea of public service broadcasting and also played a significant role in generating initial support for public broadcasting in Canada.

PUBLIC BROADCASTING AND DEMOCRACY

There are three distinct ways in which a broadcasting organization can serve democracy. The first is by contributing to the education of citizens for the performance of democratic responsibilities. 'It is obvious,' wrote John Watson, emeritus professor of moral philosophy at Queen's University in 1926, 'that education is the necessary complement of an enlightened democracy.'[3] For Watson, educating citizens for democracy meant a greater role for universities, which were attended in his day by only a small minority of those Canadians who managed to complete high school. But for some of his younger colleagues at Queen's, such as R.C. Wallace, it also called for new methods of education, including the use of radio. Wallace was impressed by developments in Britain and Germany which pointed to the 'vast possibilities' of radio as an aid to both elementary and adult education. In a 1931 memorandum prepared jointly with E.A. Corbett, director of extension at the University of Alberta, he noted that 'nearly a million children in the schools of Great Britain listen for a short period daily to great scientists, artists, and teachers of various subjects. In adult education the principle of group listening during evening hours has been developed to such an extent that there are now in England over two hundred study groups listening to courses of lectures on history, literature, astronomy, music, drama, biology, and other subjects.' In Wallace's view, 'no private system, however powerful or beneficent,' could undertake the educational tasks 'that radio has to perform in the future.'[4]

The educational achievements that Wallace so admired in Britain were largely motivated by John Reith, the BBC's first director-general. One of the few broadcasting authorities to think deeply about the role of public ownership, Reith saw a close connection between broadcasting and democracy. He believed that broadcasting might finally link the 'theory' of democracy to 'real life' because it was the first medium of communication capable of reaching the whole community. It could, he wrote, be 'the tempering factor that would give democracy for the first time under modern conditions a real chance of operating as a living force throughout the extended community as long ago it operated in the city-state.'[5] Reith assumed that broadcasting would thus have to be democratic in the second sense of giving a voice to various points of view. There were definite limits on how far he was prepared to extend this principle, but he argued that the newspaper press had failed to serve democracy adequately because 'the freedom it had always claimed was not necessarily accompanied by an obligation to give unconditional elucidation or points of view opposed to those of its owners.'[6]

To educate and provide an open forum broadcasting has to be free (as Caplan-Sauvageau observed) from both government interference and the pressures of the commercial system. Reith thus defended the creation of a public broadcasting corporation with wide autonomy, including financial independence, and a monopoly over programming. From *Broadcast over Britain* (1924) to *Into the Wind* (1949), he made the case for monopoly public service broadcasting. For Reith, the management and staff of a public corporation should be regarded, not as mere civil servants, but as the proprietors of an important business, motivated by a desire to serve the public interest rather than by the stimulus of profits. While acknowledging that the BBC should be accountable to Parliament at regular intervals, Reith thought that 'the nature and degree and method of accountability' should be carefully defined and 'the over-riding and essential powers of public control should only ... be felt when the body was not carrying out its obligations; had exceeded its powers; had been guilty in one way or another of offending the letter, or even the spirit, of its constitution.'[7]

Reith did not, however, take the further step of embracing public broadcasting for its ability to be democratic in the third sense of facilitating public participation. His hope that the BBC might become 'the integrator for democracy' was not accompanied by a belief that its own operations should be governed by democratic principles. He allowed that the BBC was thus placed in the ironic position of 'serving a high democratic purpose by means which in the literal sense were not democratic.' But he questioned 'whether democratic principle and purpose could best and quickest be served by democratic means as commonly understood.' Though admitting that 'the BBC might be considered autocratic or arbitrary in attitude and procedure,' he suggested that it was more important that 'it had the courage of its convictions; it did what it believed was in the public interest. Ought that not to apply to any body vested with authority and responsibility?'[8] In other words, Reith never had any doubt that it was the BBC's duty to determine for itself what was in the public interest. As a result, he was opposed not only to government interference in the management of the BBC but also to the idea of basing its programming on what the public wanted.

Reith's general approach was shared by those Canadians who advocated public broadcasting because of its democratic potential. Most accounts of the origins of public broadcasting in Canada have emphasized the nationalist argument – 'the state or the United States,' as Graham Spry put it – which was used to convince both politicians and the public of the need for public ownership. This argument was first enunciated by the royal commission set up by the federal goverment to recommend a system of broadcasting. It was later refined by the Canadian Radio League organized by Spry together with Alan Plaunt in support of public broadcasting.[9] But according to broadcasting historian Marc Raboy, many of those who supported the Radio League, including Spry himself, thought of public broadcasting as a means for a more broadly based public opinion.[10] As the brief used at the league's first executive meeting on 8 December 1930 put it in somewhat veiled language, 'Canadian public opinion, so far as it may be influenced by the radio, is in the hands of irresponsible authorities.'[11] Only as opposition arose to the concept of public broadcasting did they shift their emphasis from democracy to nationalism. 'The motion picture and the theatre have largely become the monopoly of American commercial enterprise,' a league pamphlet stated, 'and there is a grave danger that this last instrument of general culture and entertainment, radio, will fall under the control of, to some extent, the same American corporations.'[12]

THE AIRD COMMISSION'S CONCEPT OF PUBLIC BROADCASTING

In creating the Royal Commission on Radio Broadcasting in December 1928, the Liberal government of Mackenzie King made no reference to democratic considerations or even to the concept of public broadcasting. The closest option to public ownership that it mentioned was 'the establishment and operation of stations by a Government-owned and financed company.' But after hearing numerous submissions and inspecting several other systems, the principal members of the commission – Sir John Aird, president of the Canadian Bank of Commerce and commission chairman; Charles A. Bowman, editor of the *Ottawa Citizen*; and Augustin Frigon, director of the Ecole Polytechnique in Montreal and the head of technical education in Quebec – concluded that 'the interests of the listening public and of the nation ... can be adequately served only by some form of public ownership, operation and control behind which is the national power and prestige of the whole public of the Dominion of Canada.'[13]

In its report submitted on 11 September 1929 the Aird commission took it as a 'fundamental principle' that Canadian broadcasting 'must be operated on a basis of public service.' Although its discussion of this principle was neither systematic nor prolonged, it had a number of things in mind. The first was simply that radio service should be provided to all parts of the country. When Aird and his colleagues surveyed the situation in 1929, there were about 300,000 radio sets and 87 licensed broadcasting stations in Canada. However, almost half of the sets were in Ontario and the number of licensed stations was misleading. Nine of the stations were operated by amateur broadcasters; 16 were 'phantom' stations, which meant that they used the physical plant of another station; and of the remaining 62 private commercial stations, many provided only intermittent service and most had low-power transmitters.

Although Canada had exclusive use of only 6 of the available 95 channels (and shared another 11 frequencies with the United States), it was scarcely in a position to complain about this allocation. Only three stations had a power of 5,000 watts – CKAC owned by *La Presse* in Montreal, CKGW owned by Gooderham & Worts in Toronto, and CKY run by the Manitoba Telephone System. Only four others had 1,000 watts or more – CFRB in Toronto with 4,000, CJRX in Winnipeg with 2,000, CFCF in Montreal with 1,650, and CKLC/CHCT in Red Deer with 1,000. The Canadian National Railways' phantom station CNRM in Montreal operated with 1,650 to 5,000 watts, depending on whether it linked up with CKAC or CFCF.[14] In contrast, there were already 40 stations in the United States with between 5,000 and 25,000 watts. Many were located close to Canada and were listened to by Canadians on a regular basis.[15]

'To provide good reception over the entire settled region of the country during daylight or dark under normal conditions on a five-tube receiving set,' the Aird commission recommended that a new system of stations be developed and operated 'as soon as possible.' It thought that the nucleus of this system might be a chain of seven 50,000-watt stations, one in the Maritimes and one in each of the other six provinces, with additional local stations being added as needed. The high-power stations, which would cost an estimated $3 million, should be 'so modelled as ultimately to provide for two programs being broadcast simultaneously on different wavelengths.' While they were being built, the company could provide provisional service by taking over with compensation a private station in each area. Under this scheme, 'all remaining stations located or giving a duplication of service in the same area should be closed down' – as would the stations taken over on a temporary basis once they were no longer needed.[16]

For the Aird commission, however, public service meant more than serving all Canadians. It also entailed the production of Canadian programs. While not ruling out the provision of some foreign programs, the commission stressed that there was 'unanimity on one fundamental question – Canadian radio listeners want Canadian broadcasting.' Moreover, not just any Canadian programming would do. If programming was to serve the public, it needed to be 'an instrument of education,' albeit 'education in the broad sense, not only as it is conducted in the schools and colleges, but in providing entertainment and of informing the public on questions of national interest.' Only then would broadcasting 'become a great force in fostering a national spirit and interpreting national citizenship.'[17]

The Aird commission did not explain how its proposed Canadian Radio Broadcasting Company could be 'vested with all the powers of private enterprise' and at the same time have the 'status and duties ... of a public utility.' Nor did it make clear how the company could foster national consciousness if the provinces were to have full control over programs. At the very least, the administrative structure which it recommended – a national board consisting of three federal and nine provincial members – assumed that a high degree of cooperation was possible. But its most serious failing, from a democratic standpoint, was its limited conception of public participation. To be sure, each province was to have an advisory council made up of representatives of 'the responsible bodies interested in radio broadcasting.'[18] The stated purpose of the councils was to provide the provincial representatives with advice on programming. But beyond this, the Aird commission gave no thought to the question of how to ensure that those in charge of the Canadian Radio Broadcasting Company were in touch with the needs of the listening public.

ASHCROFT, GIBBON, AND THE UNKNOWN AUDIENCE

During the subsequent debate over the Aird report, this question was raised by a number of opponents of complete public ownership. In a debate with Graham Spry in *Saturday Night* in January 1931, R.W. Ashcroft, general manager of the Trans-Canada Broadcasting Company, argued that the objective of broadcasting should be 'to please *most* of the people, *most* of the time' and that this was impossible with a monopoly, whether public or private. Ashcroft thought that this argument was borne out by the lamentable failure of the BBC, whose motto might well be 'The public be damned!' He saw no merit in turning radio in Canada 'over to a group of Civil Service employees' who were 'untrained and inexperienced as impressarios and showmen.'[19]

A few months later, in a controversial article in *Canadian Forum*, John Murray Gibbon made the case that a private commercial system was better suited to serving the wants of audiences, because 'the sponsor of a radio programme which does not please the listener cuts his own throat.' 'Under private ownership,' he wrote,

radio entertainment is governed by the rules of demand and supply. The objective of the programme sponsor is to gain the goodwill of the unseen audience. Different types of programme are created by the realization of sponsors that it is impossible to please every one with one type of programme and that therefore it is advisable to please a specific type of audience with a specific type of programme. Competition on this Continent has resulted in providing a great variety of programmes, far greater than is available through the B.B.C. or Continental European systems, and from the nature of things better adapted to North American mentality.[20]

Gibbon also made the point that 'if the advocates of Government monopoly of radio hope to monopolize the attention of Canadian radio listeners, they will have to secure a much larger subsidy for talent than is allowed for in the recommendations of the Aird Commission.'[21]

These were arguments that warranted discussion, but regrettably, attention was deflected away from them by the fact that Gibbon, who was the director of publicity for the Canadian Pacific Railway, also accused the BBC of being, among other things, 'a machine for propaganda.' This statement brought howls of protest from the BBC, which was determined that the CPR make a public denial of any association with the article. The CPR equivocated, however, and the BBC was eventually forced to issue its own statement to the press, which was based, it said, on correspondence from the railway dissociating itself from Gibbon's remarks. Recounting these events, E. Austin Weir, the rival CNR's director of radio, told CNR vice-president W.D. Robb that the final sentence of the BBC's statement ('the article is a unique combination of inaccuracy and malevolence') was 'the hottest that has ever been issued officially from Savoy Hill.'[22]

To say that some of Gibbon's remarks merited consideration is not to endorse his belief that the public would be served best by competition between private commercial stations. On the contrary, there were two basic problems with his position when applied to Canadian broadcasting in the early 1930s. The first, which was emphasized by the Canadian Radio League, was that most of the private stations in Canada were in no position to compete against the powerful American stations. As Graham Spry pointed out in 1931,

the United States is the largest advertising market in the world, and is at least ten times as important as Canada. The corporations financing broadcasting there represent a combination of resources with which no Canadian group of companies could compare. Behind the National Broadcasting Company stand the Radio Corporation of America, the General Electric Company, the Westinghouse Electric, General Motors Radio, Radio-Victor, Radio-Keith-Orpheum theatres and motion pictures, several transoceanic communication services, sheet music companies, tube and other equipment manufacturers, and associated interests.[23]

Applied to Canadian broadcasting, the principle of supply and demand meant that areas which were 'not profitable from an advertising point of view either are not served or are served by small, weak and poorly financed stations.'[24]

The second problem with Gibbon's position is that it assumed that it was possible for broadcasters to determine which programs were most liked by audiences. But at the time it was impossible to do so. The first radio broadcast in Canada originated from the Marconi station XWA in Montreal in 1919, about the same time that broadcasting began in the United States. But for the next decade, broadcasters had virtually no idea how many people were listening to their programs, let alone what they thought of them. As an American radio publication noted in the late 1920s, estimating the size of audiences was 'equivalent to determining the number of crickets chirping at any instant in a swamp on a foggy summer evening.'[25] In 1930 the Crawford-Harris agency did conduct a survey of listeners in southern Saskatchewan and reported, among other things, that the radio was on for seven hours and twenty-two minutes a day in the average household.[26] But as Merrill Denison wrote the following year, 'very little is actually known about the radio audience, either its likes or dislikes, its desires, or even its numbers. And so one may reach knowingly for the salt cellar when he reads forthright statements purporting to tell what the radio audience likes and what it dislikes. No one knows and no one can know for there is no means of finding out.'[27]

Stations did make use of a number of crude techniques for estimating circulation or coverage, which was variously defined as the number of people who listen to a station habitually or the area in which a station has a significant share of regular listeners. One method was simply to count fan mail. Another was to draw a circle with a hundred-mile radius around the station on a map and then calculate the population within it. But as a later work on audience measurement pointed out, this procedure was 'entirely meaningless' since 'differences in power, interference between stations, overlapping of stations, local geology and geography, station programming, wave length, and numerous other factors are known to influence the size of the population habitually reached by each station.'[28] In any event, the circulation of a station provided no indication of audiences for particular programs.

This was also a problem for public broadcasting, of course. Spry was correct up to a point when he argued that only through public broadcasting would Canadians 'have the opportunity of hearing Canadian programmes of great variety.'[29] But the challenge of serving Canadians was not simply one of finding adequate resources for high-quality programming. It was also one of knowing what Canadians needed in the way of programs. Spry offered no suggestions as to how public broadcasters could ascertain programming needs. He simply took it for granted that public-spirited broadcasters would know what kinds of programs were required.

THE CANADIAN RADIO LEAGUE'S CASE FOR PUBLIC SERVICE BROADCASTING

Spry and his colleague Alan Plaunt were necessarily concerned first and foremost with establishing the primacy of public ownership of broadcasting in Canada. For in their view, 'on an advertising basis Canadian radio and Canadian public opinion pass out of Canadian control.'[30] While supporting the continuation of small, local stations, they explicitly rejected a balanced system of public and private enterprise. As a submission prepared for a parliamentary committee in 1936 emphasized, 'we cannot have the best of both worlds. Canadian radio must be established on a primary basis of public service or on a primary basis of advertising.'[31] The campaign for public broadcasting was thus preoccupied with the dangers of advertising rather than the potential for public involvement.

Spry and Plaunt believed, like the Aird commission, that broadcasting should do more than entertain. It is, said Spry, 'primarily ... an instrument of education in its widest significance, ranging from play to learning, from recreation to the cultivation of public opinion.' Treated as such, it would also serve as 'a majestic instrument of national unity and national culture.'[32] Or as the Canadian Radio League's constitution stated, one of its goals was 'to ensure that radio broadcasting is developed on the broadest educational and national basis and used as an instrument for strengthening Canadian unity, for binding the different sections of Canada together into one nationality, and for creating harmonious and healthy relations between the races composing the Canadian people.'[33] The concern of the Radio League was not only to protect Canadians against what would come to be known as American cultural imperialism but also to overcome internal obstacles to nationhood. 'Radio is a means of breaking down narrow sectional prejudices and of creating a better understanding of the problems which confront us as a nation as well as those which are peculiar to the provinces individually,' said Radio League supporter E.A. Corbett on a national broadcast on 13 November 1931.[34]

Although the Radio League's constitution emphasized that public ownership was to provide 'for the broadcasting of programmes in the French language and for the protection of minorities in Canada from alien [American?] influences,'[35] its vision of Canada was essentially federalist; the purpose of public broadcasting was to promote Canadian nationalism while maintaining regional and cultural differences. Spry and Plaunt wanted not merely to placate but to genuinely embrace French Canada, but they were not ideologically prepared, or even able, to contemplate the use of public broadcasting to promote a Quebec nationalism that would take precedence over Canadian national unity. At the same time, however, they wanted 'public' rather than 'government' broadcasting to ensure that national values were achieved through consensus rather than disseminated by the political elite. They believed that national unity required the prior expression of a wide range of viewpoints, including those which challenged the status quo. This was the implied meaning of the Radio League's stated objective of making 'full use' of broadcasting 'for the stimulation of healthy and well informed public opinion in Canada.'[36]

It was for these reasons in part that the Radio League rejected the Aird commission's proposal to eliminate the private stations. Despite its belief that commercial broadcasting represented special interests, it maintained that small, short-range private stations were still necessary to satisfy local programming needs. It was influenced by people like the general manager of the *Halifax Herald*, who wrote to Plaunt that 'smaller powered stations located at various points in the Maritime Provinces are much more flexible than a large station and ... are in a position to meet the local needs of their constituencies much better than the large stations could do it.'[37] This modified approach to the question of station ownership was adopted by the Special Committee set up by Prime Minister Bennett in 1932 'to advise and recommend a complete technical scheme of radio broadcasting for Canada.' The Morand committee recommended that stations of 100 watts or less, of which there were thirty or so at the time, remain under private owner-ship, thus reducing the burden on the public broadcaster to satisfy all the programming needs of Canadians.

THE FALSE START OF THE CRBC

The report of the Morand committee was hailed by Spry as 'a complete victory for the Canadian Radio League' and a triumph for the public.[38] But this reaction proved to be premature. The Canadian Radio Broad-casting Commission, established by the broadcasting act of 1932, was intended to be both national and public in character. But during its brief and troubled life-span, it fell far short of achieving either of these goals in their most meaningful sense. Even with the assistance of pri-vately owned affiliates, many of which were paid to carry its programs, it was only able to reach about 60 per cent of the population during the day and even fewer people at night. Much of the programming that it provided was indistinguishable from the commercial fare on the unaf-filiated private stations and contributed little to a shared national experience. Its administrative structure was inherently unrepresenta-tive, and provisions in the broadcasting act for advisory councils were largely ignored. And despite a series of controversies arising from poor programming decisions, it made no attempt to find out what Canadi-ans wanted in terms of radio service.

Heading the tripartite commission was Hector Charlesworth, known mainly for his work as a music and drama critic and two volumes of 'Candid Chronicles' – a third volume of which, entitled *I'm Telling You* (1937), related his tribulations as chairman. At the time, he was editor-in-chief of *Saturday Night* and, though not unsympathetic to the Conservatives, was insufficiently political to be considered a partisan appointment. The same could not be said, however, for the vice-chairman of the commission. Despite an earlier understanding among the parties that the commission was to be a non-partisan body, Bennett deferred to his Quebec cabinet ministers and named Thomas Maher to this position. A forestry engineer and director of radio station CHRC, Maher had worked as a Conservative organizer in Quebec, run unsuccessfully as a Conservative candidate in the 1930 election, and founded and edited the Conservative paper *Le Journal.* Like Charlesworth, he had little experience to draw upon for running a broadcasting organization. The only commissioner with a technical knowledge of radio was Lt. Col. W. Arthur Steel, who had been in the Signal Corps in the Department of National Defence and had served as technical adviser to the 1932 radio committee. But he also lacked the administrative expertise necessary to carry out the broad mandate of the commission.

The commissioners made matters worse by their managerial style. According to Austin Weir, who served for the first few months as the commission's director of programs, 'they felt the irrepressible urge to be active in day-to-day operations and could not, or would not, delegate managerial authority to others. They proceeded to departmentalize operations under three heads, with each of them in charge of a section.'[39] By May 1933, Maher had taken over responsibility for all programming from Weir, and in June he unilaterally dismissed him while Charlesworth was on a trip to western Canada. Weir had arranged for transmission circuits for four hours each evening, which enabled the commission to broadcast programs simultaneously across the country for one hour each night (from 9:00 to 10:00 p.m., EST), with the rest of the time being devoted to regional programming. Without consulting Charlesworth or Steel, Maher proceeded to schedule French-language programs for three and sometimes four of the seven national hours available weekly. He even temporarily overrode Charlesworth's instructions to restrict French-language programming to eastern Canada.

The result was a predictable explosion of protests, especially in Ontario and western Canada. But in Weir's opinion, much of the opposition was motivated not by antagonism to the French language as such, but rather by hostility towards Roman Catholicism, which was closely associated with it. In his view, a more gradual approach to the introduction of French-language programming in English Canada might have avoided the bitter reaction of 1933 and helped to create a mutual understanding of the French and English viewpoints.

Tactfully handled, the occasional routing of French programs over the national network held real possibilities for the greater appreciation of French talent and the French way of life. Later, as understanding grew and prejudice lessened, such broadcasts might have been judiciously increased without arousing any serious agitation. But Maher was in a hurry; the CRBC was inadequately equipped, and the staff inexperienced. What was of potential value was ruined through ambition and sheer awkwardness.[40]

The commission later tried to make Weir the scapegoat for this sordid affair. 'They claimed,' he wrote, 'that it was not that too many French programs were being broadcast but too few English. It was suggested that this was my fault, but the contention was absurd. At the time, there was only one hour (from 9:00 to 10:00 P.M.) available daily on the full national network, and it was completely filled.'[41]

During the next year, Maher did little to overcome English Canada's negative impression of CRBC programming. Although the commission began broadcasting two five-minute news reports on a daily basis, their content was controlled by the Canadian Press, which prepared them at no charge and ensured they were scheduled at times that would not undermine newspaper circulation. The commission also instituted daily weather forecasts and a popular northern messenger service on Saturday evenings between November and May. But the bulk of its programming consisted of popular music. There were very few talks, dramas, or special broadcasts initially and scarcely any educational programs of the kind envisaged by Wallace and Corbett.

As a result of growing criticism of the CRBC in various newspapers and magazines as well as in the House of Commons, a parliamentary committee was appointed in February 1934 to review its operations. It recommended that the post of general manager be created with responsibility for day-to-day operations, but nothing came of this until a new broadcasting act was passed in 1936 and the commission was replaced by the Canadian Broadcasting Corporation. However, the CRBC's programming did improve somewhat after Maher resigned in

July 1934. Although he was replaced by Jacques Cartier, another active Conservative from Quebec, responsibility for programming was placed in the hands of Ernest L. Bushnell, former manager of CKNC in Toronto. Under Bushnell's direction, the number of talks, special events, and international broadcasts was substantially increased and the field of drama was considerably expanded. Among the new dramatic productions were 'Forgotten Footsteps,' based on ancient relics in the Royal Ontario Museum; 'And It Came to Pass,' a biblical series produced in Montreal; and 'The Young Bloods of Beaver Bend,' a serial drama written by Tommy Tweed of Winnipeg.

Despite these improvements, the programming of the CRBC still suffered from the cumbersome and costly means by which it was distributed. In this regard, the commission was hindered by the fact that it could not expropriate, purchase, or construct stations without parliamentary approval; the only free hand that it had initially was to lease existing stations or work out affiliation agreements, although Bill 99 (1933) Amending the Act of 1932 enabled the commission to lease or purchase stations with the approval of the Governor-in-Council instead of Parliament. In March 1933 the CRBC acquired stations in Moncton, Ottawa, and Vancouver, along with studio facilities in Halifax and Montreal, from the Canadian National Railways for $50,000, and the purchase was ratified by Parliament on 25 April. But the Moncton station was so decrepit that it soon had to be closed down. And except for a small station in Quebec City purchased in 1935, these were the only stations that the commission ever owned, and none had 50,000 watts of power as recommended by the Aird commission. The government steadfastly refused to provide any funds for station construction and actually withheld a substantial portion of the monies collected through radio licence fees. To serve the Toronto area, the commission had to take over CKGW, change the call letters to CRTC, and lease studio space from CKNC. It also leased the 100-watt station CRCS in Chicoutimi and a 5,000-watt transmitter from CKLW in Windsor. But beyond this, it was forced to distribute its programs through a string of low-power affiliates.

This was not necessarily a bad arrangement in principle. But the twelve affiliates that were initially integrated into its 'basic' network were paid to carry its programs – at the outset, for three hours each evening. During the 1933–4 fiscal year, these payments accounted for almost a fifth of the CRBC's expenditures; by the time of its demise, its total distribution costs (wire lines plus station payments) actually exceeded what it had spent on programming. The fact that a large number of 'supplementary' stations agreed to carry a substantial proportion of its programming without payment made this a questionable practice.

The commission's handling of the 'Mr. Sage' programs during the federal election campaign of 1935 was the low point of its judgment on programming matters. The programs in question were produced on behalf of the Conservative party by the J.J. Gibbons advertising agency using a CRBC studio in Toronto. They consisted of conversations between 'Mr. Sage' and an ordinary citizen called Bill in which the policies and personalities of the Liberals were forthrightly criticized.[42] Carried over a network of private stations with the CRBC's approval, the first two programs neglected to mention their sponsor and, when the CRBC insisted that the sponsor be named, it was given as R.L. Wright (a Gibbons employee) rather than as the Conservative party.[43] Beyond this, the broadcasts did a disservice to public broadcasting as an instrument of democracy by failing to provide for all parties equally and by manipulating listeners through their dramatic format.

On 24 June 1932 Lee de Forest wrote to Plaunt that 'all who believe that radio is primarily for the people and not a mere sales medium will wish to see the Canadian plan a great success.'[44] But being 'for the people' did not necessarily mean being influenced 'by the people.' For the people were too likely to be like 'Pro Radio Publico,' who simply wanted to listen to 'the Palmolive hour, the Coca Cola Dance Orchestra, to say nothing of Amos and Andy,' and who declared that 'frankly, for one, I don't want to be educated. I don't want to be informed, via the radio. In so far as entertainment is concerned, the idea of the government doing it through twelve of its leading citizens simply gives me a pain in the neck.'[45]

In the fall of 1932, Spry and Plaunt expressed fear not only that 'there is no real and effective buffer between the paid commission and the Government' but also that 'there is no real and effective buffer between the commission and the public.'[46] They thus overlooked the possibility that public involvement might be the surest protection against government control. The commission undermined its relationship with the government by the distance that it created between itself and the public. Brooke Claxton, who provided the Canadian Radio League with legal expertise, wrote to Plaunt in 1935 that the CRBC had 'done nothing whatever to use the potentialities of the radio for enlightenment or for the development of national unity and consciousness of national problems.' And he added that 'in the criticism of the present Commission, I would place first its failure to recognize the potentialities of radio and its failure to do anything to develop Canadian public opinion in support even of the idea of national radio.'[47] But if the CRBC failed in this respect, it was partly because of the paternalistic attitude to programming that it shared in common with many of the supporters of public broadcasting.

Some of the poor decisions made by the CRBC might conceivably have been avoided had it adhered to the provision in the broadcasting act for establishing advisory groups. In addition to three salaried commissioners, the CRBC had nine unsalaried assistant commissioners, each of whom was to organize and chair provincial or local advisory committees. The commission was supposed to convene periodic meetings of a general council, which was to be composed of the commissioners and assistant commissioners and could include representatives of the advisory committees as well as the private stations. The general council was expected to advise the CRBC on policy, 'including the general composition, character and co-ordination of national and local programmes, the apportionment of time and any other matters which the Commission or the Minister may refer to the General Council.' In a report prepared for the government on the CRBC's early progress (or rather lack thereof), Gladstone Murray, who had left Canada to work for the BBC, wrote that 'in the early stages of a broadcasting service, Advisory Committees are of special importance.'[48] However, no provincial advisory committees were actually formed,[49] and they would not, in any event, have constituted an adequate substitute for audience research.

The failure of the CRBC was the result of several factors, including the inexperience of its commissioners, its inadequate degree of autonomy, the scarcity of resources available for broadcasting in the midst of the depression, and the lack of support which it received from the government. But underlying the gap between the vision of its founders and the reality of its achievements was an ideological factor. Neither the government nor the commission conceived of national public broadcasting in democratic terms. Or, to the limited extent that they did, they took few if any of the steps necessary to make the CRBC a truly democratic institution.

3

Divergent Approaches to Audience Research in the United States and Britain

Think of broadcasting as a ship. Its final destination is determined by consider-ations of policy. The course it takes is affected by many factors, including its available fuel and the likelihood of the presence of icefields. But the task of the helmsman will be made infinitely easier by good charts. It is the job of Listener Research to prepare those charts.

Robert Silvey, 1938[1]

There were two possible incentives for trying to find out more about audiences and, more particularly, for developing a method of audience measurement. The first was to enable broadcasters to serve their audi-ences more effectively by providing an objective indication of program popularity. Initially, however, this was not a major consideration for either public or private broadcasters. In the case of public broadcast-ing, it seemed to run counter to its educational and cultural objectives for programming. It was only after private broadcasters became com-mitted to audience measurement that public broadcasters began to follow suit. And initially, private broadcasters were too hard pressed to provide a schedule of programs and stay afloat financially to worry much about whether audiences actually liked their programming. For private broadcasting resources to be expended on audience measure-ment, there had to be an economic advantage to knowing which pro-grams were attracting the largest audiences, and the only advantage of this kind was to be able to obtain more advertising.

THE ECONOMIC INCENTIVE TO AUDIENCE MEASUREMENT

It was not until advertisers started to become interested in radio that any attempt was made to measure audiences regularly and scientifically. From the beginning, therefore, audience measurement – or what quickly became known as the production of ratings – was intended first and foremost to serve the needs of advertisers, not those of the listening public. But before audience measurement could link advertising and broadcasting closely, several other developments had to occur.

The first was the removal of both formal and informal restrictions on direct advertising. In Canada, a set of radio regulations issued by the Department of Marine and Fisheries in 1922 provided for the licensing of 'private commercial broadcasting stations.' But the term 'private' was intended to mean that these stations were not available for 'public correspondence'; that is, they were not to be operated as outlets for messages by any member of the public, including advertising messages. They were to be 'commercial' only in the sense that owners would derive a certain promotional value from the use of their names in station identification. At the same time, the regulations allowed for the licensing of 'public commercial broadcasting stations' whenever it became clear that there was a demand for 'toll-type' broadcasting. A situation was envisaged in which an advertiser would call a station by telephone, read a commercial message for transmission over the air, and then be charged a toll according to its length.[2] Although this scenario never materialized, the Radio Branch of Marine and Fisheries decided the following year to allow the so-called private commercial stations to undertake advertising, both direct and indirect, on an experimental basis to see whether it could be 'handled in such a way as to make it popular with the broadcast listener.' 'An example of direct advertising,' it explained in a report submitted by the deputy minister in March 1923, 'would be an automobile salesman renting a station for ten minutes to extol the virtues of his particular make of car. An example of indirect advertising would be a departmental store renting a station for an evening, putting on a first class programme, and announcing its name and the fact that it was contributing the programme before and after each selection.'[3] It was argued that because the stations could refuse to accept any particular message, they were still essentially private.

On 23 May 1923 Ernest Lapointe, the minister of Marine and Fisheries, tabled amended licence conditions in the House of Commons allowing stations to transmit direct advertising before 6:00 p.m. and indirect advertising without restriction. However, this permissive policy did not last for long. A year or so later, after it was found that stations were not engaging in much direct advertising, Marine and Fisheries laid down the rule that 'direct advertising is not allowed except with the express permission of the Department in writing; such permission will only be granted in special cases.' Although a number of stations ignored this rule and began to solicit direct advertising more aggressively,[4] the official regulations hindered the growth of radio advertising. As a result, only a few stations were able to operate profitably, leading Graham Spry to tell the Royal Commission on Railways and Transportation in early 1932 that 'the real problem of Canadian broadcasting is financial. The problem is, where is money to be found for financing stations and producing programmes and paying wire charges?'[5]

A more permissive policy towards direct advertising was not the only requirement for the growth of radio advertising. In the United States, where there were no formal restrictions on direct advertising, there was still a psychological barrier that had to be overcome before advertisers could embrace radio. During the 1920s, the prevailing view was that radio should be used as a means of cultural elevation and refinement, and the advertising industry shared this view, at least for the first few years. It was concerned that the debasement of radio by commercial messages might lead to public resentment and ill will towards all advertising.

While commending the sponsorship of radio programs as a public service, advertisers initially disapproved of making direct sales pitches for products. It was in this context that musical groups such as the Ipana Troubadours and A & P Gypsies made their debut on radio; they served to publicize trade names without any accompanying promotional message. Of course, this attitude proved to be short-lived. 'Let us realize once and for all,' one advertising agency representative wrote with typical bluntness in 1938, 'that radio is a powerful medium of advertising, not a means for Mr. Sponsor to take on the role of a philanthropist offering free entertainment to a nation.'[6] Still, as Roland Marchand has observed, 'the advertising industry did not set out in the early 1920s to capture this new medium. Quite the contrary. The overwhelming majority of advertising leaders held just as lofty a view of radio as anyone else. Eventually, most agencies had to be ardently wooed before they took up with the new medium.'[7]

Station owners were assisted in this task by a growing feeling among advertisers that a saturation point for commercial messages was being reached within the print media. At the same time, the growth of networks increased the attractiveness of radio to advertisers by making it easier to reach a national market. Upon its creation in 1926, the National Broadcasting Company formed the Red Network, based on a line-up of stations first linked together by the American Telephone & Telegraph Company. The next year, NBC acquired a chain of five Westinghouse stations and organized these into the Blue Network. And in 1928 the Columbia Broadcasting System formed a third American network and began to compete for advertising. In addition, radio audiences were – as far as one could tell – growing rapidly, especially once the Great Depression began reducing the amount of family income available for entertainment.

Despite these developments, advertisers remained sceptical about radio. For there was still no evidence that radio advertising was effective and no way of determining how many listeners a given commercial might reach. In the depressed conditions of the 1930s, radio needed the support of advertisers; but advertisers were not immediately convinced that they needed radio.

While many advertisers offered coupons or prizes in an attempt to measure response to particular commercials, the question of the effectiveness of radio advertising was mainly tackled by the networks. For example, CBS hired Robert Elder to conduct a comparative study of product use in radio and non-radio homes and later published the results in a pamphlet entitled *Does Radio Sell Goods?* (1931).[8] In the case of audience measurement, the initiative came from outside the networks and was supported at first by the advertisers alone. In 1928 NBC did commission an extensive survey of radio ownership. On the basis of over 17,000 personal interviews, Dr Daniel Starch, a Harvard professor and pioneer market researcher, estimated that nearly 35 per cent of American families owned a radio.* But the Starch survey did not provide any indication of how many people were listening to particular networks, stations, or programs.[9] It was thus of limited value to the networks in terms of their relationship with advertisers and their agencies. The same was true of an on-the-air mail survey conducted by

---

* A decade later, a study conducted by the Joint Committee on Radio Research estimated that 82 per cent of US families had radio sets, 69 per cent of rural families and 91 per cent of urban families. About 15 per cent of all families had two or more sets.[10]

CBS in 1930 in which a free map was offered to anyone who would write the station to which they were listening. It was not until A.M. Crossley developed a method for measuring radio audiences through sampling that advertisers were freed from the necessity of making radio-time purchases on faith.

Sampling is now a highly developed and widely used statistical technique for obtaining reliable data about a population rapidly and at a low cost. It is based on the well-established principle that a small number of items selected at random will reflect with a known degree of precision the characteristics of a large group of items. Although the results of all sampling operations are approximations, the economic viability of sampling arises from the fact that a sample representing a relatively small fraction of a population can yield results that will apply to the whole with an acceptable degree of reliability for most research purposes.

The reliability of data based on sampling is determined by three main considerations: the size of the sample, the procedure used to draw the sample, and the instruments used to collect data. A large sample does not in itself provide a guarantee of reliability. Regardless of how large the sample, estimates from a biased sample will always be potentially erroneous. Moreover, even when a sample is sufficiently large and carefully drawn, it may still be unrepresentative because of the method used to collect data. And while the degree of error associated with a given sample size can be calculated mathematically, this is not the case with error resulting from the procedures used to draw samples or collect data. During the early years of audience measurement through sampling, the size of samples used by various ratings companies was often called into question. But the main problems actually lay in the ways that they drew their samples and collected their data.

A.M. CROSSLEY AND THE COOPERATIVE ANALYSIS OF BROADCASTING

The unprepossessing head of a small American market research company, Archibald M. Crossley can rightly be called the father of audience ratings.[11] He first got involved in radio research in 1927 when he was hired by S.H. Giellerup of the Frank Seaman Advertising company to check which stations on a particular network were actually carrying a program sponsored by one of the company's clients. Two years later, the Crossley Business Research Company undertook a similar project on Giellerup's behalf for Eastman Kodak, but this time Crossley also conducted a telephone survey to find out what percentage of radio families had listened to the program. The results brought an enthusiastic response from both Giellerup, who wrote an article proposing that advertisers support an ongoing mail survey of station listening,[12] and Carleton Healy, the advertising manager of Eastman Kodak. Healy generated further interest in Crossley's telephone survey by describing it to the members of the Association of National Advertisers (ANA), about a dozen of whom hired Crossley to do further radio research.

The matter might have rested there had it not been for John Karol, a Harvard graduate who had joined Crossley's New York staff in the summer of 1929. Karol, who later became director of research for CBS, urged Crossley to try to interest the ANA in sponsoring a regular survey of radio audiences by telephone. Together they met with the ANA, prepared a report entitled 'The Advertiser Looks at Radio' which illustrated the potential value of such a survey, and drew up a detailed operating plan whereby the ANA would provide support for a year at a cost of $21,600. Influenced no doubt by the stock market crash, the ANA rejected this plan in November 1929. But it offered to endorse the formation of a radio audit bureau – to be called the Cooperative Analysis of Broadcasting – if Crossley would assume responsibility for its costs. Hopeful that he could secure enough subscriptions from advertisers to cover his budget, Crossley agreed to this stricture and received the ANA's official endorsement on 7 February 1930. To ensure maximum control in return for this minimal commitment, the ANA required Crossley to work under the direction of a governing committee and consult with an advertising agency advisory committee. It also excluded the networks from joining the bureau.

In March 1930 Crossley's interviewers began a twelve-month study of 17,000 radio families in fifty cities. In return for paying $70 a month ($60 for ANA members), which more than covered Crossley's costs, forty-nine subscribers received three four-month reports. These set forth what came to be known, to the ANA's dismay, as the Crossley ratings or estimated percentages of listening households tuned to particular network programs (what is now called a share). Crossley also hoped to provide his clients with breakdowns of the audience composition for various programs. As *Printer's Ink* reported optimistically, 'the listening habits of the different sexes, the different age groups and the different financial classes will be compared. Fluctuations in public preference for programs will be studied closely in the hope that answers to questions will indicate what are the factors that make pro-grams popular.'[13] Although the early reports issued by Crossley failed to live up to this advance hoopla, it should be noted that from the very beginning the intention was to provide advertisers with audience demographics.

Crossley developed what became known as the telephone recall method to produce monthly and later biweekly audience estimates for all national network programs. This method consisted of selecting numbers at random from telephone directories and asking respon-dents to recall what they had listened to the previous day. As Eileen Meehan has shown, this had two main benefits for the advertisers who made up Crossley's clientele.[14] First, because telephone ownership was still largely restricted to the upper and middle classes, Crossley's sample was clearly biased in favour of the so-called commodity audi-ence (those with the means and desire to purchase consumer goods). According to his own data, the lowest socio-economic sector had only one-quarter of the number of telephones necessary to represent it ade-quately. Crossley eventually altered his sampling procedure to com-pensate for this fact, but another benefit for advertisers remained. This arose from the fact that the rather onerous task of recalling the names of programs and their sponsors for an entire day's listening encour-aged people to underreport their listening or simply say that they had not been listening at all. In addition, if no one answered after four or five rings, this was taken as evidence that no one was at home and therefore no one was listening – but of course some people might not answer the phone precisely because they were listening. The result was to give advertisers more listeners than they actually paid for, since advertising rates varied in direct proportion to audience size.

During the last six months of 1931, the advertising revenues of NBC and CBS increased by 37 per cent over those of the same period the year before.[15] Between 1930 and 1935 their advertising revenues nearly doubled,[16] and by 1938 they passed the $100 million mark.[17] Not all of the increase was due to Crossley's ratings; after all, between 1929 and 1930, radio advertising had increased from $16½ million to almost $29 million.[18] But it is not surprising that Crossley helped to create 'adver-tiser confidence in the audience delivery of radio' and thereby 'ensured rapid growth in future radio investments.'[19] For as Meehan has observed, Crossley 'produced ratings limited to the type of audi-ence that advertisers wanted and delivered a quantity of audience that suited advertisers' interest in depressing network prices.'[20]

In 1931 the ANA decided to allow advertising agencies as well as individual advertisers to join the Cooperative Analysis of Broadcasting. But the networks were still specifically barred from its ranks; although they were allowed to look at its reports, they could not use them officially. Concerned by the fact that the number of individual advertisers began to decline as their agencies became clients, Crossley proposed in October 1932 that networks and stations be accepted as members. But the ANA turned down this proposal and a year later assumed even more control over the bureau's operations. While Crossley's company continued to perform the survey work, the formulation of policy was vested firmly in the ANA.

CBS RESEARCH AND THE STANTON-LAZARSFELD PROGRAM ANALYZER

When the first Crossley ratings were published in mid-1930, they were dominated by NBC programs. As expected, NBC's 'Amos 'n' Andy,' which was so popular that movie theatres piped it in before their first show, led all programs with a rating (actually, a share) of 53.4. Several other NBC programs also obtained impressive scores. For example, 'Rudy Vallee Varieties' was given 36.5 and 'Lucky Strike Dance Orchestra' had 27.8. In contrast, the highest figure for a CBS program was 12.0, and only one other CBS program got more than 3.3. One reason for the difference may have been that it was easier for listeners to recall NBC programs, most of which had been on the air for a longer period of time. But this was little consolation for CBS. As William S. Paley later recalled, 'that first Crossley rating hit us like a blow in the solar plexus. There were cries of anguish in the CBS offices, but most of us were angry with disbelief. It just could not be so. We were certain that at least some of our programs were more popular than those of NBC.'[21]

Fearful of the impact of the Crossley ratings on its advertising, CBS responded by hiring the prestigious accounting firm Price Waterhouse to conduct an independent study of radio network popularity. Instead of attempting to measure the audience for specific programs, Price Waterhouse decided to focus on the popularity of particular stations. Several hundred thousand postcards were sent to homes in cities where CBS had affiliates, asking listeners simply to name their favourite station. According to Paley, 'the results were reassuring. In the ten largest American cities, the survey showed CBS stations were favored seven to three over one of the NBC networks and five to four over the other. In all sixty-seven cities covered by the CBS network, we rated 34 to 31 over the first NBC network and 32 to 31 over the other.'[22]

During the next few years, Crossley made several alterations to his sample design to reflect the relative popularity of NBC and CBS programs more accurately. But CBS remained distrustful of the Crossley ratings, partly because it could not join the Cooperative Analysis of Broadcasting but also because its programs continued to trail those of NBC. It decided, therefore, to set up its own research department and develop new ways of determining what makes programs popular. In 1935 Frank Stanton, who later became president of CBS, was hired to head the new department. He had only just graduated from Ohio State with a PhD in psychology and had written to the network about some market research he was conducting.

Together with Paul F. Lazarsfeld, a professor at Columbia University and director of the Bureau of Applied Social Research, Stanton developed a system for predicting a program's popularity. The CBS Program Analyzer originally came in two sizes – affectionately known as 'Little Annie' and 'Big Annie.' For 'Little Annie,' ten to fifteen people were invited off the streets to listen to a pilot program in specially designed seats. The seats were equipped with green (for like) and red (for dislike) buttons which enabled their occupants to indicate their reactions to a program as it progressed; not pressing either button was interpreted as indifference. The buttons were connected electronically to capillary pens which recorded the second-by-second reactions of each listener on a moving tape. Afterwards, the participants completed a questionnaire and were interviewed by a member of the research staff. This procedure was usually repeated until seventy-five to one hundred people had reacted to the program. 'Big Annie' used two synchronized devices to record and total the 'like' and 'dislike' reactions to a program. It could handle as many as one hundred listeners at once, but did not enable analysis of individual reactions and later fell into disuse. The CBS Program Analyzer could also be used to see whether programs were losing their appeal, assess program strengths and weaknesses, determine the limits of good taste, and study audience demographics. CBS used it to pretest all of its package shows and with good results: a 1952 issue of *Variety* indicated that the first nineteen programs out of twenty on the American networks were CBS shows.[23]

The pretesting of programs was only part of the CBS research operation. Much of its time was spent analysing ratings data. The same was true for NBC, which conducted a number of nationwide surveys in the early 1940s asking people to identify the station they listened to most frequently at particular times of the day. It then examined the relationship between its data and those of the ratings services and developed a formula for converting 'most listening' into 'share of audience' percentages.

C.E. HOOPER AND THE TELEPHONE COINCIDENTAL

By the 1935–6 season, the Cooperative Analysis of Broadcasting was conducting surveys in all thirty-three cities with stations carrying CBS and the two NBC networks. But its exclusion of broadcasters together with its underestimation of audiences for certain types of programming left the door open for a second ratings service in the United States.[24] Once again, the initiative did not come from the networks themselves, but rather from a group of magazine publishers who believed, albeit incorrectly, that the Crossley ratings overestimated radio audiences. In the fall of 1934, they hired Montgomery Clark and Claude E. Hooper to conduct an independent survey of network listenership. Webster and Lichty explain that although the survey was specifically designed to 'capture certain unremembered listening, the publishers hoped that Clark-Hooper would show that many people were not at home, and many others at home were not listening to the radio.'[25] Clark and Hooper, who had recently quit the market research organization of Daniel Starch to set up their own company to study magazine advertising readership, introduced a new survey technique which came to be known as the coincidental telephone method or telephone coincidental. It was 'originally presented' to them by Dr George Gallup,[26] who had observed that a telephone survey of programs being listened to 'coincidentally' or at the time of the call yielded similar results to a survey conducted in the home. In 1932 Gallup had left Drake University in Iowa, where he had been teaching journalism, to undertake a weekly telephone coincidental study for Young and Rubicam, a major advertising agency in New York.[27] Other pioneers of the telephone coincidental were Percival White, John Karol, and Pauline Arnold. In a comparison of the telephone recall and coincidental methods in 1933, Arnold had found that 'some programs which were listened to by many listeners, were reported the next day by only a few. In general, dramatic programs were better remembered than musical programs.'[28]

Instead of asking respondents to recall their listening during the previous day, interviewers simply asked what was being listened to at the time of the call (as well as fifteen minutes earlier). The Hooperatings, as they were dubbed by Walter Winchell after Clark withdrew to the print field in 1938, were expressed as percentages of *all* radio households tuned to network broadcasts, whereas the Crossley ratings were calculated as percentages of *listening* households. According to Meehan, the Hooperatings were attractive to the networks because they were generally higher than Crossley's audience estimates, allowing for the different objects of measurement. However, Webster and Lichty state that the Hooperatings 'were lower than CAB's for some programs but higher for others. As Hooper would argue later, people were better able to remember programs that were longer, more popular, and those that had been on the air for a longer period of time. Respondents were also much more likely to recall variety programs, and most likely to forget having listened to the news.'[29] In any event, Hooper counterbalanced any advantage for the networks with a comparable benefit for advertisers. This took the form of targeting the consumer-oriented middle class even more precisely by drawing his sample exclusively from urban telephone directories and asking respondents for simple demographic information about themselves and other listeners in the household. As Meehan points out, 'the big cities, although seriously hurt by the Great Depression, remained centres of consumption, especially when compared with small towns or rural areas. The concentration of people in cities meant that the cities housed more potential consumers, more members of the middle class with sufficient disposable income who were willing and able to purchase name-brand goods.'[30]

Because his sampling was restricted to urban areas and his customers included the networks, Hooper – or 'Mr. Ratings' as he became known – was able to charge less for his service than Crossley could for his. He secured valuable publicity by giving the press a list each month of the fifteen highest-rated evening programs and, later, of the top ten daytime programs. He also conducted a series of studies designed to show the superiority of the coincidental telephone method and began to produce local radio ratings by combining the figures obtained for a given metropolitan area over several months. As a result, the Hooperatings soon began to rival the Crossley ratings.

The situation forced the Cooperative Analysis of Broadcasting to make several changes in its approach. From 1937 onwards, NBC and

CBS were accepted as subscribers, though without representation on the governing board. The recall period was shortened by subdividing the listening day, first into four parts and later into eight. In 1944 the recall method itself was abandoned in favour of Hooper's coincidental method. These moves enabled Crossley to compete with the less-expensive Hooper service for a time, but a study of the two ratings operations conducted by Dr Hans Zeisel in late 1945 reflected unfavourably on Crossley's methodology. Faced with the withdrawal of the networks, the Cooperative Analysis of Broadcasting folded in July 1946 and sold its subscribers to Hooper.

A.C. NIELSEN AND THE AUDIMETER

Hooper's victory was short-lived, however. During the Second World War, a new competitor with a mechanical device for measuring radio audiences had joined the fray. The earliest patent application for an audience meter was made in 1929 by Claude E. Robinson, a student at Columbia University, who was later so hard up for money that he sold his patent to RCA for a few hundred dollars. And for his dissertation at Ohio State, Frank Stanton had built and tested a number of devices for recording set operation. But the first meter capable of recording station tuning was developed in 1933–4 by Robert Elder, an assistant professor of engineering and business administration at the Massachusetts Institute of Technology, and his colleague, Louis F. Woodruff, an associate professor of electrical engineering. Their device, which Elder called an audimeter, used a stylus to draw a line indicating where a radio dial was tuned. After receiving permission from RCA, they tested it in the Boston area in 1935. They ran into difficulties partly because they could only finance the manufacture of 110 meters (at $100 each), an insufficient number for obtaining an acceptable degree of statistical accuracy. But the audimeter's potential was clear to Arthur C. Nielsen, who aproached Elder shortly after hearing him speak about it at a meeting of the Market Research Council in New York. The head of a successful market research business, Nielsen had the capital to develop the audimeter commercially. In the spring of 1936 the Nielsen Company acquired the rights to the device and launched a major research and development campaign. According to Nielsen, his company spent more than $9 million developing the audimeter.[31]

Born the son of a Danish immigrant in 1897, Nielsen graduated from the University of Wisconsin with the highest grades ever attained by any engineering student. In 1923 he formed a company to test the efficiency of industrial equipment and began to acquire a growing list of clients. After a major set-back during the early years of the depression, the company rebounded by developing a consumer survey and food index and quickly became one of the largest marketing research firms in the world. Following acquisition of the audimeter, Nielsen spent two years on preliminary research and another four years on a pilot project. It was not until 1942 that the first regular measurement of radio audiences began with a sample of 800 homes in the eastern and central states.[32] Within a few years, however, Nielsen was producing national ratings and challenging the Hooperatings.

Nielsen hoped to displace Hooper from the network radio ratings field by providing figures that had additional advantages for both broadcasters and advertisers. Like Hooper, he maintained that his measurement technique adhered to the principles of scientific sampling, and he produced in-house studies to prove that it was superior to any other available method. During the early years, however, the audimeter suffered from defects of timing and station calibration; it could not be used in non-electrified areas; and it could not measure listening on battery-operated radios, including those in automobiles. Even when these problems were overcome, meters still suffered from the fact that they measured tuning rather than listening per se.

By including households in small towns and rural areas, Nielsen's sample was more representative than that of Hooper. According to Meehan, however, this feature was no longer disadvantageous for advertisers, because 'as more categories of people became bona fide customers, advertisers sought media with greater coverage of the general population than ever before.'[33] At the same time, however, the advantage of broader sampling for advertisers was counterbalanced by the fact that the audimeter measured tuning rather than actual listening, thereby artificially inflating audience estimates in the networks' favour. In addition, both advertisers and broadcasters benefited from the meter's ability to provide a minute-by-minute account of tuning over a twenty-four-hour period. This capacity became increasingly important as advertisers moved from the sponsorship of complete programs to the use of spot commercials and as the networks took over control of their schedules.

By adopting a method of measurement that reflected the growth of consumerism and changes in broadcasting, Nielsen was able to acquire a solid footing in the ratings industry and move rapidly

Services provided or promised in connection with main US audience measurement methods, 1939

Measurement service	Crossley	Hooper	Nielsen
1. Average number of sets tuned in	No	Yes	Yes
2. Peak number of sets tuned in at any one time	No	No	Yes
3. Total number of sets tuned in at any time during period	Approx.	No	Yes
4. Extent to which people remember a program	Yes	No	No
5. Composition of audience	No	No	No
6. Number of people listening	No	No	No
7. Identification of sponsor	No	Yes	No
8. Sample covers all income groups	In cities	No	Yes
9. Sample includes rural population	No	No	Yes
10. Adequate sample for individual cities	No	No	?
11. Length of time program tuned in	No	No	Yes
12. Tuned to commercial	No	No	Yes
13. Increase or decrease of sets tuned in during program	No	No	Yes
14. Amount of switching	No	No	Yes
15. Covers all hours of day	Yes	No	Yes
16. Turnover of audience on individual programs	No	No	Yes
17. Checks sales effectiveness	No	No	Yes

Source: Adapted from L.D.W. Weld, 'Radio Checking Methods Are Here Evaluated and Analyzed,' *Printer's Ink,* 188 (18 August 1939), 15–17, 71–3.

towards dominance at the network level. The fact that the audimeter was able to produce ratings more quickly than did telephone surveys also contributed to Nielsen's rise. By 1945 Nielsen had acquired forty-seven subscribers, including the networks, and was steadily approaching the goal of projectable national ratings. Faced with this competition, Hooper began to combine data from telephone interviews and household diaries, but the results met with limited acceptance. By 1949, when the Nielsen Radio Index (NRI) had achieved 97 per cent coverage of American households, the writing was on the wall for Hooper's national radio ratings service. The final blow came when CBS decided to cancel the Hooperatings service and rely on the NRI. In March 1950 Hooper sold his national ratings service to Nielsen for several hundred thousand dollars and withdrew to the local ratings field. Ironically, this action proved to be a blessing in disguise for Hooper since television quickly transformed American radio from a national to a local market medium.

Nielsen's victory was prefigured in a comparison of the recall, coincidental, and electronic measurement methods carried out by McCann-Erickson's research director in 1939 (see the table). For, despite its higher cost, the audimeter promised to provide more useful and accurate data than were provided by either the recall or coincidental methods.

REITH'S HOSTILITY TO AUDIENCE RESEARCH

Because of its monopoly over broadcasting and secure funding through licence fees, the British Broadcasting Corporation had no economic incentive to engage in audience measurement. But its public service philosophy provided an alternative motivation for listener research, as it was called in Britain. At the time of the creation of the CBC, however, the BBC was just starting to take a few hesitant steps in this direction, owing in large measure to the scepticism of its first director-general, John Reith. At the outset, therefore, the BBC did not provide the CBC with a clear alternative to the American networks' reliance on independently produced ratings.

Reith had no objection to setting up a facility for answering audience mail and preparing summaries of correspondence for the various programming departments, especially since letters from listeners tended to be overwhelmingly supportive. For example, the BBC *Handbook* for 1929 reported that one set of letters consisted of 3,067 positive replies to only 108 negative ones. But Reith saw no need to take any further steps to determine whether audiences were satisfied with BBC programming. The same year as these consoling statistics were published, members of the Central Council for Broadcast Adult Education proposed that the BBC create a listening research post, and the idea attracted some support within the corporation. 'It must be a source of considerable disquiet to many people besides myself,' productions director Val Gielgud complained in 1930, 'to think that it is quite possible that a very great deal of our money and time and effort may be expended on broadcasting into a void.'[34] Gielgud was particularly critical of the practice of relying on audience mail for clues about reactions to programs. Letters from listeners, he suggested a few years later, were written for the most part by 'ego-maniacs, cranks, axe-grinders or the incorrigibly idle who can find nothing better to do.'[35] But despite the case against audience mail, the idea of listening research went nowhere. Reith identified it with the 'nose counting' undertaken for American commercial broadcasters and worried that it would end up dictating program policy.

Upon his appointment as head of public relations in 1935, Sir Stephen Tallents renewed the effort to organize a scheme of listener research. He was careful to distinguish between the study of listeners' preferences, which was thought to characterize American audience research, and the study of listeners' habits and tastes, which he wanted to be the focus of BBC audience research. The BBC, he argued, needed to know much more about its audience if it was to fulfil its listeners' many and varied needs. Still, his proposals met with a lukewarm response from the BBC's General Advisory Council, and Reith himself remained unconvinced of the need for audience research. In 1935 he apparently told King Edward VIII that 'water engineers could provide a pretty clear indication of the popularity of broadcast items. When there was anything specially interesting, water consumption fell; immediately afterward there was a sudden, sometimes alarming, peak load.'[36]

Reith's conviction that the public shared his ideas about suitable programming was belied by the popularity of foreign radio programs, which were received from France and Luxembourg through the operation of relay exchange companies and which were often sponsored by leading British advertisers. Despite attempts at suppression by the BBC, the Post Office, and even the Foreign Office, listening to these foreign commercial programs flourished during Reith's tenure from 1927 to 1938. A committee established by British advertising interests in 1938 found that on Sundays, when BBC programming was at its most elevated, listening to these programs was 'of the same order of magnitude as that to the stations of the corporation.'[37] Despite such evidence, Reith continued to believe that the masses 'would learn in time to enjoy what was good. To offer them what *they* wanted would have turned the BBC into a spiritual whore-house, himself into a cultural pimp.'[38]

THE BBC'S LISTENER RESEARCH DEPARTMENT

If anything was to be done to ascertain listeners' habits, Reith commented in January 1936, 'I do not think that it need be very much, and certainly nothing formal.'[39] As Mark Pegg has observed, he 'visualised the audience to be so infinitely divided and separated by taste, so capricious in instinct, so limited in artistic appreciation and so selfish that it would be impossible to learn anything more from a more objective survey.'[40] By then, however, this attitude was being questioned both within and outside the BBC. In 1936 the Programme Revision Committee pointed to the need for information about the social composition of the audience and its listening habits, tastes, and preferences. And though supportive of public broadcasting, W.A. Robson complained in *Public Enterprise* (1937) that the BBC had 'only the vaguest and most remote contact with the world of listeners. It does not really know who they are, to what they listen and what their views are.'[41]

Reluctantly, therefore, Reith gave Tallents permission to form a listener research committee and conduct some small-scale audience studies on an experimental basis. In March 1936, moreover, the BBC Control Board agreed to the appointment of a special BBC officer to deal with all research problems. The first person to occupy this post was C.V. Salmon, but the moving force within the small audience research group that began to develop was Robert Silvey, who had joined the BBC in mid-1936 after seven years at the London Press Exchange. On 1 October 1936 Silvey became the first head of the BBC's Listener Research Department, or Audience Research Department, as it was renamed in 1950 when it was expanded to include television. (It later became the Broadcasting Research Department.)

Until recently, the department conducted its own measurement of audiences, producing what was called a 'listening barometer' – so named because it showed the rise and fall in the size of audiences for programs. In its orginal form, some 500 persons were paid to conduct daily personal interviews with a group of over 2,000 listeners (and later viewers) using the telephone recall method, with different samples being interviewed each day. The main reason for this approach, according to a later account, was that 'at little extra cost the same procedure provides ratings' for both radio and television.[42]

In addition, the department also set up a 'listening thermometer' to assess reactions to programs. This consisted of panels of volunteers who recorded their 'likes' and 'dislikes' on cards over a period of several months. The results were presented in the form of an 'appreciation index.' Initially, there were separate panels of 500 members each for different categories of programming: music, features, talks and discussion, light entertainment, and daytime women's programs. But permanent regional panels were later instituted to study reactions to programming overall; there were eventually six panels consisting of 600 rotating members each.[43] During the early years, panelists awarded each program a mark out of ten, which was then multiplied by ten to give a score out of one hundred. After the war, this system was abandoned in favour of a five-point alphabetical scale (A+, A, B, C, and C–), with verbal explanations provided for each score. However, the results were still presented in terms of a hundred-point scale by awarding points to each position from four down to zero. This system was also applied to television, although the product was called a reaction index (RI) rather than an appreciation index (AI).[44]

There were two main problems with early BBC audience appreciation measurement. First, the measurement of 'likes' and 'dislikes' was extremely broad, covering only programs as a whole and one or two of their features. As a result, the BBC undertook special surveys for a more-intensive examination of audience reactions. In 1950, for example, it conducted a survey on the intelligibility and interest of a series of fifty Armed Forces Educational Broadcasts.[45] Second, members of the panels were recruited postally from people interviewed on the daily survey. Thus the door was opened to biases of all kinds, as volunteers tended to be more literate, up-scale, and appreciative of BBC programming. In addition, because of the low level of telephone ownership in Britain in the 1950s, the daily survey itself was not based on a representative sample.*

Despite these shortcomings, social historians Paddy Scannell and David Cardiff regard the creation of the Listener Research Department as a turning-point in the history of the BBC. In the first place, it settled program planning on a rational basis.

If much of the data seemed to confirm what common sense might have predicted, that does not undercut its importance. It enabled the structural framework of broadcasting – the arrangement of programme output through the days of the week, through the seasons of the year – to be arranged on a rational basis. Programme schedules could now be more confidently planned in rela-

---

* Since the early 1980s, audience appreciation measurement in Britain has been conducted under the auspices of the Broadcasters' Audience Research Board (BARB), which was established by the main broadcasting institutions in August 1980 to provide both quantitative and qualitative data. However, the fieldwork for BARB's Audience Reaction Measurement Service is actually carried out by the BBC's Broadcasting Research Department.[46]

tion to reliable information about who was available for listening, where and when.[47]

In addition, it provided 'criteria for arbitrating between the competing claims' for time and money of the various production departments.[48] Although its initial impact was limited, the commitment to audience research was, for Scannell and Cardiff, 'the clearest acknowledgment of the necessity of basing the activities of broadcasting on real knowledge and understanding of their audiences, not on what the broadcasters thought they might want or need.'[49]

If anything, there was an even greater need for such knowledge and understanding in Canada, with its numerous cultural and regional divisions. But the CBC lagged behind the BBC by almost two decades in terms of creating a separate audience research unit. In fairness, the CBC lacked the resources to produce both quantitative and qualitative audience research in the fashion of the BBC. But a modified approach might have been tried by the CBC at a much earlier date had there been a greater appreciation of the role of audience research in a public broadcasting organization.

4

Early Audience Measurement Services in Canada: Elliott-Haynes, ISL, and BBM

> No entirely satisfactory method of measuring audiences ... has yet been de-
> vised although years of work and millions of dollars have been expended in the
> effort.
>
> Canadian Facts report for CBC, 1948[1]

Neither Hooper nor Nielsen showed any interest in expanding their audience measurement services to Canada in the 1940s. Nielsen did respond to overtures from American branch plants by opening the A.C. Nielsen Company of Canada in 1944, but its activities were confined to traditional market research functions; it was simply too uneconomical to use the audimeter in Canada. It remained, therefore, for enterprising Canadians to produce marketable audience data for the far-flung Canadian broadcasting industry on a profitable basis – or, failing that, for the industry to undertake the task itself.

THE ELLIOTT-HAYNES RATINGS REPORTS

On the morning of 1 October 1936, one month before the CBC began operations, a young graduate from Loyola College by the name of Walter Elliott boarded a streetcar on the west side of Montreal and set off for the city's financial district in search of an office. After working for a short time as an insurance investigator and credit analyst, Elliott had decided to set up his own credit reporting company.[2] For working capital and additional expertise, he had approached his university friend Paul Haynes, who was currently involved in professional hockey but was interested in a career in market research when his playing and coaching days were over.[3] Together they had established

Elliott-Haynes Reg'd, capitalized at $500, with the understanding that Haynes would likely remain a non-operating partner for several years. Accompanied by seventeen-year-old George Kennedy, the company's first employee, Elliott leased an 8 by 10 cubicle on the mezzanine floor of the Transportation Building on St James Street for $15 a month in advance. He spent another $4 for a sign on the door, $5.10 for a second-hand desk and chair, and $7.50 for a month's telephone service. Weekly salaries came to $33 – $8 for Kennedy and the rest for himself.[4]

Though Canadian business was still suffering from the depression, the company grew steadily. It took in less than $200 during its first month, but by the end of the first year had billed for almost $5,000 in services. Buoyed by this success, it was formally incorporated as Elliott-Haynes Limited on 1 October 1937 and soon began to expand its operations into the area of market research. Among its early clients were Murray's Lunch, Canada Steamship Lines, and Pepsi-Cola. By 1959 it had exceeded a million dollars in annual billings and employed over 2,700 field workers across Canada. Although Haynes later left to form International Surveys Limited, the company continued to be called Elliott-Haynes until 1965, when it changed its name to Elliott Research.[5]

At the time of Elliott-Haynes's formation, there was only one private company in Canada engaged in audience measurement – Canadian Facts Limited. It had been set up in 1932 by Ethel Fulford, a senior staff operator for Bell Telephone, and was originally called Ethel Fulford and Associates. Fulford had been convinced of the need for reliable data on audiences for sponsored radio programs by Frank Ryan, who worked in the media research unit of the Cockfield Brown advertising agency. After learning about the coincidental telephone method developed by Hooper, she hired and trained interviewers to conduct coincidental surveys of the audiences for imported soap operas on behalf of sponsors like Proctor & Gamble and Lever Brothers.[6] However, Canadian Facts did not offer a comprehensive or continuing audience measurement service. The door was thus open for Elliott-Haynes to provide Canadian broadcasters with the kind of service offered by Hooper and the Cooperative Analysis of Broadcasting in the United States.

In 1939 Elliott-Haynes was given a contract by Pepsi-Cola to conduct a survey of soft-drink dealers in Montreal and Toronto. To assist with this, Elliott hired J. Myles Leckie from Canadian Facts and through him became aware of the development of radio research in the United States. In 1940 he travelled to New York, where he spent six weeks studying the coincidental telephone method under Hooper, and the same year set up an audience measurement service in Toronto under Leckie's supervision.[7] It began by producing monthly radio reports for Montreal (English and French), Toronto, Winnipeg, and Vancouver using a version of the telephone coincidental.

During the 1940s, Elliott-Haynes steadily augmented both its broadcasting and non-broadcasting operations. In 1941 it conducted the first national mail ballot survey of radio audiences in Canada on behalf of CBS, and the next year undertook a similar survey for the newly organized Bureau of Broadcast Measurement. In 1943 it set up an affiliated company to publish a composite of current radio program schedules called *Radiotime*, which was issued every two weeks and sold on a subscription basis to national advertisers, advertising agencies, and broadcasters. (A television equivalent called *Teletime* was started in 1954.) In 1944 it began semi-annual national surveys of attitudes towards Canadian business and industry using in-home personal interviews. During the 1950s, it continued to use the coincidental telephone method to produce radio program ratings and in 1952, after two years of experimental research, began issuing television ratings as well.[8] It also developed a sponsor identification index, which represented 'that percentage of the listeners or viewers to a given program who are able to correctly name the sponsor or the program and/or the product advertised.'[9]

The early E-H rating reports provided three types of information for each market surveyed: i) the number of sets in use on a daily basis (together with a weekly average) for each thirty-minute daytime period (from 9:00 a.m. to 6:00 p.m.) and each fifteen-minute evening period (from 6:00 to 10:30 p.m.); ii) program ratings (the percentage of total households listening) for each thirty-minute period; and iii) station shares (the percentage of sets in use tuned to each station) for each thirty-minute period. The surveys were conducted during two weeks of each month, one week being used for the daytime periods and the other for evenings. A certain number of calls were made in each market for each time period. The results were supplemented by periodic surveys of the early-morning (7:30 to 9:00 a.m.) and late-evening (10:30 p.m. to midnight) periods using the recall method. In addition, a national ratings report for both daytime and evening commercial programs was produced by combining data from individual markets across Canada.[10]

In principle, telephone surveys are well suited to random sampling; that is, to gathering a sample in such a way as to ensure that every member of the population to be measured has an equal chance of being selected. But in practice, they suffered from certain basic weaknesses when applied to the Canadian situation in the 1940s. The reliability of such surveys is closely related to both the level and distribution of telephone ownership, each of which was quite different then than it is today. When most households have a telephone, it does not matter a great deal whether listening habits (or socio-economic levels) are the same in telephone and non-telephone homes. But this consideration becomes important when a substantial proportion of homes are without telephones, especially if the level of ownership also varies by region or place of residence.

During the first two decades of radio broadcasting in Canada, the number of telephones per 100 population grew quite slowly, increasing from 10.4 in 1921 to only 13.5 in 1941, the year after Elliott-Haynes began its radio-listening surveys. In fact, during the depression the number had actually decreased. It was not until the postwar period that telephone ownership began to grow rapidly, increasing from 16.3 per 100 population in 1946 to 69.6 in 1981.[11] Moreover, while a surge in household leasing of phones occurred between 1941 and 1947, there remained several important disparities in the distribution of telephone ownership.

One disparity was between urban and rural Canada. In the mid-1940s nearly 50 per cent of Canadian households were still on farms or in small towns and villages of under 10,000 population. And the level of telephone ownership was substantially lower in rural areas than urban. This meant that to survey rural areas about radio listening, the same telephone numbers often had to be called repeatedly. Because these numbers were used for other kinds of surveys as well, there was a tendency for rural-dwellers to become annoyed and uncooperative. In addition, it was more economical to conduct telephone surveys in large urban centres. As a result, there was a tendency for companies like Elliott-Haynes to ignore rural Canada.

TABLE 1
Percentage of households with telephones

	1941	1947	1960
Maritime Provinces	30	35	
Newfoundland			34
Prince Edward Island			57
Nova Scotia			72
New Brunswick			71
Quebec	33	44	84
Ontario	52	62	91
Prairie Provinces	31	38	
Manitoba			83
Saskatchewan			76
Alberta			74
British Columbia	48	55	84
Canada	40	50	83

Sources: Robert Pike and Vincent Mosco, 'Canadian Consumers and Telephone Pricing: From Luxury to Necessity and Back Again?' *Telecommunications Policy,* March 1986, 21; Dominion Bureau of Statistics, *Annual Survey of Household Facilities and Equipment, May 1960* (Queen's Printer 1961), Table 25.

Within urban areas, there was a further disparity between home-owners and renters. As a report prepared in 1952 pointed out:

It has been suggested by D.B.S. that in Canadian cities of 30,000 or greater, over one-third of the dwellings possessing radios have no telephone. In a study of the relationship between home tenure and telephone subscription, it was found that 37 percent of the renters as compared with 73 percent of the home owners were telephone subscribers. Since stability of residence is much greater among people who own their own homes than among families who rent, the sample of telephone subscribers would be biased in favour of the more stable groups in the population.[12]

A third disparity was between regions within Canada. This was particularly marked during the 1940s and remained a factor into the 1950s, as illustrated in Table 1. To the extent that radio listening differed between telephone and non-telephone households, this meant that listening patterns were less likely to be fairly represented in some regions than in others.

Although these disparities tended to diminish as telephone owner-

TABLE 2
Telephones in Canada, 1950

Total households	3,600,000
Residential telephones	2,015,521 (56%)
Single party lines	464,270 (23%)
Local 2-party	970,607
Local 4-party	49,227
Private branch	127,665
Rural (5-party or more)	403,752
Business telephones	901,659
Total telephones	2,917,090

Source: H.F. Chevrier, 'Telephones in Canada 1950'
(February 1952) [DMC Files].

ship increased overall, the form which this increase took in the early postwar period created another problem for telephone surveys. While the number of households with individual telephones increased steadily, an even greater number of households acquired a telephone on a party line. The situation in Canada in 1950 is set forth in Table 2. In Toronto 70 per cent of telephone households were on party lines in 1951. This figure was higher than in Winnipeg (50 per cent), but lower than in Montreal (73 per cent) or Vancouver (95 per cent).[13] The problem from the standpoint of telephone surveys was that party lines increased the number of busy signals. According to some investigations, as many as one-third of the calls made fell into this category.[14] Following the lead of C.E. Hooper, Elliott-Haynes treated 'busys' (and also refusals) as if the listening habits in these households were identical with those of respondents; they did not attempt to reach busy households through call-backs.* This practice served to maintain the effective sample size, but produced a potential bias because the demographic make-up of households on party lines was different than that of households with individual telephones. As one survey research expert pointed out, '"busy signals" provide a bias that may be quite

* Hooper found that calls were divided as follows: disconnects, 10 per cent; no answer, 30 per cent; busys and refusals, 10 per cent; declared not listening, 20 per cent; and declared listening, 30 per cent. He dropped the disconnects from his sample, but the busys and refusals were assumed to be listening in the same proportion as declared listeners. C.E. Hooper, 'How Program Ratings Are Computed' (unpublished report, c. 1952) [DMC Files].

serious ... due to the fact that party lines are more prevalent among certain economic groups than others. The probability of getting a busy signal is obviously greater when several parties share the same line than when only one party is on a single line.'[15]

INTERNATIONAL SURVEYS AND THE PANEL-DIARY TECHNIQUE

From the standpoint of advertisers, the principal weakness of the coincidental telephone method was that it provided no practical way of linking media exposure to consumer behaviour. What was required was a method by which data could be gathered on both radio usage and the purchase of retail commodities. It was necessary to know, among other things, the date, price, brand, type, size, and retail outlet of each item purchased. And it was simply not feasible to expand telephone interviews to the degree required to gather this kind of detailed information.

Part of the solution to this problem was provided by the American market researcher Samuel G. Barton, who organized a fixed household panel in which participants recorded their buying behaviour in diaries. The panel was operated by Industrial Surveys, set up by Barton in 1938, and later renamed the Market Research Corporation of America. Barton was not alone in using panels comprising a representative sample of households. Panels were also used by Nielsen, Pulse, and the BBC. But in each case the panel was combined with a different technique for gathering information. Nielsen combined it with the audimeter, Pulse with in-home interviews, and the BBC with telephone interviews. Although Barton's panel was only used to gather data on consumer purchases, it could in principle accommodate the collection of information about media exposure as well. It made it possible, therefore, to measure the impact of different commercial messages on purchasing behaviour.

The potential of Barton's panel-diary technique was recognized in Canada by Paul Haynes, who resigned from Elliott-Haynes in 1945 and set up a market research firm of his own called International Surveys Limited (ISL). For the first few years, Haynes worked in association with Barton and two of his partners, each of whom owned one-third of ISL. But from the outset, Haynes operated the firm, and later he ended up as the sole owner.[16] By linking up with Barton, he was able to use his copyrighted procedure to organize a Consumer Panel of Canada. Intended to gather information about buying habits for manufacturers and distributors, it consisted of 2,000 households of various types and stratified by region, community size, education, and economic standing. As an incentive to participate, panelists were given points each month for keeping a diary and returning it on time. A quarterly bonus could also be earned by mailing diaries on time for three consecutive months. The points were redeemable for merchandise, such as a set of china or a magazine subscription.[17]

In 1948 Haynes created the Radio Panel of Canada using the same sample and similar incentives. He claimed that the panel-diary technique was the only one that could measure actual listening. 'In multiple radio homes the diary follows the principal listening from room to room throughout the day (morning and afternoon in the kitchen; evening in the living room; at night in the bedroom).'[18] Although ISL did not initially estimate audiences for individual stations, it claimed that its ratings were projectable; that is, they could be applied to different regions and city-sizes. With the advent of television, however, advertisers wanted more accurate estimates of audiences in Montreal and Toronto, which contained about one-fourth of Canadian households. At the end of 1952, therefore, ISL set up separate radio and television panels for the Montreal and Toronto areas (and not long afterwards for the Vancouver-Victoria area) to measure the total audience as well as the audience share for each station.

During the 1940s, CBS experimented with diaries and Hooper added diaries to his sample in areas that could not be reached by telephone. But the main proponent of diary-based measurement in the United States was a company known as the American Research Bureau (ARB). In 1949, a year after Haynes's radio panel commenced, ARB began using diaries to produce local market reports for television. Founded by James Seiler, who had left NBC after a half-hearted response to his proposal to use diaries to measure radio, ARB later became the prime contender to Nielsen in the local television audience field, especially after 1955 when it took over Hooper's television ratings service. In the 1970s ARB took control of the local radio ratings business as well.[19] In contrast, ISL's reports were not of much use to local broadcasters and advertisers because of their limited information at the station level. They were subscribed to mainly by national advertisers and the CBC, both of whom were interested in their demographic data, albeit for quite different reasons. The CBC wanted audience breakdowns for various programs, not in order to place commercial messages with greater

effectiveness, but rather to know how well it was serving different segments of the Canadian population.

The panel-diary method made it possible to obtain a more representative sample than by the coincidental telephone method since it
was not restricted to urban areas served by toll-free telephone coverage. But because of the burden of keeping a diary, cooperation was
greatest among those with higher education and socio-economic status. As a CBC research report explained, the diary requires 'a definite
set of characteristics among its respondents. One member of the family must be willing to keep a diary and must be able to read, write and
have ... a sense of responsibility for detail.'[20] For its monthly city
reports, ISL designed its sample to yield 500 participating households
in each area, selecting city blocks at random and taking a uniform proportion of homes in each. It found that it had to contact between four
and five thousand households to obtain 500 participants since only 10–
13 per cent of those contacted by mail agreed to take part.

Members of the panel were expected to keep a diary of listening for
each fifteen-minute period of the day from 6:00 a.m. to 12:00 midnight
for the first full week of each month. New members were added to the
panel only after a three-month training period during which their diaries were scrutinized to ensure that the reporting was being done correctly. While any member of the family who listened to the radio was
supposed to record the program and station at the termination of the
broadcast, overall responsibility for taking care of the diary was placed
with one person, usually the female head. In addition to a bias towards
those with more education and higher socio-economic status, therefore, the panel-diary method had a bias towards female listening,
which was also a bias towards the commodity audience. Two current
studies did conclude, however, that the advent of a diary in the home
does not significantly alter listening habits.[21]

FORMATION OF THE BUREAU OF BROADCAST MEASUREMENT

The ratings produced by Elliott-Haynes and ISL were of little use to
most of the smaller radio stations in Canada in this period. Few of
these stations were covered in their reports, and many had no need of
rating or share data since they were the only station in town. What they
needed, in order to compete with the print media for advertising, were
reliable circulation figures. In the United States, the CBS research

department developed a method of measuring station coverage through a questionnaire distributed by mail to a cross-section of the population in each county. The returned ballots gave a listening picture of the entire family unit. CBS also hired Elliott-Haynes to conduct a mail ballot survey to determine the coverage for three of its affiliates – WGR Buffalo, WJR Detroit, and CFRB Toronto – and the value of this kind of survey was quickly recognized by Canadian advertisers and broadcasters.[22]

At the annual meeting of the Canadian Association of Broadcasters (CAB) in 1942, a committee was created jointly with the Association of Canadian Advertisers (ACA) and the Canadian Association of Advertising Agencies (CAAA) to determine the best way of measuring radio coverage.[23] The joint committee was chaired by Jack Kent Cooke, who was working at the time for Roy Thomson's Northern Broadcasting & Publishing Co. and was in the process of purchasing CKEY Toronto. The other members of the committee were Ray Barford (J.J. Gibbons Limited), Henry Gooderham (CKCL), Adrien Head (J. Walter Thompson), Tom McReynolds (Young & Rubicam), L.L. Phenner (Canadian Cellucotton Products), Harry Rimmer (Canadian General Electric), and Arthur Evans (CAB secretary). After investigating and testing various systems for two years, they presented their recommendations at the annual meeting of the CAB in Quebec City on 14 February 1944.

The committee rejected both the mail response and contour methods of estimating station circulation. By way of illustrating the defects of the latter, it noted that

the 1/2 MV/M contour of WTAM Cleveland includes the city of Detroit, yet in a city of Detroit's size a 1/2 MV/M contour would be of practically no value whatsoever. The noise level would simply drown out the signal. Yet on consulting a contour map, the uninitiated, the individual who relies entirely on this type of map would believe that WTAM Cleveland is serving Detroit with a primary signal. Of course, nothing could be further from the truth.[24]

In place of these methods, it favoured the use of a controlled mail ballot survey similar to the one developed by CBS. It also recommended that a cooperative, non-profit organization similar to the Audit Bureau of Circulations be established to conduct the surveys. The Bureau of Broadcast Measurement (BBM) was set up on 11 May 1944 and granted a government charter a year later. A set of rules and regulations was established 'to benefit the industry as a whole by maintaining a high ethical level among its subscribers and by eliminating the confusion which has arisen in the past from conflicting and occasionally unsubstantiated claims for station audiences.' Ironically, Cooke and CKEY decided against joining the organization, which began with no paid staff, though the ACA provided administrative assistance. Advertisers, advertising agencies, and station representatives paid $25 a year, while the fee for radio stations was set initially at two-thirds of their peak half-hour rate per month. Under this arrangement, BBM was financed largely by broadcasters; over the next fifteen years, about 90 per cent of the financial support for BBM came from radio and television stations. At the same time, however, it was controlled by advertising interests. Of the nine positions on the original board of directors, three were filled by advertisers, three by advertising agencies, and only three by broadcasters.

The original, limited purpose of BBM was to measure the size and location of radio station 'audiences' in the way that the Audit Bureau of Circulations estimated the number of readers for publications. Even from this perspective, the term 'audience' is relative, since it may or may not be taken to include occasional listeners, which may in turn be variously defined. For the first BBM survey, which was conducted by Elliott-Haynes and released in October 1944, ballots were mailed to a cross-section of households in 220 counties or census subdivisions asking them to list the call letters of all stations to which they listened at least once a week during the daytime and evening periods.

BBM used the 'unaided' rather than the 'aided' ballot technique; that is, respondents had to compile their own list of stations listened to, instead of checking stations from a prepared list. The aided ballot technique tended to produce higher coverage figures, but according to the BBM's research director, John K. Churchill, it was 'not more truthful' because it led respondents accordingly. As he pointed out, 'this has been shown in tests where fictitious stations have been carried on the check list and they nonetheless received quite a sizeable listening audience.'[25] As an incentive to complete the ballot, participants were sent a packet of safety pins. The ballots were coded to each name on the mailing list to permit a mail follow-up on delinquent respondents. According to Walter Elliott, it cost 25 cents to send out one ballot and 40 cents for each one returned; although this was more expensive than conducting personal interviews in urban areas, it was the most economical method in rural areas.[26]

Shortly after the creation of BBM, a similar organization called the Broadcast Measurement Bureau (BMB) was established in the United States.[27] As a result of the efforts of Horace Stovin, chairman of BBM's technical committee, the two organizations worked in concert for a few years, using the same mail ballot technique and running their surveys simultaneously. This enabled advertisers to operate on either side of the border with equal facility.[28] However, the BMB did not last very long. It was harassed by criticism of its methods, plagued by high costs, challenged by privately owned measurement services, and thrown into disarray by the resignation of its president, Hugh M. Feltis. In 1950 it threw in the towel and left the station coverage field to Nielsen.[29] Nielsen used what was called the interview-aided recall method; during personal interviews, participants were shown a list of stations normally heard in their area and asked to identify the stations listened to within a specified time period. This method was also used in Canada by Elliott-Haynes.

In the spring of 1945 Lew Phenner, who served as BBM president and chairman of the board in 1944–51, wrote to CAB president Glen Bannerman that 'the future prospect' of BBM was 'most disturbing' and that BBM was 'not adequately financed to deliver what its members ... expect of it.'[30] Of the CAB's sixty-eight members, only thirty-six belonged to BBM; altogether BBM had only fifty station members. Bannerman suggested that more stations might be willing to join BBM if its surveys were organized on the basis of urban areas rather than county or census divisions.[31] During the next year, the number of station members rose to sixty-one and it was decided that 'a consistent campaign should be started with the objective of securing 100% membership of all Canadian stations.' BBM's finance committee also decided to approach the leading radio advertising agencies and stress the necessity 'of their insisting upon the use of BBM information when buying time.'[32] By the end of the 1940s, BBM had 114 broadcasting members – 80 per cent of the industry – including the CBC.

Little mention is made of the CBC in accounts of the origins of BBM, but without its cooperation, it would have had a difficult time maintaining its surveys. In the early 1950s about a quarter of BBM's annual income of $60,000 came from the CBC. The CBC also provided considerable technical assistance through the statistics branch of its commercial department. This helped BBM to increase the number of areas surveyed, introduce bilingual ballots in some areas, distinguish between daytime and evening coverage, and provide each station with its own individual report and map.[33]

Despite these improvements, BBM's surveys did not meet the needs of the CBC very well. In the first place, they were limited to station coverage. As the 1944 survey report pointed out, its figures were 'not to be interpreted as reporting the actual number of radio homes reached by an individual *program* on this station, or the probable coverage of a proposed program, but rather the average potential or maximum audience obtainable by a station within a given area.' Moreover, there was a long delay between the collection and publication of BBM data. For example, the report for the second BBM survey in March 1946 was not available until June 1947, which meant that it could not be used in the promotion of the CBC's commercial business.[34] In addition, the surveys were not conducted with a great deal of rigour. In a memo explaining why the 1950 BBM survey results were not ready yet, H.F. Chevrier of the CBC's commercial department recounted that 'throughout the operation of the tabulation and computation of survey data, there has been a lack of proper organization, improper supervision and most serious of all the failure to carry out checks on all work undertaken.' Indeed, although the CBC had provided 'all possible assistance,' most of its instructions 'were never followed to the letter' and much of the work 'had to be done over again.'[35]

THE BBM RATINGS STUDY OF 1952

In 1950 the Canadian Association of Broadcasters asked BBM to conduct a study of the coincidental services and suggest a way of finding something better. BBM set up a research and development committee, chaired by C.W. McQuillan of Cockfield, Brown, which submitted a report to the annual meeting of the CAB in 1952. The report included discussion of ISL's panel-diary method and the Nielsen audimeter as well as the coincidental telephone method which was used in Canada by both Elliott-Haynes and another less-well-known company formed by J.D. Penn McLeod in 1947. The same year as BBM's report, the Advertising Research Foundation in the United States created a ratings review committee under the chairmanship of E.L. Deckinger, vice-president and director of research of the Biow Company. It was specifically concerned with the lack of uniformity in audience measurement and drew up a set of standards for the ratings industry to follow. However, the BBM committee did not go nearly so far; while it did suggest that standards should be laid down for telephone surveys and that auditors should be appointed to see that they were met, it failed to produce any standards of its own.

On the basis of a questionnaire circulated to all Canadian users of ratings, BBM's research and development committee found that none of the Canadian services, or even any combination of them, satisfied the various needs of broadcasters and advertisers for audience data. For example, Elliott-Haynes left out of consideration a large part of the coverage of most stations, while ISL provided no measurements of listening to programs on individual stations. It also questioned practices such as the presentation of ratings to the decimal point (which encouraged broadcasters to treat ratings as if they were exact numbers, rather than estimates); the accumulation of samples for particular programs; using the same sample size for all cities regardless of the number of stations; and the assignment of entire columns or pages of the local telephone book to individual interviewers.

In the BBM committee's view, there had been 'very little change or refinement in measurement surveys' and hardly any 'planned internal research.' Still, it refrained from criticizing any of the services excessively. 'It must be stated emphatically,' it said, 'that no part of this report is to be interpreted as a criticism of any business organization, its integrity or manner of operation.'[36] It also refused to endorse any one method as the best. The CBC's Austin Weir speculated that 'possibly there was good reason for this inasmuch as it was probably afraid of possible legal reprisals.'[37] But it was difficult if not impossible to determine which service produced the most accurate estimates. This determination could not even be made in the case of Elliott-Haynes and Penn McLeod. Although both conducted telephone coincidentals, they used different samples, carried out their surveys at different times, asked respondents different questions, measured different time segments, and presented their data in different forms.

Later in 1952, BBM hired Professors A.H. Shephard and K.S. Bernhardt to examine the 'co-recall' method which Gruneau Research had developed for measuring radio and television audiences. On the basis of their report, BBM's research and development committee concluded that, although the method held some promise, 'much more development and testing would have have to be done before it would be possible to arrive at a set of known standards, and before any positive action could be taken.'[38]

THE POVERTY OF EARLY RATINGS DATA

BBM's research and development committee did not question the utility of ratings data. From its standpoint, the problem with audience measurement was that it had not yet become sufficiently scientific. It had no doubts about its potential usefulness, basically because it considered this from the perspective of the advertising industry. But for program producers and planners, the value of ratings was less obvious. Leaving aside the methodological problems associated with the various measurement techniques, early ratings data were often too fragmentary to be of much help to programmers. This shortcoming was especially noticeable in the case of the CBC, given the special nature of its programming, but it affected the private broadcasters as well.

For confirmation of this point, one need only dust off a few of the old Elliott-Haynes reports currently stored in the National Archives of Canada. Then imagine consulting them with an eye to improving a particular CBC radio program – say 'CBC Wednesday Night,' which went on the air in December 1947. This was not a typical CBC program at the time in that it consisted of an entire evening of drama, music, talks, and readings. But it was a program for which audience feedback was especially important. The producers of this daring and innovative program received many letters of encouragement for their efforts. But while not as esoteric as the BBC's Third Programme, 'CBC Wednesday Night' was also criticized in some quarters as being too elevated for most Canadians. Because it used up a substantial portion of the program budget, it was essential for the CBC to know whether this was a valid complaint and what might be done about it.

After a five-minute introduction at 7:25 p.m., 'CBC Wednesday Night' usually began with a half-hour segment which set the stage for the main feature of the evening at 8:00 p.m. At 10:00 there would be a break for the 'National News Bulletin' and 'CBC News Roundup,' after which there was a closing segment devoted to a 'distinguished artist.' The program did not, however, adhere to a rigid format. As Harry Boyle, the program director for the Trans-Canada network, explained on its first anniversary, 'it was decided that the taboo of definite time periods, often regarded as a tyranny because it required the compression of programs which by their very nature should have been allowed more scope, would be abolished on this one evening of the week.'[39]

The richness, diversity, and artistic quality of 'CBC Wednesday Night' are clear even from a brief synopsis of some of the programs which were broadcast. For example, during the first three months of 1949, listeners were treated to the following:

'CBC WEDNESDAY NIGHT' (JANUARY–MARCH 1949)

January 5 – English folk ballads; two-hour performance of Shakespeare's *Twelfth Night* adapted by Lister Sinclair; pianist Aline van Barentzen

January 12 – music by Canadian composer Barbara Pentland; Griller String Quartet; first of three talks on the English language by W.H. Brodie, CBC supervisor of broadcast language; Rupert Caplan's production of J.M. Synge's comedy *The Well of the Saints*

January 19 – Roth String Quartet; second talk by W.H. Brodie; adaptation of Henry Kreisel's Canadian novel *The Rich Man*; recitals by Hungarian, Australian, and Canadian artists

January 26 – McGill String Quartet; final talk by W.H. Brodie; recording of the BBC's production of *British Agent* starring Eric Portman; Handel and Britten music

February 2 – 'A Day in the Life of Dr. Samuel Johnson,' a two-and-a-half hour re-creation of a day in the golden age of English letters written by Lister Sinclair and produced by Esse Ljungh; violinist Eugene Kash

February 9 – James Joyce's short story 'A Painful Case' read by Frank Peddie; two-hour performance of *La Traviata* by the CBC Opera Company; pianist Jan Cherniavsky

February 16 – Walter Kaufmann concert; two recordings of BBC programs on British society and music; Lloyd Roberts's vignette 'Winter' produced by J. Frank Willis; feature on Sir John Boyd Orr, the first director-general of the Food and Agriculture Organization of the United Nations

February 23 – songs of the Gay Nineties; talk on American theatre around 1900; production by J. Frank Willis of the classic melodrama *East Lynne*; violinist Donna Grescoe

March 2 – ballet music; talk on ballet; Canadian Ballet Festival; poetry of A.M. Klein; pianist Gordon Manley

March 9 – talk on human rights by Eleanor Roosevelt; Arthur Benjamin's one-act opera *The Devil Take Her*; adaptation by Tommy Tweed of one of Stephen Leacock's anecdotes in *Sunshine Sketches of a Little Town*; violist William Primrose

March 16 – talk by Canadian historian Arthur Lower; Irish songs and verse; Sean O'Casey's *Juno and the Paycock* produced by Esse Ljungh; soprano Carmen Torres

March 23 – music of the eighteenth century; two-hour production of Shakespeare's *Julius Caesar*; piano recital

March 30 – Maxim's Gorki's story 'The Affair of the Clasps' read by Larry McCance; BBC symphony orchestra; talk by historian Arnold Toynbee; Tolstoy's *The Power of Darkness* adapted by Len Peterson and produced by J. Frank Willis; songs of Russia

TABLE 3
E-H data for 'CBC Wednesday Night' on CBL Toronto, January–March 1949

	Program rating		Audience share	
	8:00 p.m.	9:00 p.m.	8:00 p.m.	9:00 p.m.
January 5	4.0	3.0	9.5	6.4
January 12	–	–	–	–
January 19	–	–	–	–
January 26	–	–	–	–
February 2	2.9	1.8	7.3	3.9
February 9	–	–	–	–
February 16	–	–	–	–
February 23	–	–	–	–
March 2	5.1	5.4	11.6	11.5
March 9	–	–	–	–
March 16	–	–	–	–
March 23	–	–	–	–
March 30	–	–	–	–

In this situation, audience research might have been expected to provide programmers with information about who was listening to the program, what they thought of it overall, and which aspects were most or least appreciated. Lacking its own research department, the CBC did not have any such information. What it had were ratings produced by Elliott-Haynes. While it would be incorrect to say that these were of no help whatsoever, their value was quite limited.

As already noted, Elliott-Haynes's surveys were only conducted once a month, even for cities like Montreal and Toronto. For the three months of 'CBC Wednesday Night' outlined above, the Elliott-Haynes reports provided the data compiled (by myself) in Table 3. The gaps indicated in this table would not matter a great deal in the case of programs where the content was reasonably consistent from one week to the next. However, in the case of 'CBC Wednesday Night,' there was considerable variation from one week to the next. While there are ratings and shares for things like *Twelfth Night*, 'A Day in the Life of Dr. Samuel Johnson,' and the Canadian Ballet Festival, there are no data to indicate the size of audiences for Synge's comedy *The Well of the Saints*, the BBC drama *British Agent*, the opera *La Traviata*, the turn-of-the-century American theatre program, the talks by Eleanor Roosevelt, Arthur Lower, and Arnold Toynbee, or indeed any of the three talks by W.H. Brodie. In addition, the Elliott-Haynes reports usu-

TABLE 4
E-H program ratings and audience shares for Toronto, 8:00–10:00 p.m., 5 January 1949

Time	CBL	CFRB	CJBC	CKEY	WBEN
8:00	Wednesday Night	Mr. Chamberlain	Blondie	Mickey Lester	Blondie
Rating	4.0	15.8	4.1	8.9	2.6
Share*	9.5	39.5	10.2	22.5	6.5
8:30	Wednesday Night	Take a Chance	Opportunity Knocks	Mickey Lester	The Great Gildersleeve
Rating	(4.0)	21.0	7.0	5.5	6.4
Share	(9.5)	47.7	15.9	12.4	14.4
9:00	Wednesday Night	Mr. & Mrs. North	Mildred Morley	Music & Talks	Duffy's Tavern
Rating	3.0	15.8	9.7	4.0	10.2
Share	6.4	33.5	20.5	8.7	21.6
9:30	Wednesday Night	John Fisher & TBA	Curtain Time	Scotland Yard	Mr. District Attorney
Rating	(3.0)	9.3	11.6	7.0	11.3
Share	(6.4)	20.5	25.6	15.4	25.1

*Shares do not total 100 per cent because of listening to other stations as well.

ally gave data only for the 8:00–8:30 p.m. and 9:00–9:30 p.m. time slots, which made it difficult to assess longer program segments and left the first and last half-hours of the program unreported.

To see how 'CBC Wednesday Night' was doing in comparison with competing programs, it would have been necessary to construct a chart such as that set forth in Table 4 (for Toronto) and then maintain it over an extended time period. The same would have to be done for other cities as well, where the results were often quite different. In Ottawa, where the CBC station CBO competed with CFRA and CKCO, 'CBC Wednesday Night' got a 33.7 share on the same date. But in Halifax, where CBH's main competitors were CHNS and CJCH, its share was only 13.8 according to Elliott-Haynes. Even if all of the data supplied by Elliott-Haynes for 'CBC Wednesday Night' were reorganized in this manner, however, it would still be impossible to estimate the total audience for the program on any given evening.

The producers of 'CBC Wednesday Night' might conceivably have

TABLE 5

Program ratings and audience shares for 'CBC Wednesday Night' on CBL Toronto, January 1949 to June 1950

	Program rating		Audience share	
	8:00 p.m	9:00 p.m.	8:00 p.m.	9:00 p.m.
1949				
January	4.0	3.0	9.5	6.4
February	2.9	1.8	7.3	3.9
March	5.1	5.4	11.6	11.5
April	3.8	5.9	8.7	12.7
May	2.7	3.9	7.1	9.1
June	3.6	4.5*	11.6	11.2*
July	1.4	1.4*	5.9	5.8*
August	2.6	1.3	12.6	5.9
September	2.6	3.3	8.8	10.9
October	2.3	2.9	7.1	8.4
November	4.2†	2.3	11.4†	5.8
December	2.3	4.2	5.6	9.2
1950				
January	3.9	6.1	9.4	13.3
February	2.6	3.8	6.1	8.1
March	2.0	4.9	4.9	10.4
April	3.9	5.1	9.1	10.8
May	2.4	3.7	6.4	8.3
June	3.0	3.7	9.3	10.2

*Given for 9:30–10:00 p.m.
†Given for 8:30–9:00 p.m.

benefited from plotting audience-size data in particular cities over an extended period of time (Table 5). When set forth in this manner, however, it is difficult to imagine how such data could assist the production of the program. Despite considerable variety in its cultural offerings, 'CBC Wednesday Night' seems to have consistently achieved ratings in the 2–6 range. To improve its ratings beyond this, it would clearly have had to become a different kind of program. This does not mean, however, that it could not have improved its performance for the kind of audience it was attracting. It only means that the data in question provided little if any indication of how to do so.

5

The E-H Ratings and the Missing CBC Audience: Origins of the Bureau of Audience Research

The CBC is the only national broadcasting authority of which we have any personal knowledge that has not established a reasonably qualified Research Department.

Austin Weir, 1 November 1952[1]

When the CBC began operations on 2 November 1936, no thought was given to the creation of an audience research department. Section 8(q) of the new Canadian Broadcasting Act stated that the CBC could, for the purpose of carrying on a national broadcasting service, 'do all such ... things as the Corporation may deem incidental or conducive to the attainment of any of the objects or the exercise of any of the powers of the Corporation.' Although this mandate would presumably have justified engaging in audience research, no steps were taken in this direction. This is not surprising since even programming had to take a back seat initially to the development of a national network. Yet even after the completion of several high-power stations and the rapid expansion of programming,* very little was done to learn more about audience needs and desires.

---

* During its first year, the CBC spent less than a million dollars on programming, compared to nearly three million dollars per year by the end of the Second World War. As capital expenditures decreased and more resources became available for production, the programming output increased rapidly. For the first year or so, the CBC was on the air for only eight or nine hours daily; by the outbreak of the war, it was broadcasting to a widely scattered population in English and French for over nineteen hours a day and producing 7,000 hours of programming a year.

THE LOW PRIORITY OF AUDIENCE RESEARCH WITHIN THE CBC

The CBC was certainly not as negligent in this regard as its ill-fated predecessor, the Canadian Radio Broadcasting Commission. The CBC's commercial department, which was set up in 1940 under the supervision of Austin Weir, purchased the Elliott-Haynes reports and later those of ISL and BBM. It also made periodic assessments of audience mail, which totalled 14,000 pieces annually by the mid-1940s. And the press and information service, which was organized in 1938 and also managed by Weir for a brief span, spent part of its time gathering statistics on things like sales of radio sets. In addition, the CBC arranged for a few special surveys.

Yet even though its staff increased from twenty-six in 1939 to forty-five in 1948, the commercial department lacked the resources as well as the expertise to analyse ratings data from a programming perspective and was certainly in no position to engage in the kind of program testing being undertaken by CBS. Letters from listeners (and telephone calls) made up a self-selected sample and thus could not be regarded as representative of the audience as a whole. Statistics on equipment purchases revealed nothing about reactions to programming. And the occasional polls tended to be exercises in self-promotion; one conducted by Opinion Surveys in central Canada in 1940 concluded, for example, that 'the C.B.C. is giving people more of what they desire than are independent or American stations.'[2]

It might be thought that the CBC simply did not have the resources in this period for even a small audience research unit. In 1948 management asked E.C. Stewart in the engineering department to assess the value of the existing ratings data. Stewart concluded that there was 'an apparent lack of confidence' in the available services, that 'there seems to be no certainty that the information is adequate, and in fact there seems to be some doubt whether it is of sufficient value to warrant the expenditure involved.' But he still concluded that the CBC's 'requirements for audience data can be met most economically by an outside organization.'[3] He estimated that a research department would cost $25,000 a year for salaries alone, at a time when the CBC's yearly expenditures came to about $6.5 million.[4]

The Massey commission concurred with this assessment a few years later when it observed that 'the limited financial resources of the C.B.C. do not permit systematic listener research on an adequate scale.'[5] But by this time, the budget for the press and information department was close to $200,000 a year. It was, therefore, a question of priorities rather than finances. Certainly, it could be argued that finding out what the public thinks about the CBC is no less important than telling the public what the CBC is doing. Audience research that seeks to give the public a say in programming is actually the most important form of public relations.

THE MIXED BLESSING OF ELLIOTT-HAYNES FOR THE CBC

The E-H reports provided the CBC with its first regular data on the size of radio audiences. In principle, they constituted one mechanism by which to assess the popularity of its programming. But the early data supplied by Elliott-Haynes were of dubious value for the CBC. In addition to their fragmentary nature, discussed in the previous chapter, they suffered from two basic shortcomings as a guide to audience behaviour. In the first place, the E-H reports left large sections of the country uncovered. Although thirty-six cities were included by the end of the 1940s (and another ten a decade later), for many years only the original four markets were surveyed on a monthly basis. This meant that rural areas, where the CBC was usually the pre-eminent service, were only covered to the extent that their inhabitants listened to stations in larger urban centres. Secondly, even in the urban areas which Elliott-Haynes purported to cover, its surveys did not adequately reflect the listening of different socio-economic groups. In particular, they underrepresented those at the lower end of the socio-economic spectrum.

It was to be expected that Elliott-Haynes should encounter certain procedural problems in conducting its surveys during this period. For example, because it had to rely on published schedules, it sometimes reported ratings for programs which had not actually been broadcast. On one occasion, 'Ford Theatre' was given a rating even though it had been cancelled after an explosion disrupted CBC operations in Montreal.[6] Moreover, the E-H reports did not explain precisely which geographic areas were sampled, how the calls were distributed, or what weighting methods were used. Elliott-Haynes boasted at one point that its records were open to the inspection of clients. But when the CBC challenged the company on this score in 1948, it refused to allow the corporation to examine its procedures. The CBC subsequently tried a number of times to determine the degree of accuracy and area applicability of Elliott-Haynes's data, but met with little or no success, which left the corporation to draw its own conclusions about the applicability of the data provided.

In fairness to Elliott-Haynes, the fees that it charged for its reports were, as the CBC's commercial manager himself later acknowledged, 'ridiculously low.' 'Until Canadians are prepared to pay more for this [service],' Weir observed in November 1952, 'they can expect it to remain in the same generally undependable and contradictory position.'[7] Yet the fact remained that, because of the urban/rural and regional disparities in telephone ownership, the E-H reports were biased in favour of the private commercial stations. This circumstance diminished the early success of the CBC and played into the hands of private broadcasters seeking to enlarge their presence at the CBC's expense.

To understand why the disparities in telephone ownership affected the CBC adversely, it is necessary to recall that in the 1940s the CBC attracted a substantial proportion of its audience through its 50,000-watt regional stations in Quebec, Ontario, the Maritimes, and the Prairies. CBF Montreal and CBL Toronto had been completed in 1937, followed by CBK Watrous and CBA Sackville in 1939. Further progress was delayed by the fact that Canada's three remaining clear channels were in private hands. In 1948, after the 1946 Parliamentary Committee on Radio recommended that these frequencies be relinquished to the CBC, the corporation added CJBC Toronto, CBW Winnipeg, and CBX Alberta to its chain of high-power stations. Even with this system in place, however, the CBC was unable to reach many areas of Canada. As a result, it still had to rely on a number of privately owned affiliates on its Trans-Canada and Dominion networks to carry its programs.

Elliott-Haynes's reports were particularly unfavourable to the CBC in Saskatchewan, where CBK Watrous operated on the 540-kc clear channel. The station blanketed Saskatchewan and reached far into Alberta, Manitoba, and the United States. Even parts of British Columbia could hear it well. But according to Elliott-Haynes's reports, it attracted only a small number of Saskatchewan listeners. Most people were said to be listening to the seven private stations, five of which had recently received power increases from 1,000 to 5,000 watts.

During the 1940s, Saskatchewan was still primarily rural. In 1947 agriculture accounted for 84 per cent of the value of provincial production. But Elliott-Haynes made no attempt to measure audiences outside the main urban centres. In fact, it did not even survey the urban population very well. It surveyed Regina every two months and Yorkton and Prince Albert every four months. It did not survey Saskatoon, Moose Jaw, North Battleford, or any other urban centre. Indeed, about 90 per cent of the population of Saskatchewan lived outside its survey area. In effect, the listening habits of those living in Regina were projected to the entire province. As a result, CBK scarcely appeared in Elliott-Haynes survey results, except occasionally in Yorkton. In the eyes of Elliott-Haynes, CBK virtually did not exist.[8]

THE SASKATCHEWAN SURVEY OF 1948

By the mid-1940s, Austin Weir was convinced that there was an 'underground campaign' to 'disparage the size of the audience of CBK,' especially 'among Eastern advertisers and their agencies.'[9] To counter 'anti-CBK propaganda,' Weir arranged for Canadian Facts to conduct a thorough survey of radio listening in every part of Saskatchewan. In August 1948 Canadian Facts carried out a study of the seven leading cities in the province together with fifty separate rural areas. It used a mail ballot, rather than the coincidental telephone method, and followed an approach developed by NBC during the war. That is, the main question was: 'Which station do you and your family listen to *most* frequently before 12:00 noon, between 12:00 noon and 2:00 p.m., between 2:00 p.m. and 6:00 p.m. and after 6:00 p.m.?' Some 7,560 ballots were distributed to radio homes using BBM's quota allocation procedure. Of these, approximately 5,200 (68 per cent) were returned and 4,509 (59 per cent) were acceptable for analysis.[10]

The main results of the Saskatchewan survey, released in March 1949, are set forth in Table 1. CBK was clearly the 'most listened to' station in the mornings, early afternoons, and evenings. Only during the 2:00 to 6:00 p.m. period, when it broadcast public service and minority-audience programming, was its audience less than one-third. During the lunch-hour, when it carried the farm broadcast and daytime serials, it was designated the 'most listened to' station by half of those surveyed.[11]

In response to the further question 'What is your favourite radio station for news?' CBK was chosen by 35 per cent in the morning, 42 per cent at noon, 31 per cent at supper, and 41 per cent in the later evening. Of those surveyed, 61 per cent also thought that CBK provided the best farm market and farm news service. It is 'easy to see,' the Canadian Facts report concluded, '... how woefully inadequate

TABLE 1
1948 Saskatchewan survey: station 'most listened to' (percentages)

Station	Before 12:00 noon	12:00 noon to 2:00 p.m.	2:00 p.m. to 6:00 p.m.	After 6:00 p.m.
CBK Watrous	33.9	49.2	21.2	36.9
CKCK Regina	9.8	10.3	15.5	10.5
CKRM Regina	7.3	7.9	8.4	7.3
CHAB Moose Jaw	23.1	8.6	22.5	11.7
CFQC Saskatoon	9.5	7.5	7.6	8.7
CJGX Yorkton	4.1	3.9	3.5	3.4
CKBI Prince Albert	6.5	3.4	6.7	7.3
CJNB North Battleford	1.8	1.0	2.8	0.7
Others or not stated	4.0	8.2	6.8	13.5

coincidental telephone surveys in a few urban centres can be in such an area as Saskatchewan, or for that matter in many other parts of Canada.'[12]

Upset by the Saskatchewan survey, CKCK Regina issued a pamphlet entitled *Come Hell or High Water*, which, according to Weir, 'challenged the CBC report, suggesting that it was unintelligent, based on an antiquated technique and inadequate samples.' CKCK was not alone in this regard; a number of other stations complained to BBM that the CBC had used BBM data 'in such a way as to contravene regulations' and that the ballot designed for the survey had involved 'flagrant suggestiveness' in favour of the CBC.[13] But CKCK went even further and hired Elliott-Haynes to conduct a rural telephone coincidental survey in the southeastern corner of Saskatchewan. The survey was undertaken in late March and April 1949 and the results were published in June in a report entitled *Acres or Listeners*. Unfazed by the findings of the Canadian Facts survey, CKCK trumpeted its supposed dominance over the entire province. When Weir requested a copy of the report, he was sent an incomplete version. 'Essential pages setting forth the quotas of calls made were missing,' he noted in the first draft of a letter sent to advertising agencies and sponsors on 2 September 1949. However, 'a complete copy finally was secured ... from one of the advertising agencies to which it was circulated.'[14]

In his letter to advertisers, Weir criticized the CKCK-commissioned study on four grounds. First, it ignored Hooper's dictum that the results of telephone coincidental surveys apply only to homes listed in the telephone directory. Weir quoted Hooper's statement in his 'Code of Practice' that 'projections or other suggestions of applicability beyond this scope are not permissible.' Second, although its surveys were only conducted on Mondays and Tuesdays (when CKCK carried such popular imported programs as 'Fibber McGee and Molly,' 'Bob Hope,' and 'Lux Radio Theatre'), Elliott-Haynes estimated CKCK's audience for the entire week. Third, it only surveyed 'a comparatively localized group of subdivisions in the Regina area.' And finally, even within this limited framework, it based its surveys on an inadequate number of calls per quarter- or half-hour in the districts outside Regina. As Weir summarized the matter, 'no so-called rural coincidental survey based on an average of one or two calls per quarter-hour or per program in each subdivision, confined to two selected days of the week and projected to all homes in these areas, can be regarded as either soundly based or thorough.'[15]

SIFTON, THE CAB, AND CBC'S OVERALL AUDIENCE SHARE

Undeterred by such arguments, the private stations and their lobbying agency, the Canadian Association of Broadcasters, continued to point to the Elliott-Haynes ratings as supposed proof that Canadians overwhelmingly preferred their programs to those of the CBC. They also commissioned additional studies from Elliott-Haynes to bolster their case. Late in 1951, for example, Clifford Sifton arranged for Elliott-Haynes to conduct a study of the average share of the Canadian audience reached by programs produced by the CBC. In addition to his newspaper interests, Sifton owned several private radio stations and was a director of the CAB. He gave a copy of the Elliott-Haynes study[16] to the CAB, which redistributed it, with added comments, to the press and other parties in Canada and elsewhere.

Drawing on its regular ratings reports, Elliott-Haynes examined the twelve-month period from 1 November 1950 to 31 October 1951. According to its figures, CBC programming (on both its own stations and the private affiliates) could be subdivided as follows:

(a) Non-commercial programming produced by CBC   72%
(b) Commercial programming produced by CBC   17.8%
(c) Commercial programming imported by CBC   10.2%

The non-commercial programming produced by the CBC, which was taken to include news and special events, was described by the CAB as 'what the Canadian people receive for radio subsidies paid to the CBC.' Elliott-Haynes calculated that it accounted for only 16.5 per cent of sets-in-use at the time it was broadcast and had a meagre 11.8 per cent average share of radio listening in Canada.[17]

In conveying these figures in a newsletter, the CAB crowed that 'by their free choice, Canadians have demonstrated an 8 to 1 listening preference for programs produced on advertising revenue over the programs produced on taxpayers' subsidy. Thus, $12 million taxes imposed on Canadians provided 1/9 of their radio listening.'[18] But once again, the method used by Elliott-Haynes was extremely faulty. In the first place, the commercials carried on CBC-produced programs did not necessarily pay for them any more than the commercials on the private stations covered the original costs of the programming which they acquired from the United States. Second, if the important consideration was Canadian-produced programming, then the proper comparison would have been between programs produced by the CBC and those actually produced by the private stations – rather than between CBC-produced programming and *all* private station programming.

Beyond these points, however, there was a much more serious problem with the method used by Elliott-Haynes, one that went to the heart of its ratings procedure. This was dealt with at length in a report which H.F. Chevrier of the statistics branch of the commercial department prepared in 1952 at Weir's request. Chevrier did not question the legitimacy of asking what share of the Canadian radio audience was obtained by non-commercial CBC programming. Nor did he undertake to gather any additional data by which to ascertain this share. Rather he checked how Elliott-Haynes had extracted data from its regular radio reports, and he then considered the validity of using these reports to determine the CBC's average overall audience share. 'The CBC has usually paid little attention to mischievous propaganda,' he observed, 'but such flagrant and deliberate mis-representation based on the findings of a so-called "independent research agency" made it necessary for the CBC to at least check the contents of this report.'[19]

Elliott-Haynes claimed that it had done a thorough job of examining Canadian listening in both urban and rural communities. But this assertion was clearly unfounded. While it used data from its quarterly area reports as well as its semi-monthly city reports, its sample of CBC programming was heavily oriented towards the latter. For example,

Chevrier found that during the time period in question, Elliott-Haynes's city reports listed 7,217 CBC non-commercial programs. Of these programs, 70 per cent were from CBC stations in four cities (Montreal, Toronto, Winnipeg, and Vancouver), which collectively amounted to 26 per cent of radio homes in Canada. In fact, 85 per cent of the CBC listings in the city reports were from eight of the largest cities containing only 30 per cent of radio homes in Canada.[20] The main problem was not that it neglected rural areas, but rather that it neglected smaller urban communities.

This bias in sampling CBC non-commercial programs would not have mattered a great deal if radio listening had followed much the same pattern everywhere in Canada. But CBC programming had a much greater audience share in smaller cities (as well as in rural areas) than in Canada's major urban centres. This situation followed quite naturally from the fact that its stations and those of its affiliates usually faced much less competition in rural and small-town communities. Indeed, the CBC had an almost complete monopoly of listeners in areas that could only be reached by its low-power repeater stations, of which there were about two dozen at the time of the Elliott-Haynes survey. In effect, less than 15 per cent of the audience-share figures for CBC non-commercial programs were drawn from situations in which the CBC was predominant.

To demonstrate this point, Chevrier compared audience-share figures for various programs (including commercial and imported programs) in two basic situations: i) when broadcast by a CBC-owned and -operated station in a major Canadian city with several independent private stations; and ii) when broadcast by a CBC-owned and -operated station or private affiliate in a smaller Canadian city without private-station competition. In the early 1950s there were some sixty single-station markets across Canada in which the local station was affiliated with one of the three CBC networks (Trans-Canada, Dominion, and French) and carried CBC non-commercial programs. Yet as Chevrier calculated, 'in 12 months a grand total of only 175 listings [from these markets] appeared in EHL reports, less than 15 monthly, among the whole 60 stations, or .25 of one listing per station per month. Still, EHL suggests that their report is representative of Canadian listening.'[21]

The listening pattern differed markedly between these two situations. Whereas a CBC-produced program such as 'Wayne and Shuster' might get 95 per cent or more of the listening audience when broad-

TABLE 2
Percentage of listeners to various programs on CBC or affiliated stations in main cities compared to smaller cities, December 1951

Time	English programs	CBL Toronto	CKWS Kingston	CJOC Lethbridge
11:45 a.m.	Laura Ltd.	19	91	99
1:15 p.m.	Happy Gang	30	89	100
1:45 p.m.	Musical Kitchen	22	87	100
2:00 p.m.	Brave Voyage	17	84	93
3:15 p.m.	Ma Perkins	30	90	97
3:30 p.m.	Pepper Young	30	91	93
2:00 p.m.	Metropolitan Opera	12	69	–

Time	French programs	CBF Montreal	CJBR Rimouski
6:15 p.m.	Radio Journal	26	98
7:00 p.m.	Un homme et son pêche	53	100
8:00 p.m.	Beni fut son berceau	24	92
8:30 p.m.	Mosaïque canadienne	25	98
8:30 p.m.	La Chanson 57	29	95
9:00 p.m.	Théâtre lyrique	35	95
9:00 p.m.	Radio Carabin	46	98
9:00 p.m.	Théâtre Ford	29	96
9:00 p.m.	French Hockey	38	94

Source: H.F. Chevrier, 'Examination of a Report on Canadian Listening to CBC Non-commercial Programs Prepared for Clifford Sifton by Elliott-Haynes Ltd.' (nd) [Weir Papers, vol. 11, file 1].

cast on CKGB Timmins or CJOC Lethbridge, it would do well to get 25 to 30 per cent on CBL Toronto. The same was true of popular American programs, some of which were carried on unaffiliated stations in large cities and on affiliated stations in smaller ones. The situation is illustrated in Table 2. It is interesting to note that CBC non-commercial programs (e.g. 'Un homme et son pêche' and 'Radio Carabin') sometimes drew larger audiences than did CBC commercial ones.

WEIR'S PROPOSAL FOR AN AUDIENCE RESEARCH UNIT

At the end of his dissection of Elliott-Haynes's survey for Sifton, Chevrier recommended that the CBC discontinue its subscription to Elliott-Haynes. But the CBC did not act upon this recommendation in the short run because there was still no satisfactory alternative; Penn

McLeod also used the coincidental telephone method, BBM only provided circulation data, and ISL was even more restricted geographically than Elliott-Haynes. And as long as it lacked its own research department, it was impossible for the CBC to do very much about this situation.

It was also difficult to deal with the more general surveys conducted periodically by Gallup and Elliott-Haynes. In 1949, for example, the Canadian Gallup Poll asked people to assess the overall performance of the CBC. While it was possible to cast the results in a favourable light by stressing that 45 per cent of those polled thought that the CBC was doing 'a good job,' critics could just as easily point out that 40 per cent rated the CBC's performance either 'fair' (24 per cent) or 'poor' (16 per cent). (Presumably the rest had no opinion.) Even more damaging were the results of questions about Canadian broadcasting which Elliott-Haynes began to include the same year in its annual surveys on public attitudes. According to its figures, 60 per cent of Canadians favoured complete private ownership of broadcasting, 20 per cent favoured 'all government ownership and operation,' and only 14 per cent favoured the existing system.[22]

In the late 1940s Weir began to agitate for a separate audience research department, but his efforts met with no response from senior management.[23] It was not until the Massey commission recommended that the CBC re-establish regional advisory councils that management gave any thought to its relationship with the Canadian public. When the commission tabled its report in Parliament on 1 June 1951, Donald Manson was serving as general manager of the CBC. He had replaced Augustin Frigon, who had been forced by ill health to step down to the new post of director of planning. Like Frigon, Manson was nearing the end of a distinguished career in broadcasting. He had been chief inspector of radio in the Department of Marine, secretary of the Aird commission and later of the CBC board of governors, and Frigon's executive assistant. On 9 July he wrote to Sir William Haley, director-general of the BBC, asking for information about the operation of the BBC advisory councils. His recollection was that 'early in our existence we had such councils but they were dropped for one reason or another.' He also explained that the CBC board of governors was 'interested in listener surveys and it has occurred to us that you might also be in a position to give us some information, with a rough estimate of cost, on this point.'[24]

Manson did not wait to hear from Haley before taking further action.

The same day he also sent a memo to Weir, asking him to 'prepare a report on a plan of listener survey [sic] for the CBC indicating an estimate of costs' by 15 August.[25] Weir was actually several steps ahead of Manson at this point. In 1950 he had arranged for Gruneau Research to conduct a study of radio listenership throughout Ontario using listening diaries for a seven-day period. It was completed in May 1951, two months before Manson's request for a listener survey plan.

With Manson's further endorsement, Weir proceeded with arrangements for a similar project in Quebec. Both studies reached into areas that had never been surveyed previously. As the report for the Quebec study noted, 'seventy-one areas in the province were entered and sampled. It should be remembered that many of these areas, in rural parts particularly, measured upwards of twenty-five square miles, within which it was necessary to criss-cross back and forth along concession lines in order to locate the sample homes according to a pre-determined sampling ratio.'[26]

Weir also hired Gruneau Research to conduct a general survey of public opinion about radio and the CBC. It was intended in part to provide a basis for dealing with the Massey commission's recommendation that the CBC publicize itself better. The Massey commission had spoken of 'the general ignorance of the Canadian public about the control, the finances and the Network outlets of the CBC.'[27] According to Weir, 'it was felt that before money was appropriated to correct this situation some measurement should be made of the nature and extent of public ignorance referred to in the Massey report.'[28]

Completed in the spring of 1952, the Gruneau Research study[29] sampled homes by province, community, language, age, sex, education, and socio-economic level. It confirmed the Massey commission's impression of pervasive ignorance about public broadcasting in Canada. It found, for example, that three-quarters of Canadians had no knowledge of what was done with the money collected from radio licences. Only one in ten knew that it was used to finance the CBC; the rest had only a vague idea that it was somehow used to improve radio. The CBC itself had never been heard of by 13 per cent of Canadians (mostly public-school pupils and lower-income families), while more than a third of those who knew of its existence did not know for sure that it produced its own programs.

More encouraging was the finding that three-quarters of those who knew about the CBC had no criticism to make about its performance. Moreover, the criticisms which were solicited were generally quite mild. In addition, almost 90 per cent of those surveyed approved the expenditure of money from taxes or radio licences on the production of Canadian programs.[30] After reading the report, Neil Morrison wrote to Donald Manson: 'we have every reason to be encouraged by what this survey reveals about public attitudes towards the CBC and its work. While it is obvious that more information is required in various directions it seems equally apparent that the Corporation is well and favourably established in the minds of Canadians as an important national institution.'[31]

In March 1952 Weir reported to Manson on these various undertakings and took the additional step of recommending that 'an Audience Research Division or department be set up within the CBC to direct all audience studies.' His main argument was that it would make for better and more-effective programs. It would not, he said, be necessary to create a large department, since outside research organizations could still be used for research requiring extensive fieldwork.[32]

Weir pointed out that the CBC was spending 'somewhat less than $50,000 annually' on audience research, that this was 'largely on services over which the CBC has little or no control,' and that 'the value of much of this is quite limited.' This was in stark contrast to the BBC, which Weir estimated was spending about $375,000 a year on audience research, or about 2.5 per cent of its domestic program expenditures. Weir calculated that if the CBC devoted only 1 per cent of its program expenditures to audience research, this would still mean a budget of about $100,000 a year. He also suggested that 'even $30,000 a year in addition to present expenditures would accomplish a vast amount of direct value to the CBC.'[33] But he was probably just being cautious at this point; he did not want Manson to rule out the idea of an audience research department simply on the grounds of cost.

Although Manson's response was initially noncommittal, he gave Weir the go-ahead to investigate the matter further and prepare a proposal for management's consideration. On 1 November 1952 Weir forwarded a revised plan in which he offered a more realistic assessment of what it would take to do the job properly. 'Further studies,' he wrote, 'have now convinced me of the necessity of raising our sights on the matter of annual expenditures for this purpose so as to place the proposed organization in a position to do competent work on a continuing basis.'[34] He had recently talked to CBS's director of research in New York and learned that CBS was spending over half a million dollars annually on audience research.

While revising his estimate of BBC costs downward to about $275,000 a year or 2 per cent of the domestic program budget, he now argued that CBC expenditures on audience research should conceivably be higher than those of the BBC. Unlike the BBC, the CBC had to serve two languages; it had to deal with a 'more constant and insistent' barrage of propaganda; and it had 'little or no accumulated background of research on which to draw.' At the very least, the CBC 'should envision annual expenditures at least as great percentage wise as those of the BBC.' Weir also expressed the hope that the new research department would 'not have to conduct a more or less continuous battle for funds. Such would dull its efforts and impair its usefulness.'[35]

SEARCH FOR A DIRECTOR OF AUDIENCE RESEARCH

On 1 January 1953 Alphonse Ouimet, who had coordinated the introduction of television, was rewarded for his efforts by being appointed general manager of the CBC. As an administrator, Ouimet had a penchant for consolidation and also anticipated a greatly increased need for audience data with the advent of television. He was thus predisposed to the idea of bringing the scattered research functions within the CBC together under one umbrella. With his authorization, Weir began an extensive search for a suitable director of audience research. In addition to Canadian universities such as Queen's, he visited Columbia, the University of Chicago, and the Institute of Social Research at Michigan. He also attended meetings of organizations such as the Canadian Political Science Association.

In August 1953 Weir sent Ouimet a report on his efforts to find a director. He had earlier thought that the post should be filled by 'a psychologist of unquestioned ability, specialized training and with a Doctor's degree,' who 'should not be over-academic but have a sense of practicalities.'[36] He now abandoned the emphasis on psychology, but still thought that the director 'should have such academic standing as would enable him to take his place competently among any academic group of sociologists or research people and thus secure their cooperation.' For this reason, he continued to regard a PhD degree as 'almost the minimum requirement.'[37] But he also thought that it was more important for the director to have a general knowledge of survey research methods than to be an expert on sampling techniques or data analysis. 'Almost any qualified statistician with an adaptable mind can undertake limited quantitative analysis,' he observed, 'but qualitative program evaluation and the study of the impact of programs for their success or failure and their social implications require a different approach, different training and generally a different type of mind.'[38]

Among the Canadians Weir considered were Angus McMorran, chief of the Bureau of Special Surveys at the Dominion Bureau of Statistics; Gerald Mahoney, director of the Survey Research Centre at Michigan University with a PhD from McGill; H.F. Chevrier, who was still in the statistics branch of the CBC's commercial department; and William B. Baker, a native of Saskatchewan with an MA from Michigan. Of these, Weir ranked Baker the highest, but ruled him out on the grounds that he was currently serving as chairman of the Royal Commission on Agriculture and Rural Life in Saskatchewan. The others were eliminated for a variety of reasons: McMorran was not really interested in the position, Chevrier's 'basic training' was considered to be 'inadequate,' and Mahoney's experience was mainly in the field of industrial research rather than mass communication. The only Canadian to make Weir's short list was Alex Sim, an assistant professor of sociology at the University of Toronto and one of the founders of the CBC's 'Farm Forum.'

Weir also gave consideration to Dallas Smythe and David Riesman. Smythe, who was born in Canada, later taught at Simon Fraser and wrote the first critical history of communication in Canada, *Dependency Road* (1981). But in the early 1950s he was a research professor in the Institute of Communications (and also a professor of economics) at the University of Illinois. He was described by Weir as 'an outstanding, brilliant and energetic man who knows his way around.' (A few years later, he was hired by the Fowler commission to conduct an analysis of Canadian radio and television programs.) But Weir did not contact him because he believed that 'it would take more money than CBC would pay to interest him.' Moreover, he also had 'some doubts as to whether he might have all the patience necessary to such a position in the CBC.' Riesman, who was author of the popular work *The Lonely Crowd* (1950), was considered to be 'beyond this position except possibly at some time in a contributive capacity.' Like Smythe, he was also 'already earning [a] much larger salary than CBC could pay.'[39]

Weir's 'number one choice for the position of Research Director if he will accept the position' was Seymour Martin Lipset. Born in New York in 1921, Lipset had spent a year in Saskatchewan doing research on the agrarian movement in Western Canada for his PhD thesis at Columbia

University, which was later published as *Agrarian Socialism* (1950). Upon completing his degree in 1946, he had emigrated to Canada and lectured for a year in the Department of Political Economy at the University of Toronto. In 1948, however, he returned to the United States, taking up positions in sociology first at the University of California and then at Columbia University. At Columbia he came in contact with Paul Lazarsfeld and became a research associate in his Bureau of Applied Social Research. In Weir's opinion, he was well suited to the position of research director. '[He] already has a very thorough knowledge of Canadian social and political conditions and of our educational institutions. I believe he has a sympathetic understanding of the purposes of the CBC and of how research could best serve those purposes.'[40]

Neither Sim nor Lipset was chosen for the position of research director, however. Sim was interviewed by Alphonse Ouimet in Ottawa in October. But shortly after the interview, Ouimet informed Weir that neither of his candidates was to be considered for the position. 'There is one point I forgot to mention to you, this morning, when discussing the appointment of the director of Audience Research,' Ouimet wrote in a rather terse memo to Weir. 'Would you be kind enough to advise Mr. Lipset and Mr. Sim that we have decided to appoint someone from the Corporation to this job. Until we make an announcement to this effect, I believe it is not necessary to mention to them who it will be.' Ouimet reminded Weir that 'we do not normally pay expenses of candidates for positions with us, whether they are eventually selected or not' – Sim had apparently asked Ouimet 'to send him the necessary forms so that he could submit his expense account.'[41]

6

Organization and Development of CBC Research under Morrison, Laird, and Kiefl

The symbols of contemporary culture are more than anything else the products of complex organizations. To understand these symbols, it is necessary to understand among other things the organizations producing them.

James S. Ettema and D. Charles Whitney, 1982[1]

Unlike many areas within the CBC, the research department has experienced remarkable stability and continuity since its formation in 1954. During that time, it has had only three directors: Neil M. Morrison from 1954 to 1961, Arthur J. Laird from 1962 to 1983, and Barry Kiefl from 1983 to the present. Each brought something special to the task of running the department which was needed at the time. And all adopted an approach to audience research which reflected their different educational and occupational backgrounds as well as changes within the CBC and the broadcasting environment. Under Morrison the department adopted a broad definition of audience research but lacked some of the tools necessary for its fulfilment; under Laird it narrowed its approach somewhat but expanded its methodological repertoire; and under Kiefl it has widened its interests again while continuing to develop new research techniques. Each director has viewed audience research as a channel of influence from the public to the CBC, though more in terms of specific programming matters than overall program policy.

MORRISON'S BACKGROUND AND PHILOSOPHY

In assessing the qualifications desired in a CBC research director, Weir included 'an appreciation of the importance and place of public service broadcasting and the part research could play in its maintenance.'[2] It was a significant consideration and one that helps to explain why CBC management chose as the first director a Canadian with little research experience over an American with impressive scholarly credentials. Through his work as supervisor of talks and public affairs, Neil Morrison had acquired not only a first-hand knowledge of programming but also an understanding of the role that the CBC could play in the lives of Canadians.

Born in 1914, Morrison was raised initially in the small town of Elbow, Saskatchewan, on what is now Lake Diefenbaker, where his father, a bank manager from Amherst, Nova Scotia, had been sent to open a branch of the Bank of Commerce (formerly the Bank of Halifax). The family later moved to Treherne, Manitoba, and then in the mid-1920s to Winnipeg, where Morrison studied arts and sciences at the University of Manitoba. Among his professors at United College was Arthur Phelps, who taught English and indulged in what was considered in some university circles to be the nefarious and not very respectable business of broadcasting. Through Phelps, who appeared quite frequently on the CBC, Morrison came to think of radio talks as a form of literary expression.

While at Manitoba, Morrison was active in student politics and became friends with Harry Avison, a United Church minister and former secretary of the Student Christian Movement. Avison urged Morrison to pursue a masters degree at McGill and helped to line up a part-time job for him at about $100 a month as assistant secretary of the Student Christian Movement. Morrison arrived at McGill in the fall of 1935, hoping to learn more about French Canada and follow in Phelps's footsteps by combining academic pursuits with occasional talks and interviews for the CBC; by his own recollection, he conducted the first radio interview of André Laurendeau in English. It was as a graduate student in economics and political science at McGill that Morrison was first introduced to formal research methods. McGill was one of the few Canadian universities at the time with a sociology department and had recently set up a social research laboratory under the direction of Leonard Marsh from the London School of Economics.

Morrison began the research for a masters thesis on the taxation of industry and the growth of nationalism in Quebec, but it was too large a topic and he never completed it. In 1939, when it appeared that he would be in the army shortly, he was offered a job in the CBC's talks department by Gladstone Murray. Although the position failed to materialize because of the commotion associated with the first royal visit, Ned Corbett, head of the Canadian Association for Adult Education and a friend of his fiancé's family, arranged for him to work jointly for the CAAE and the CBC investigating the possibility of organizing listening groups in Canada. In this capacity, he travelled across the country conducting interviews and doing research on the use of radio.

In 1940 Morrison joined the CBC on a full-time basis and was assigned to the talks department. After experimenting with a program called 'Community Clinic,' he proposed a listening group program called 'Farm Radio Forum.' When Orville Shugg, the supervisor of farm broadcasts, heard about the proposal, he persuaded Morrison to move the program to his own department and become his assistant. Together they wrote the program scripts, combining dramatization with studio and group discussions. Morrison's specific task was to adjust the cast of farm characters, originally created for eastern audiences, so as to make it more suitable in the west.

In 1943 he was asked to replace Hugh Morrison as supervisor of what soon became the talks and public affairs department. While a firm believer in the educational value of radio talks, he thought they should be delivered in a manner that the average listener could readily understand.[3] Among those whom he enticed on to the air were Leonard Brockington, John Fisher, Blair Fraser, Clyde Gilmour, Matthew Halton, and Lister Sinclair. During his tenure as supervisor, he was instrumental in developing such programs as 'National Farm Radio Forum,' 'Citizens' Forum,' 'Capital Report,' 'Critically Speaking,' 'Cross Section,' and 'Couchiching Conference.' He also served as chairman of the program committee of the Canadian Institute on Public Affairs for several years and, at the time of his appointment as director of audience research, was working on television programming problems.

Morrison was well known to senior CBC management by the early 1950s. In addition to his duties as supervisor of talks and public affairs, he had conducted a job and wage analysis for the programming division at the end of the war and had helped to prepare material for the CBC's submission to the Massey commission. When Alphonse Ouimet undertook centralization after becoming general manager, Morrison was among those who agreed to come to Ottawa. Dissatisfied with Weir's candidates for director of audience research, Ouimet offered Morrison the position on a Friday afternoon in the fall of 1953. Morrison was under the impression that the job had been turned down by several others and did not consider it to be a step up the corporate ladder. But he agreed to go home and think about it over the weekend and, after talking it over with his wife, told Ouimet that he would accept the post if he was given adequate resources. He would need, he said, a good statistician, a sociologist, a political scientist, and a social psychologist among others. A look of dismay came over Ouimet's face and he asked, with his usual concern for bureaucratic efficiency, whether it might be possible to combine some of these positions. But Morrison insisted that there was no point in setting up a research department without the staff to do the job properly and Ouimet concurred. In 1956–7 the department's budget was about $200,000 – $126,000 for salaries and $74,000 for surveys and ratings. By 1960–1 this had more than doubled to $459,000 – $301,000 for salaries and $158,000 for surveys and ratings.[4]

Underlying Morrison's approach to talks and public affairs was a belief in the value of public participation, whether through organized listening groups, the use of a more conversational speaking style, or the development of program formats capable of accommodating a cross-section of public opinion. He thought of public affairs as a vehicle through which Canadians could communicate their views to the governing powers, rather than as means of indoctrinating the public with the ideas of the elite. In the same manner, he came to see audience research as a way of enabling the CBC to be more reponsive to the needs and desires of the Canadian public.

Morrison liked to think of himself less as an employee of the CBC than as a citizen representative, working within the corporation on behalf of those outside it. During his years in talks and public affairs, the CBC maintained a close working relationship with farm organizations, adult education groups, universities, women's organizations, and departments of education. But as the CBC expanded to meet the demands of television, this approach became less feasible and the corporation tended to become more remote from the public. For Morrison, audience research offered a way of re-establishing connections with the public, albeit in a less direct way than in the case of public affairs broadcasting.

EARLY STAFFING AND ORGANIZATION

Morrison assumed the post of director on 1 January 1954. At the time, the CBC's head office in Ottawa was located in the Victoria Building on

Bank Street. The Bureau of Audience Research was given space in the Lord Thomas Building, but in 1957 moved to the Cooper Building where it stayed until the CBC's new head office on Bronson was opened on 31 March 1964.[5] Morrison spent the summer of 1954 taking courses on survey research techniques at the University of Michigan and then settled down to the task of hiring staff. This proved to be more difficult and time-consuming than anticipated. During the Second World War, Morrison had been approached by John Marshall of the Rockefeller Foundation with the intention of funding a research project on 'Farm Radio Forum.' He had travelled to New York, where he was introduced to Frank Stanton at CBS and Paul Lazarsfeld and his staff at the Bureau of Applied Social Research, but the project had fallen through when he was unable to find a qualified Canadian researcher to direct it. Ten years later, the situation was much the same; there were still relatively few graduate programs in Canada and none in the area of mass communication. 'One of our most difficult and persistent problems,' Morrison told the Royal Commission on Government Organization in 1961, 'has been the recruitment and retention of qualified and experienced social science research staff.'[6]

The early members of the department had quite diverse backgrounds and training. Lois Rae, mother of the future premier of Ontario and Morrison's assistant, graduated from Cambridge in history and worked at the British Library in New York and the National Film Board. Patricia Cockburn, the department's first research assistant, had a commerce degree from the University of British Columbia and research experience with the BC Department of Health and Dominion Bureau of Statistics. Raymond Lewis, the department's statistician, graduated from McGill in economics and statistics and developed expertise in survey research theory and sampling techniques at DBS. And Kurt Lang, who was hired as a research associate, had a doctorate in sociology from the University of Chicago. For his dissertation on how television alters reality, he had conducted an imaginative study comparing crowd reactions to MacArthur's 1951 parade through the city with the reactions of viewers at home. An essay based on the study was awarded the Edward L. Bernays Foundation prize for 1952, while the finished thesis paved the way for an assistant professorship at the University of Miami.[7]

The same kind of diversity characterized those who joined the department a few years later. Sy Yasin had studied sociology at McGill and the University of Chicago. After graduating from Carleton University, John Johnstone – an accomplished jazz musician who studied with Oscar Peterson – had also obtained a PhD in sociology from Chicago. Irwin Shulman from Montreal had a BSc from McGill, an MS from the University of Wisconsin, and research experience at the Massachusetts Institute of Technology. John Twomey had a masters degree from a short-lived communications program at the University of Chicago; for his thesis, he had examined the current crusade against comic books. Kenneth Purdye, the department's specialist in sampling and statistical analysis, had studied in London and Stockholm. After graduating from McGill with an honours degree in sociology, Constance McFarlane had worked for Steinberg's research department and Cockfield-Brown in Montreal and then McCann-Erickson Advertising in London. The first member of the department with a PhD in mass communication was Ken Adler. After studies at the University of Montreal and in Paris, Anthony Boisvert had done research for the Quebec government, worked as a journalist, served as director of studies at a college in Montreal, and lectured in psychology and statistics at the University of Montreal.

Many members of the department went on to distinguished careers in other countries and research fields. Yasin joined the Social Science Research Council in Britain; Johnstone became a professor at the University of Illinois; and Adler worked for the United States Information Service. Among those who remained in Canada, Purdye went to MacLaren Advertising and then to BBM, Twomey and Boisvert rose up through the ranks within the CBC, and Soucy Gagné left to work for the B & B commission and founded the Sorecom public opinion research company in 1969. Yvan Corbeil founded C.R.O.P. Inc. in 1965, while Ray Whalen became the head of market research at Nestlé and later served as president of the Professional Market Research Society.

Organizing this disparate group into an effective research team was also a challenging task. Because the structure of the CBC was undergoing substantial change, Morrison tried to maintain as much flexibility as possible; he did not want to force the department into a rigid mould which would make it difficult to adapt to new research needs. At the same time, it was by no means obvious what form of organization would work best. 'It is not easy to establish clear divisions between the areas of our work,' Morrison wrote to some of his staff in 1956, 'because it is all so closely related.'[8] Or as he reiterated a year later, 'a division of functions is not easy to work out in dealing with research problems because areas of work overlap and several different skills or techniques may have to be brought to bear on one particular subject area.'[9]

Weir had advocated that the statistics section of the commercial division, which had a supervisor, three clerks, and a draftsman, be absorbed by the Bureau of Audience Research. Ouimet also wanted to centralize and coordinate all statistical and research work. However, H.F. Chevrier, the supervisor of statistics, thought it would be better to wait a few years before shifting statistical operations from Toronto to Ottawa. In 1955 a compromise was reached whereby the five positions in statistics were incorporated into the bureau, but the actual staff remained in Toronto. Under the guidance of Raymond Lewis, who took over from Chevrier as supervisor of statistics, the relocated statistics unit developed improved statistical procedures which resulted in higher volume of output, greater statistical reliability, and lower unit production costs.

Three areas of responsibility gradually emerged within the department's Ottawa operation: one was concerned with analysing ratings data and conducting studies on such things as the economics of advertising and comparative programming costs; another focused on audience behaviour and the social effects of broadcasting; and the third concentrated on providing basic statistical information, designing and selecting samples, and evaluating the quality of statistical material purchased from commercial research organizations. However, the boundaries between these areas were not rigid, and personnel from all often collaborated on specific projects.

Although the original directive from Ottawa stated that the department was to be located in Ottawa, it did not specifically rule out the creation of regional offices. For reasons of both economy and efficiency, it made sense to have certain functions performed in the main production centres. As a result, small research offices were set up in Toronto and Montreal to conduct program evaluation studies, carry out fieldwork for other projects, and respond to limited requests for audience information. The Toronto office, which began regular program evaluation in the summer of 1955, was originally located in the basement of a brothel before moving to more conventional office space in the Hospital Memorial Building on Sheppard Street. It was first headed by J.A. Patton, who had served in the Canadian Navy and taught psychology at Queen's University and the University of Michigan, and later run by John Johnstone, John Twomey, Edward R. Lyons, Constance McFarlane, and Brian Stewart, among others.

The organization of a regional office in Montreal proceeded less expeditiously. In August 1954 Morrison met with Ouimet while attending the annual conference of the American Statistical Association in Montreal. Ouimet suggested that he should try to keep developments in Toronto and Montreal parallel, and Morrison agreed that this was desirable. Though admitting to Ouimet in September that 'we have not had time yet to do as much as I would like,' he reaffirmed a short time later that setting up a research office in Montreal was a 'most urgent requirement.' However, it proved difficult to find an experienced person to run the unit.[10]

Marc Perron, a producer in farm broadcasts for ten years, was finally chosen to supervise the Montreal office, which was located in the Castle Building on Stanley Street, but as with Joe Patton in Toronto, who had poor rapport with program people, the appointment did not work out very well. The purpose of the Montreal office was primarily to evaluate French-language radio and television programs. But Perron informed Morrison that program evaluation was not a very good idea; there was, he said, a general belief within the French-language network that it was producing extremely good programs, superior to those of the private stations as well as those made in the United States and Europe. While producers would be happy to have program ratings, they would be suspicious of qualitative assessments of their programs. Perron also thought that program studies should be undertaken only after consultation with program directors.[11] Perron was soon transferred back to farm broadcasts and, after a short period during which Raymond Lewis acted as temporary supervisor, Tony Boisvert was placed in charge of the Montreal office. Among his successors were Soucy Gagné, Jean-Paul Kirouac, and Yvan Corbeil.

From the outset, there was a tendency for the Montreal and Toronto offices to grow at the expense of the office in Ottawa. 'During the past year,' Ray Lewis wrote to Morrison in 1956, 'I have become progressively convinced that a more satisfactory structure for AR would be obtained by a concentration of research personnel and procedures in Ottawa.'[12] But during successive waves of 'de-centralization' within the CBC, the Montreal and Toronto offices gained staff at the expense of the Ottawa office. By the early 1970s, half of the staff were in Montreal and Toronto, and today only about a quarter of the staff are located in Ottawa.

EVOLUTION OF THE DEPARTMENT'S NAME

In announcing the creation of the department, CBC management stated that it was to have responsibility for 'conducting scientific research about the size, composition and characteristics of listening and viewing audiences' and for 'investigating the reactions and preferences of the Canadian public about radio and television programs.' It was also to make 'special opinion and market surveys about broadcasting in Canada.' But no mention was made of the larger significance of these responsibilities in terms of providing a vehicle of communication between the public and the CBC. Instead of being seen as central to the operation of the CBC, the department was depicted as a service unit for other areas within the corporation. It was expected to 'act in an advisory and service capacity to Management, the Program Division and other related Divisions such as Commercial, Press and Information, Station Relations and Broadcast Regulations.'[13]

The idea of serving various departments became a source of some tension, especially with regard to the sales department. 'At present,' Morrison's assistant director, Arthur Laird, complained to the director of sales in 1960, 'all we have is a kind of "I-ask-the-question–you-tell-me-the-answers" situation which is satisfactory to neither side.'[14] Earlier that year, the assistant director of sales had suggested that Morrison allocate a portion of his budget to purchase survey subscriptions for use by sales and designate a member of his staff to provide the necessary analysis. 'Perhaps there is a certain segment of your operations that could be moved right into our department,' he added. 'At the moment, most of this analyzing is done by our salesmen. This is time consuming and so often turned out inadequately.'[15] Morrison had in fact assigned John Twomey to act as a research liaison with the sales department, but Twomey had found the experience 'a frustrating one' because of the sales department's 'short range view, lack of knowledge and willingness to compromise and distort.'[16] And Morrison assumed that it was up to the sales department to appoint someone who, in Laird's words, 'would know enough about research to be able to *discuss* sales problems with research people, as distinct from simply *asking* for certain information, which may or may not be relevant to what really needs to be known.'[17]

In general, however, neither Morrison nor Laird questioned the idea that the department existed to serve the needs of other areas within the CBC, and this corporate service conception was reflected in the evolution of the department's name. Within a few years of its creation, the Bureau of Audience Research became known as the Audience Research Division. Then, during an organizational review in 1960, management proposed dropping the term 'audience' and adding 'statistics' to the designation. In a memo to the programming vice-president, however, Laird argued against using 'Research and Statistics' on the grounds that there was 'no precedent that I know of for a title of this kind being used by a broadcasting corporation' and that the statistical approach was fully integrated into the work of the department. In Laird's view, 'Research and Statistics' would 'tend to convey the idea that there are two quite separate kinds of activity carried out in the Division – one statistical, the other non-statistical. This is quite untrue. Almost all the research we do, and certainly all the audience research we do, has a statistical basis and/or the data which it produces are subjected to statistical analysis.'[18]

Laird preferred the title 'CBC Research' and Morrison agreed with this. On 9 December 1960 the director of personnel and organization announced that management had recently approved a change in title from 'CBC Audience Research' to 'CBC Research.' But Ouimet, who was now CBC president, had not been consulted about the decision and disagreed with it. On 5 January 1961 the programming vice-president announced that the department would be called 'CBC Research and Statistics,' as Ouimet had originally desired. The personnel director asked that implemention of the change be delayed until a current organizational review was complete, but this request was ignored. In April 1961, however, there was a further announcement that the department was to be split into two units with separate directors: 'CBC Research' under Arthur Laird and 'CBC Statistics' under Raymond Lewis. The actual reorganization occurred the following July.

The change of title served to recognize the fact that some of the department's work was not, strictly speaking, concerned with audiences. But it also tended to deflect attention from the special role that audience research should play in a public broadcasting organization. Although the use of one term rather than another does not guarantee that certain functions associated with it will be performed, the deletion of 'audience' from the department's name made it less likely that it would conceive itself – or be conceived – first and foremost as a vehicle of public input into programming. And it helped to confirm the idea of research as serving the needs of other departments rather than having an important *raison d'être* of its own.

LOCATION OF AUDIENCE RESEARCH WITHIN THE CBC HIERARCHY

A major indicator of a broadcasting organization's commitment to public participation in the determination of programming priorities is the location of audience research within the bureaucratic hierarchy. Weir thought that the director of the department should report directly to the general manager. 'In the BBC, CBS and NBC,' he pointed out, 'the head of research is widely consulted by management.'[19] This advice was followed at first by the CBC; Morrison reported directly to Ouimet, sat on the senior management committee, and attended program and other meetings. But beginning in 1957, the director reported to management through the position of controller of broadcasting. Since then the organizational structure of the CBC has undergone a bewildering series of changes, but the director of research has remained one step removed from the program planning process. This is in contrast to the structure in organizations such as CBS, which has a vice-president of research.

During the 1960s and early 1970s, the director of research reported to the programming vice-president, a position filled first by Eugene Hallman and later by Marcel Ouimet. Then, during another organizational shuffle, the research department was placed under the vice-president of planning, who (as of 1980, for example) also oversaw five other departments: Strategic Planning, Corporate Program Services, Administrative Services, Corporate Development, and Management Information Systems. Thus many of the results – and especially the implications – of audience research have tended to reach programming staff through a filter of interpretation. Although program producers and planners are free to consult research staff directly, they can also ignore research findings more easily or use them in ways that fit with their own predispositions. The CBC has had a vice-president of audience relations, but until there is a vice-president of research (the most important form of audience relations) public input into programming will remain at the discretion of other jurisdictions.

Morrison always assumed that audience research had to be balanced against other considerations in program planning. 'It was never intended that Audience Research findings should dictate what should and should not be on the air,' he wrote in 1957. 'No amount of statistical analysis and scientific research can consider *all* factors involved in determining programming policies – especially for a publicly owned broadcasting system.'[20] But in accepting the post of director, it was his expectation that audience research would assume new importance within the program production and planning process. He was thus not averse to making recommendations about programming on the basis of research findings. For example, a study of CBC coverage of the 1956 Progressive Conservative convention was followed up with a set of recommendations about how future broadcasts of this kind could be improved.[21] However, Morrison sensed that management felt the department was overstepping its role in this regard, and as time went on the department tended to leave it to others to interpret the programming implications of its studies. In the process, Morrison became increasingly disenchanted with what the department was able to accomplish and by 1961 was not unhappy to leave the CBC to become the first dean of Atkinson College at York University.[22]

LAIRD'S EMPHASIS ON RESEARCH STANDARDS

Before leaving the CBC, Morrison was asked to draw up a list of candidates for the position of director. He talked to Bill Belson at the London School of Economics and Dallas Smythe at the University of Illinois, but Belson was not interested and Smythe, though hoping to return to Canada, had reservations about the proportion of 'administrative research' being done by the department and the extent to which his freedom of expression might be restricted. Among other external candidates mentioned were Canadian university professors Frederick Elkin and Edward Parker, several Canadian government officials, and Americans Thomas Coffin and George Gerbner. The main candidates within the CBC in Morrison's mind were Arthur Laird; Ray Lewis; Tony Boisvert, by then the director of information services in Montreal; Don Bennett, assistant to the general manager of English networks; Andrew Cowan, director of the Northern Service; Fred Rainsberry, supervisor of children's programs; and Pierre Charbonneau, assistant to the French policy director.[23]

Following Morrison's departure, Arthur Laird was asked to serve as acting director while the CBC underwent administrative reorganization. He was formally appointed as director of research in 1962 when the department was divided into CBC Research and CBC Statistics. Though born in England in 1919, Laird had received his early education in Glasgow and had served as a gunnery officer with the British Eighth Army during the Second World War. After the war, he returned to Scotland for an MA and BSc research degree at the University of Edinburgh. In 1950 he was awarded a research fellowship by the University of Aberdeen. While there he lectured in psychology and business management at Aberdeen Technical College and also conducted an analysis of responses of members of the BBC's Listening Panel to a request to describe the effects of broadcasting they had observed.[24] He then went to East Africa for two years as a senior research fellow. Upon his return to England in 1954, Laird went to work for McCann-Erickson Advertising and later became manager of its research department. In mid-1958 he moved to Attwood Statistics as manager of its surveys division and was hired by the CBC research department a short time later after responding to an advertisement which Morrison had placed in *The Economist.*

Laird was an applied social scientist by temperament as well as by training. Whereas Morrison liked to gather bright people about him and set them debating, running staff meetings like a graduate seminar, Laird adopted a more pragmatic, businesslike approach to research, especially with regard to preliminary theorizing. An example of his pragmatism is provided in a memo which he wrote after reading several working papers in connection with an early departmental project. 'I found all this very interesting,' he commented, 'but to me much of it reads more like an academic treatise prepared for a University seminar than the considerations of practical research people working for a particular business organization whose corporate image is to be the subject of an empirical study.' He suggested that

one way of getting high-level theorists to come down to earth is to make it clear to them from the outset that they themselves will be responsible for carrying through their conceptualizations to a practical conclusion in the time allowed and within a prescribed budget – this to include designing the project right through to writing the report. Oddly enough this often seems to have the effect of limiting the preliminary theorising to an absolute minimum![25]

Laird's commitment to scientific methodology helped to set new standards for the department and gave its research greater credibility. He encouraged his staff to use the best available methods for any project, even when he knew that others might not appreciate the work involved. One of his favourite sayings was that audience research is 'a service but not servile,' by which he presumably meant that the department was anxious to meet the research needs of other areas, but was not prepared to compromise its objectivity by tailoring the results in any way.

Along with Laird's devotion to scientific rigour went a capacity for hard work. Despite the department's relatively small resources for the work expected of it, Laird always managed to find a way of getting the job done when management called for help on a problem. This often meant working in the department in the evening or on weekends, and one anecdote had it that even on a fishing trip with a colleague, he brought along a pile of reports to read in the boat. Laird's dedication was shared by his staff – as evidenced by his explanation in a 1970 memo of why the department could not afford to lose any more positions:

To take only this past weekend as an example: Irwin Shulman and I worked almost thoughout Saturday and Sunday on the cable TV project and on the review of current ratings services – both matters of top priority. Helen McVey worked at home all day Sunday on the current program preferences study. Bob Morrison got back on Saturday morning from two days' work in Toronto, worked all day Sunday in the computer room on various projects and sent off the latest panel tabulations to Toronto late Sunday night. My secretary was in the office on Sunday afternoon typing up a report I had just completed on ratings analysis required for a meeting next week. Three of our typists were in the office on Saturday, and two of them again on Sunday, working on various aspects of the panel. Ken Purdye in Toronto was also working this weekend – on a review of audience reactions to information programs, for Knowlton Nash. So also was Jean-Paul Kirouac, preparing data for this week's radio presentation to CBC station managers.[26]

Like Morrison, Laird brought different kinds of people into the department and gave them considerable latitude in their work. But he also provided more specific goals and a clearer sense of direction and was more closely involved in project planning. Though a private man in his personal life, he loved to engage in detailed discussions of particular studies with his staff. New members of the department sometimes found his standards intimidating, and he was known to be such a stickler for detail that staff would sometimes delay drafting reports until the last possible moment so that he would not have time to start editing them. According to one member of the department, his right-hand drawer was filled with reports that had fallen into his hands and not been deemed fit to leave the department. According to another, he returned one report with a note that it contained six split infinitives, leaving it to the author to discover where they were; after a day or so, he was still searching for the sixth one. However, Laird's urge to rewrite material was motivated by a concern for clarity and precision,

Number of staff in CBC research department, 1959–1992

	1959	1969	1975	1977	1992
Ottawa	43	23	20	29	12
Montreal	8	12	14	14	18
Toronto	7	5	8	13	18
Total	58	40	42	56	48
Clerks, stenos, secretaries	29	9	12	12	–

Source: Based in part on organizational charts in CBC Central Registry, AR 2-2-1.

and his high standards inspired his staff and created departmental loyalty.

Laird's internal memoranda and public talks seldom mentioned the larger purposes of audience research. But he believed that program producers and planners needed to be in closer touch with audiences and that this could only be done through properly conducted research. 'It is sometimes possible [for programmers] to uncover the facts of a situation by sheer flashes of insight and personal intuition alone,' he observed on one occasion. 'It is possible – but it is rather rare, and it can be awfully dangerous. Objectivity is much more likely to be achieved when some orderly procedure is established for eliciting and recording the facts, and for analysing and interpreting them.'[27]

FLUCTUATIONS IN STAFFING

When Laird took over as director, very little of the department's research was known outside the CBC, a fact which he found 'appalling.'[28] But nothing came of his suggestion that the department consider starting up or sponsoring an audience research journal. For almost immediately, he was forced to deal with declining resources, especially in terms of staff. When Morrison left in 1961, the department had close to seventy members. But according to Laird, its 'future ... at that time was very uncertain,'[29] and by 1969 it had only forty positions (see the table). Part of the loss was the result of the separation of the statistics section, and many of the other positions lost were occupied by clerks, stenographers, and secretaries. But among the positions eliminated were the assistant director of research, the senior research officer, two other senior executives, and several junior research officers.

In early 1965, after eleven vacant positions within the department had been either frozen or abolished in recent months, Laird was asked to designate another two occupied positions for elimination. In an angry letter to the assistant vice-president of programming, he complained that the department was being singled out for cuts because of its high vacancy and turnover rate. Like Morrison, Laird was finding that qualified researchers were often unwilling 'to accept CBC appointments at the salary levels the Corporation feels able to offer,' while secretarial and clerical staff were always 'on the look-out for less demanding and often more glamorous duties elsewhere.' 'If one could see some preconceived design in all this,' Laird wrote,

some strange plan to reduce the Corporation's research arm to complete ineffectuality by gradually whittling away our staff, the present outcome could hardly be more frustrating, and would at least be more comprehensible. In such circumstances at least one would know what one was up against. But presumably this is not the situation at all. Rather we have suffered more than any other Department from these recent abolitions and freezes simply because we are what we are – namely, a department that has always had particular difficulty in finding and holding suitably qualified staff, and is likely to continue having this difficulty in the foreseeable future.[30]

'[O]ur strength and efficiency,' Laird wrote to the director of personnel in 1968, 'is slowly but surely being eroded as a direct result of increasing losses of senior staff and our inability to replace them.'[31] Among those who left that year was Ken Purdye, who became head of media research at MacLaren Advertising at a salary more than $2,000 above what he was making as supervisor of research at the CBC. Asked in 1970 for a formal recommendation on how further cuts could be made, Laird replied testily: 'I can only reiterate what I have already told you orally: that I can see no means of reducing Research staff; indeed, more than at any time in the past few years, we are desperately in need of additional help.'[32]

Despite further staff losses in recent years, the productivity of the department is greater today than in Morrison's or even Laird's day. This is almost entirely because of the introduction of computers, which have greatly reduced the time required for data analysis and the preparation of reports. Nonetheless, the fact remains that the CBC's commitment of staffing resources to audience research is, given the corporation's overall growth, substantially less at present than in earlier decades. This has limited the department's ability to engage in new kinds of audience research and synthesize its extensive raw data into more useful and meaningful forms.

KIEFL'S TRAINING AND RESEARCH OBJECTIVES

Barry Kiefl is the first CBC research director to have a graduate degree in the field of communication, and unlike many communication graduates, his academic work arose from prior experience in broadcasting. Born in Ottawa in 1949, he became interested in radio while doing a degree in English literature at St Patrick's College (which was part of Carleton University by the time he graduated), working on a thirty-minute student-produced current affairs program on CKOY on Sunday evenings. This helped him to land a job in the fall of 1970 as an operator-announcer for the CBC Northern Service in Churchill, Manitoba, where he later took over from Peter Mansbridge as the local CBC reporter. After less than a year in Churchill, he decided to return to university for graduate work in communication research and policy, enrolling in the School of Communication at Boston University. Among his professors was Earl Barcus, one of the founding fathers of content analysis.

While at Boston University, Kiefl was offered a summer job by Tom McPhail at the recently established Department of Communication in Ottawa and ended up working for about nine months in Richard Gwyn's division. He then took a few months off to complete his master's thesis on the effects of access to cable television on Canadian attitudes to the United States. He conducted a small-scale survey of viewers in two Ottawa-area towns, one with cable and the other without. Among those whom he consulted on policy matters was CRTC vice-chairman Harry Boyle, who was apparently so accommodating that he rewrote the entire first chapter.

While still at DOC, Kiefl approached Arthur Laird to see if there was anything available at CBC Research, but nothing came of it immediately. He accepted a CRTC contract to work on projects related to cable and community television, and in the spring of 1976 received an offer of permanent employment from the CRTC. Shortly thereafter, however, Laird also offered him a position as a senior research officer at the CBC; it was the job he had always wanted and he accepted without hesitation. In the spring of 1981 he was promoted from assistant to the director to head of a new audience and content analysis unit. Two years later, he took over as acting director on an unofficial basis, and in the fall of 1983 was formally named the department's third director.

During Laird's tenure, the department developed some of its most useful mechanisms of public input. These included large-scale national surveys of attitudes towards the CBC and its services and regular audience panels for network television programming. Under Kiefl, the department has refined these research tools and used them to gauge audience reaction to programming services. Like Laird, Kiefl has emphasized the importance of using scientific methods and procedures in audience research and has tried to keep the department independent of the decision-making process. But he has also recognized the value of qualitative research tools such as focus groups and has initiated studies of programming problems before management itself has become aware of them.

One of the department's major accomplishments under Kiefl has been the development and maintenance of a centralized data base on audience trends, schedule content, and the physical and social characteristics of the broadcast environment. The department has also played a major role in various federal task forces on broadcasting. In a time of renewed financial difficulties within the CBC, Kiefl has maintained morale within the department and kept it moving forward through increased efficiency, improved contacts with universities and external research organizations such as the Canadian Communication Association, and a number of innovative research projects. Despite the continuous threat of cut-backs, he has injected new blood into the department, placed more emphasis on the broader implications of audience research for CBC policy, and managed to elevate the general level of analysis and interpretation in project reports.

7

The CBC and the Ratings Maze, 1954–1970: The Growth and Decline of Industry Competition

To raise questions of validity assumes the existence of some absolute truth against which all imperfect measuring devices ... can be compared. The fact is that there are no such 'absolutes' in the field of media research; we merely have different data-collection techniques, each with different definitions and assumptions. Experience and experimentation increase our knowledge of the theoretical and practical advantages and disadvantages, and the relative reliability, of these various techniques of audience measurement. However, no amount of experimentation will bring us any closer to the 'holy grail' of absolute validation.

Ken Purdye, 1967[1]

One of the first tasks facing the CBC's Bureau of Audience Research was to assess the various ratings services in terms of their usefulness, reliability, and cost. Despite BBM's inconclusive study in 1952, it was not expected that this task would be particularly difficult. But it soon became clear that the department would have to review its relationship with the ratings industry on a regular basis. There were a number of reasons, including the development of new measurement techniques, changes in the composition of the market research industry, shifts of emphasis in the CBC's requirements for audience data, and questions raised by a series of American investigations of the ratings industry. But the most important factor was that the production of ratings is a business governed as much by economic considerations as by the requirements for sound research. 'None of the services that these ratings companies provide is perfect,' Arthur Laird reminded the CBC's regional sales manager in Vancouver in 1965, 'and we spend half our lives riding herd on them, threatening them, cajoling them, correcting them, and bullying them into improving what they do. If we didn't, they'd be twice as bad as they are now.'[2]

ISL VERSUS ELLIOTT-HAYNES

A preliminary investigation of International Surveys was undertaken in the spring of 1954 by Lois Rae in consultation with Austin Weir, who had been critical of ISL's failure to reach its target of 400 households for its urban panels. They were assured that ISL was working hard to reach the desired size, and in May Morrison informed senior management: 'we feel that we can now use their reports with more conviction.'[3] In a similar examination of Elliott-Haynes about the same time, H.F. Chevrier found that it still did not indicate the precise areas covered by its surveys. Only after prodding did Myles Leckie admit that it applied ratings derived from urban surveys to surrounding rural or semi-urban areas in which the stations in question had good coverage. 'We feel it is reasonably accurate to project the city ratings to the whole area,' he explained, 'because test surveys indicate that urban and rural TV audience trends are very similar.'[4] But Chevrier countered that 'urban and rural *radio listening* differ widely with many programs and especially during daytime.'[5] And Leckie inadvertently admitted to differences when he tried to put a good face on things by adding that 'sets in use figures in rural areas are slightly better than in city homes, so our city rating applications are on the conservative side.'*

On the basis of these enquiries, the CBC research department began to work more closely with ISL. It offered advice on how to improve the design of its area samples and agreed to purchase the reports for a new radio and television panel in the Vancouver-Victoria area on a trial basis, which, it turned out, gave a more favourable impression of the CBC's performance. 'We have not yet arrived at final conclusions,' Morrison reported to management at the end of 1954, 'but on the basis of investigation and experience so far it is our feeling that the audience

---

* In the case of radio, the telephone coincidental tended to produce lower sets-in-use figures and thus lower ratings than the telephone recall, panel-diary, and audimeter methods because it measured average audiences rather than total audiences. But when Chevrier compared television ratings for the Toronto area, he was puzzled to find that Elliott-Haynes's average audience-size estimates were generally higher than those of ISL. The explanation may lie in Elliott-Haynes's practice of projecting its city ratings to a wider area, which would inflate overall levels of viewing if television usage was higher in the city core than in outlying areas.

statistics being provided by the International Surveys are more reliable and more useful than those from Elliott-Haynes.'[6]

Since the areas surveyed by Elliott-Haynes and ISL were quite different, it is not surprising that their absolute audience-size estimates varied considerably. But it might have been expected that their ratings – the estimated percentages of total radio or television households tuned to particular programs – would not be too dissimilar. However, an examination of their respective ratings for six CBC television programs in Montreal, Toronto, and Vancouver during a week in October 1955 found that out of eighteen pairs of ratings only four were similar (within five percentage points). Nor was there any consistent pattern of difference.[7]

The national reports issued by Elliott-Haynes were even less reliable than its area reports. For national ratings to have any validity, they must be calculated from a nationally distributed sample. But Elliott-Haynes produced its national ratings by supplementing the calls that it made for individual station ratings with calls in a number of additional cities. As a result, its supposedly national sample was as heavily weighted in favour of urban listening as were its area samples. Nonetheless, the advertising industry preferred Elliott-Haynes to ISL because its reports covered more territory and were issued more often. In the case of television, for example, Elliott-Haynes issued its national reports (for sponsored English and French network programs) on a monthly basis and its area reports (for forty-two markets by 1960) from once a month to three times a year depending upon market size. In contrast, ISL's national and area television reports were only issued bimonthly and its national and area radio reports less frequently still. Thus it was difficult for the CBC to rely on them exclusively, and not everyone was happy with them within CBC sales. In 1959, for example, Marce Munro, the CBC's commercial representative in Vancouver, wrote to Morrison that ISL's 'methods of gathering information are wide open to criticism and the data obtained is practically certain to contain an unintentional but definite bias against CBC service.'[8]

The research department had no illusions, however, that it could conduct its own audience measurement. For its first major study, an examination of listening in the Halifax area before the introduction of television, it had used household diaries to measure audiences for a sample week along with personal interviews to gather information on individual and household characteristics, prior acquaintance with and

expectations regarding television, radio listening habits and preferences, leisure-time activities, and general attitudes related to CBC
operations and objectives. It took the department ten months to sort,
tabulate, and cross-tabulate the 140,000 entries in the listening diaries.
And it was questionable whether the sample was any better than the
ones used by the commercial ratings services. Of the 600 diaries distributed, 316 were returned and 280 of these were deemed usable. The
survey sample also excluded large rural areas which could receive the
CBC's Halifax stations reasonably well.[9]

WITHDRAWAL OF CBC FROM BBM

During the 1950s, the Bureau of Broadcast Measurement continued to
conduct radio circulation surveys, and in 1952 it began to measure
television coverage as well. But little use was made of the results within
the CBC and Morrison began to question whether it was worthwhile
remaining a member of BBM. At a meeting of the BBM board of directors in March 1955, the CBC suggested that the next survey be post-
poned so that the needs of BBM members could be re-examined. The
same point was made in writing during the summer, but to no avail, so
Morrison decided to take more drastic action. On 28 October, three
days before the deadline for giving notice of withdrawal, BBM president Charles Vint was informed that the CBC had decided to terminate
its membership, though it was willing to discuss the matter further. At
a meeting in Ottawa on 24 November, at which the research department continued to argue against yet another circulation survey, it was
agreed that the CBC would set forth its position in writing, BBM would
prepare a response, and a report containing both viewpoints would be
distributed to BBM members.

In a report forwarded to BBM on 12 January 1956, the CBC research
department called for 'a complete re-examination and revision of coverage information requirements and methods' before any further surveys were undertaken.[10] But Vint replied that the 1956 survey was 'now
in the mailing house' and it was, in any event, 'part of our obligation to
the whole industry.'[11] In the meantime, instead of waiting for BBM's
full response, the research department sent a statement to other BBM
members inferring that there were serious shortcomings in BBM's
basic techniques and methods of operation. BBM responded with a
point-by-point rebuttal, demonstrating the unfairness of many of the
research department's claims and pointing out, quite correctly, that

'few, if any, of the CBC's allegations are supported by actual research evidence.'[12]

'We feel that once you have examined the facts presented in this memorandum,' Vint wrote to Alphonse Ouimet on 1 February, 'the Corporation will reconsider its decision to withdraw from participation in BBM.'[13] But he failed to show how the CBC might benefit from remaining a member of BBM. While circulation information was still helpful to many advertisers in radio-time buying, it did not serve the programming needs of the CBC. On 7 February, therefore, Ouimet wrote to confirm the CBC's withdrawal. 'I must admit that your flat rejection of all of our suggestions ... is rather disappointing,' he said, 'but it at least has the merit of quickly resolving a mutually unsatisfactory situation.'[14]

BBM TIME PERIOD RATINGS

To serve the CBC better, BBM needed to move into the ratings field. But ironically, this idea was rejected by the CBC, even though BBM had already conducted a number of pilot studies following requests from regional associations of broadcasters and later from the Canadian Association of Radio and Television Broadcasters. 'The CBC is strongly of the opinion that BBM should not itself undertake to provide another commercial audience rating service,' an in-house position paper stated. 'Not only would this add to the existing confusion between different ratings services but the nature of BBM as an impartial, non-profit organization would be endangered.'[15] Since the CBC was also unhappy with the circulation surveys, it is not surprising that BBM was perplexed as to what the corporation wanted it to do.

The CBC was not alone in questioning BBM's methods. A number of broadcasters and advertising agencies had doubts about BBM's sample size and its treatment of the problem of non-response. Clyde McDonald, who handled Proctor & Gamble's account at Young & Rubicam, was particularly critical of BBM's methods. In 1953 the Canadian Association of Broadcasters recommended that BBM appoint a full-time research director – previously H.F. Chevrier had looked after the circulation surveys on a part-time basis – and ironically McDonald was asked to fill the post. On the basis of a series of tests in 1955, McDonald concluded that BBM's sample size was, in fact, adequate and that non-response was not a problem.

As a result of McDonald's research, BBM decided in 1956 to begin producing time period ratings for both radio and television using the panel-diary method pioneered by ISL. Surveys were initially conducted every spring and fall with each member of the participating households keeping a week-long diary of listening and viewing by half-hour periods. At the same time, the circulation surveys were increased from every other year to twice a year. To facilitate these changes, BBM moved out of the Association of Canadian Advertisers headquarters in Toronto and into its own office on Eglinton Avenue East. In 1957 McDonald left BBM to set up his own company and Wilf Hudson took over as research director.

BEGINNING OF FOREIGN COMPETITION

The fact that BBM produced only two ratings reports a year left a gap which a number of other companies tried to fill. McDonald Research, which carried out the research and estimation procedures for BBM's surveys, offered supplementary time period ratings (TPR), station profiles, and a cumograph. In addition, the American company Pulse began measuring audiences in Canada; the British firm Television Audience Measurement Limited (TAM) was hoping to offer its services; and A.C. Nielsen had finally decided to enter the Canadian audience measurement field.

Founded by Sydney Roslow, who had a doctorate in psychology, Pulse used the personal interview 'roster recall' method which Roslow had developed for radio in the 1940s with the encouragement of Paul Lazarsfeld. This involved giving respondents a list of programs or roster to help their recall of listening during the previous few hours. The method had several advantages, including being able to measure out-of-home and early-morning and late-night listening and to gather substantial demographic data. Pulse expanded rapidly after the war, including operations in Montreal and later in Toronto, and by the early 1960s was the dominant supplier of local radio ratings in the United States.

TAM had displaced Nielsen in Britain by combining data from 'tammeters' (set meters) and 'tamlogs' (diaries) to produce 'tamratings' for both commercial and BBC television programs and individual commercial messages. Its subscribers included the Incorporated Society of British Advertisers, the Institute of Practitioners in Advertising, the Independent Television Authority, three of the four program contractors, and various program producers. In early 1955 Douglas A. Brown, a member of TAM's board of directors, visited Canada to study its audience measurement needs. The following year, TAM proposed making an 'expert appraisal' of Canadian requirements for audience measurement and the best way of fulfilling them – whether by meters, diaries, telephone surveys, personal interviews, or some combination thereof. It would then draw up a plan of operation for discussion with the interested parties, including the CBC. All of this would require, it said, only a month's work.[16]

By the 1950s, Nielsen had become the dominant ratings service in the United States. In 1950, the year that it acquired Hooper's national ratings service, it also began the Nielsen Television Index (NTI) to go along with the Nielsen Radio Index (NRI). A few years later, it organized the Nielsen Station Index (NSI) to provide local ratings in both radio and television. In the local field, it competed with the American Research Bureau (later renamed Arbitron), but it had a virtual monopoly of audience measurement at the national level. Of the $1,583,000 spent by the American networks for ratings in 1962, for example, $1,363,000 went to Nielsen. For its national ratings, Nielsen used an improved version of the audimeter; tuning activity was now recorded on a 16-mm film cartidge, which could be mailed directly to sample households. At the same time, diaries (audilogs) were also used for gathering audience demographics, which the set meter could not obtain by itself. Nielsen's local ratings were based on diary and recordimeter data. The recordimeter measured the length of time a radio or television set was on, but unlike the more sophisticated audimeter, did not record the station to which the set was tuned. Instead, it sounded a buzzer or flashed a light every half-hour to remind the listener or viewer to fill in the diary. A Nielsen brochure assured clients that 'Recordimeter-controlled Audilog data, when combined with and "policed" by Audimeter data, yield results very close to those provided by an all-Audimeter operation, and at appreciably lower costs.'[17]

At first it had taken Nielsen six weeks to produce its reports; by the end of the 1950s, it had reduced the time to sixteen days and in 1959 had even begun producing day-after ratings based on a small sample of homes. By combining its meters with diaries, it was able to offer a mass of information on radio and television audiences. For many years, the CBC had tried to convince Nielsen to offer its services in Canada, but it had always declined. But in 1959, after several postponements, Nielsen launched a diary-based service called the Nielsen Broadcast Index (NBI) in Toronto, which used the audilog-recordimeter method and provided six reports a year for television and three for radio. The same year, it began a national circulation service (NCS) for radio and television. And a year later, it extended its NBI service to Montreal, Winnipeg, and Vancouver and drew up plans for another eleven markets.

BROADCAST AUDIENCE MEASUREMENT COMMITTEE

Each of these services had its own specifications, making it impossible to compare them in terms of reliability. At the suggestion of TAM, therefore, the Canadian Advertising Research Foundation (CARF) decided to form a committee to draw up a set of standards for the production of ratings in Canada. The broadcast audience measurement committee met for almost eighteen months before producing a report in 1958, in which it appraised the existing services and drew up a set of proposals for a new one. None of the five organizations escaped unscathed. Elliott-Haynes and ISL were taken to task for the lack of control over the quality of their data; BBM and McDonald Research were criticized for their small sample size, dubious sample selection procedure, and low response rate; and the coverage service provided by A.C. Nielsen of Canada was found to use too small a sample for the county reports.[18]

The broadcast audience measurement committee recommended that a version of the diary technique be used to produce a basic monthly ratings service, monthly network reports, and quarterly stations reports, all of which would include audience composition data. In addition, there was to be an annual coverage survey containing information on station popularity, among other things. While the proposed services would have fulfilled the different audience measurement needs of both advertisers and broadcasters, they provided substantially more than either party needed individually. The sample of which the panel was composed was to be one-quarter of one per cent in twenty-six designated areas, and mechanical recording devices were to be installed in 150 homes in each of Montreal and Toronto as a quality control. The committee claimed that its sample size would yield ratings with a maximum error of 10 per cent. While this was actually true only for ratings over a certain size, a 10 per cent maximum error was not needed by the industry at all levels of ratings.

According to a subsequent CBC committee, the BAM committee 'did a magnificent job, but in its search for the ideal the committee buried its head in the sands of research and failed to realize the practical considerations of cost required to implement its recommendations.'[19] It was estimated by some advertising agencies that it would cost between one and one-and-a-half million dollars to produce ratings that would meet the BAM report's specifications. Confronted with the BAM committee's demanding specifications, TAM in Britain declined to submit a proposal and Elliott-Haynes actually issued a rebuttal. Only ISL attempted to produce a sample report based on the requirements. Moreover, when Nielsen began operations the following year, its panels had 300 participants in Toronto, 350 in Montreal, and 250 in each of Winnipeg and Vancouver, which fell short of the committee's specifications. Unlike ISL, which had the entire panel keep diaries for the first complete week of each month, Nielsen divided its sample in four and had each quarter report for a different week in the month. It then averaged the results of the subsections. In the case of radio, this pattern was repeated twice before the averages were calculated. This process was followed in order to iron out any unusual trends during any particular week, but prevented the production of ratings for programs shown on one occasion only.

FURTHER REJECTION OF BBM BY CBC

The BAM committee thus resolved nothing, leaving the CBC to find its own way out of the ratings maze. In the late 1940s E.C. Stewart had questioned whether the CBC was receiving good value for the money it was spending on ratings. Ten years later, the question still remained. In 1959–60 the CBC paid $108,855 for audience measurement reports – $54,847 for ratings and $54,008 for circulation figures. Most of the CBC's ratings budget still went to Nielsen, even though the NBI radio reports for Toronto often gave nothing but hachure marks (#) for CBC programs to indicate that they were below the reporting standard. It hardly seemed necessary to pay thousands of dollars to learn that CBC radio audiences were so small that Nielsen could not report them. But the research department still saw no need to rejoin BBM, despite pressure both within and outside the CBC for it to reconsider its position.

The CBC was not the only non-subscriber to BBM in this period. In the Toronto area, for example, only one of the six AM radio stations was a member. And most BBM members subscribed to other services as well. In 1959 John N. Milne, chair of BBM's research and development committee, pointed out that his own advertising agency paid other research organizations twenty-one times what it paid BBM. The reasons, he said, were BBM's lack of frequency, lack of coverage, the form of its reports, and the inherent shortcomings of a constantly changing sample.[20]

Nonetheless, supporters of BBM argued that the CBC should co-operate with other broadcasters and advertisers in the provision of a common ratings service; its membership would help BBM eliminate its deficit and lower costs to all subscribers; and it was, in any event, losing advertising by not being a member. In a memo to Alphonse Ouimet in February 1960, however, Morrison rejected all of these arguments. With the establishment of the Board of Broadcast Governors, he said, the CBC was 'no longer responsible for general oversight or encouragement of all broadcasting activities in Canada.'

Personally, I can see little or no justification for purchase simply on the grounds of co-operation and good fellowship or assisting the industry generally. It is debateable if the Corporation should in effect subsidize the sales promotion costs of agencies, advertisers or private broadcasters. The distribution of BBM costs is such that agencies and advertisers get the complete service at a relatively low figure, although fees have been increased as compared with previous years. One of the major problems of getting good audience measurement data in Canada is that advertisers and agencies are really not prepared to pay for it.[21]

Whereas the CBC would have been charged about $75,000 for the full BBM service (without special discounts), the cost to the major advertising agencies was between $6,000 and $7,000 and to the lesser ones between $2,000 and $3,000. Finally, Morrison did not think that there was 'much solid evidence' that the CBC had lost any commercial business by not subscribing to BBM.

Morrison agreed, nonetheless, to meet with some of the BBM directors to discuss the possibility of rejoining. He later recalled that he had, at this time, 'a somewhat "laisser-faire" approach to this whole question. This may simply have been the result of a feeling of futility or fatigue after having struggled with the particular problem for so long. I was inclined to say "let's go along with the boys; what does it matter anyway."'[22] He decided, however, to have the problem re-examined by the statistics unit within the research department. It concluded that there was 'very little to be said for subscribing to BBM on the grounds of its research methods and techniques.'[23] For example, BBM's samples in rural areas were still too small for reliable reporting on radio;

the fact that its survey dates were known in advance enabled some stations to conduct publicity campaigns, which led to biased results; and there were no quality controls on its logs and no regular checks to determine differences between respondents (on average, only about 15 per cent of those receiving logs) and non-respondents.

The statistics unit also argued that there was not, as some research staff had claimed, any consistent trend for BBM to give higher ratings to CBC stations than other companies did; that the CBC could fulfil its own audience measurement needs without recourse to BBM; and that new forms of data, such as cumulative audience totals, were needed in radio. In addition, it thought that purchasing BBM data as a sales tool would be tantamount to placing a stamp of approval on its methods. It would not only put pressure on the CBC to use BBM data for other purposes but would also compromise the research department's efforts to improve the quality of ratings information in Canada. Finally, it pointed out that it would be extremely difficult to withdraw from BBM a second time, and that with the whole ratings industry in a state of flux, the CBC should maintain as much flexibility as possible. As a result, Morrison told management that it was not in the CBC's interests to re-subscribe to BBM at this time.

CBC RATINGS REVIEW COMMITTEE

In the meantime, Morrison had responded to a suggestion by John Twomey to set up a ratings review committee to evaluate the growing number of services, examine the uses made of ratings by the CBC and the advertising agencies, and make recommendations for the future. The committee was chaired by B.K. Byram and included Twomey, J.J. Trainor, Ray Lewis, Sy Yasin, Ken Purdye, and Jean-Paul Kirouac. In mid-July Byram left the CBC – in what Morrison sarcastically described as 'a blaze of glory' – for a job at CFTO-TV. Shortly beforehand, he gave instructions, without consulting anyone, for departmental staff to mimeograph, bind, and distribute a document over his signature which purported to be the final report of the committee. However, the document had not been discussed or approved by the committee as a whole. Purdye and Kirouac considered some of its assertions to be false and disagreed with several of its conclusions and recommendations. In Purdye's view, it represented 'the thinking of the chairman of the committee alone.' At his urging, Morrison stopped distribution of the document so that the committee and other members of the department could read and revise it. After looking at sections of it, Morrison wrote Kirouac: 'Quite frankly, I am appalled. It is going to have to have a lot of drastic revision and re-writing.' Ray Lewis was given the unenviable task of producing 'a more objective, detached and concise' report.[24] It does not appear that this task was carried out as envisaged, although Purdye completed a detailed appraisal of the Canadian ratings services before leaving the CBC for Proctor & Gamble in 1962.[25]

Despite its repudiation by Morrison and several members of the committee, the document circulated by Byram contained a refreshing challenge to the assumption that ratings are essential for program evaluation. It began by criticizing the research department for its previous dealings with the ratings industry. 'Our policies towards the ratings services as well as our uses of them are vacillating and ineffectual,' it stated. 'We have lacked initiative and allowed the agencies to call the tune too long and too often.' Nielsen, in particular, was singled out for its hegemony. 'Like a giant boa constrictor, it slowly moved into position, mesmerized the CBC and some of the agencies with its electronic computors [sic] and flashing lights, and wound its statistical coils around the Canadian markets.'[26]

The report then proceeded to examine the uses made of ratings in terms of four functions: research, programming, public relations, and commercial operations. It argued that 'except in a very few cases,' ratings are 'not absolutely essential' for most audience research projects; that they are 'of hardly any use' for general problems such as the image of the CBC and frequently unavailable for problems relating to specific programs. It even suggested that for research purposes, it would be cheaper to carry out or purchase special surveys as the need arose.[27]

Looking at specific areas of programming, the report stated that ratings were of little use for school broadcasts because they measured listening or viewing in the home; of little value for assessing children's programming since they reported the behaviour of adults; and of little interest to what were known as 'outside broadcasts,' except for major events such as a royal visit. Moreover, while the religious broadcasts department expressed great interest in ratings, the report said that it exaggerated their importance as a guide to scheduling. It also found no evidence that ratings affected the programming decisions in talks and public affairs, even though the department used them for comparison purposes. Only in the sports and variety departments, where there was a close relationship with advertisers and their agencies, did ratings play a substantial role. But all of the programming departments denied that they would take important programming decisions based mainly on ratings.[28] Where the ratings seemed to be of greatest use was in information services and the commercial department. But the report said that even these departments were not making the best possible use of what was available. 'An aggressive campaign of media conducted research directly aimed at helping the selling of the broadcast media would be a great boost to the commercial activities of the Corporation.'[29]

It is not surprising that this analysis was rejected by other members of the research department. It overlooked the fact that ratings can be re-analysed to help provide answers to many different kinds of questions about program performance and audience behaviour. In subsequent years, this kind of analysis was further facilitated by the acquisition (from BBM) of the raw data used to produce ratings. Nonetheless, the unauthorized report of the ratings review committee pointed to the fact that many areas of programming were poorly served by the audience data priorities of advertisers.

THE 1963 HARRIS COMMITTEE

During the late 1950s and early 1960s, ratings services generally were in a state of turmoil. In the United States, the Senate Committee on Interstate and Foreign Commerce held a one-day hearing on ratings in 1958.[30] Another hearing was conducted by the House of Representatives' Committee on Interstate and Foreign Commerce in 1961. The report of the so-called Madow committee concluded that the ratings services were, 'on the whole, doing a reasonably good technical piece of work for the purposes to be served,' but raised questions about the effect of non-cooperation on the results of audience research.[31] It was suspected that higher educational and socio-economic groups had a lower rate of cooperation. Interestingly, a study published two years later found that, while the relationship between cooperation rate and income was inconclusive, those with more education expressed greater willingness to cooperate. 'People with higher cultural tastes,' it suggested, 'may be overrepresented in the ratings.'[32]

In 1961 both the Federal Trade Commission and the House Commerce committee's Special Subcommittee on Investigations, chaired by Oren Harris (Dem., Arkansas), began further investigations of ratings. In January 1963 the FTC won a small victory when three of the largest services – Nielsen, Pulse, and C-E-I-R, Inc. (the parent company of the American Research Bureau) – agreed to emphasize in their reports that ratings are estimates which are subject to sampling error.[33] However, none of the companies admitted to any transgressions, and Nielsen in particular remained unrepentant two months later when the Harris committee began more than five weeks of hearings on the ratings.

The Harris committee, which produced more than 1,700 pages of testimony,[34] provided a shock to the American broadcasting system comparable to the revelation of rigged quiz shows two years earlier. As a CBC report noted bluntly, its hearings 'lifted the lid off a veritable garbage can of technical incompetency, concealment and lack of cooperation on the part of some companies and downright dishonesty on the part of others.'[35] Day after day, committee investigators Rex Sparger and Robert E.L. Richardson paraded the accumulation of evidence that they and the Federal Trade Commission had gathered during the previous eighteen months. The broadcasting industry watched in disbelief as they attacked the credibility not only of small companies like Robert S. Conlan Associates but of the giant Nielsen firm as well. By the end of the hearings, the entire ratings industry had been stripped of its reputation for infallibility.

The Harris committee began by considering how ratings were being used. But despite evidence from several television producers and performers that ratings meant life or death for programs, executives from NBC, CBS, and ABC insisted that ratings were not the only factor that determined their programming. Attention then shifted to the methods by which ratings were produced, and it soon became clear that hardly any of the ratings services lived up to their claims. In one extreme example, the 'staff' which one company's brochure described as consisting of 'verifiers, program editors, tabulators, and calculators' turned out to consist of one woman, who also did the bookkeeping.

Nielsen's local market ratings, especially in radio, were badly tarnished during the hearings, and there was speculation that it might abandon the local ratings field entirely, together with all radio research. The president of the McLendon Corporation, which owned six radio stations, called them 'a collosal and meaningless absurdity' and pointed out that one of the company's stations, 'which at times approaches first place in the Chicago market in both Pulse and Hooper, is not even listed by the Nielsen report.'[36] In the case of television, Nielsen witnesses were handed a list of seventy-one names from the supposedly top-secret national panel, with assurance from Richardson that the rest were discoverable by methods available to any ingenious broadcaster interested in influencing Nielsen homes.[37] But the Nielsen Television Index for network programs emerged less scathed than did Nielsen's local ratings. When questions were raised about the adequacy of using a sample of 1,110 homes drawn from 1940 census data, Warren Cordell, Nielsen's vice-president and chief statistician, replied condescendingly:

Businessmen have a difficult time undertanding sampling. In fact, I continually see comments made by laymen who have some intuitive feeling that sampling just can't work. I have heard comments, what can 1,100 homes measure? This is somewhat amazing to me in an environment where we talk about landing a man on the moon or we make probes into Venus and where we put a man into orbit. I am amazed that someone will claim that you can't sample the United States with 1,100 homes.[38]

While the Harris committee was drafting its report, one commentator attempted to inject some humour into the situation with an 'immodest proposal' for a new ratings system in which 'the viewing habits of only *one* outstandingly typical American family would be studied to make a projection for the entire country.' Each member of this family

would take a thorough examination on what he viewed the past day. If he didn't view the past day, the examination would be less thorough. But no matter which exam he took on his TV habits – the viewer's or the non-viewer's – his answers would always be truthful because he'd be under permanent oath by a federal court. You can already see what an improvement this system is over Nielsen and Trendex, which are often inaccurate because they have no power to arrest.

The viewer's exam would contain 930 penetrating questions that could easily be answered during the commercials of the late movies. Here are some samples (note the clever use of essay questions to prevent guessing):

– Do you remember any program you saw today? If so, name it. (This question is optional.)
– Give the plots of any three commercials you particularly enjoyed today. What was the influence of Emerson and Thoreau on each? ...
– If your children had to live under educational television or Communism, which would you choose for them and why?[39]

The report of the Harris committee questioned whether those who cooperated in ratings surveys were a representative sample, and concluded that the ratings services claimed much greater precision for their figures than warranted by the facts. Even though it came off fairly well during the hearings, the American Research Bureau announced that it would double the size of its national sample. And in the mid-1960s Nielsen introduced computerized sample selection and more rigid interviewing controls. However, the basic system remained in place, and there were no further congessional investigations of broadcast ratings.

CRISIS AND REVIVAL IN BBM

The situation was not much better in Canada. At a meeting with CBC head office sales staff in November 1961, Laird pointed out that Nielsen had no mechanical recorders in many sample homes and that

it had proved very difficult in recent months for Research & Statistics to get adequate information from Nielsen on various aspects of their service to us – past and proposed. This applied not only to their use of Recordimeters but to such other important considerations as sample distribution which affects the reliability of the data produced, and to the procedure which Nielsen allegedly use to adjust the measurements that they get from non-Recordimeter homes in line with the measurements they get from homes that are metered in this way.[40]

As a result, the research department 'could not properly evaluate the service they proposed to sell us.' In fact, as Ken Purdye concluded the following year, it was impossible to assess any of the available ratings services in terms of reliability, 'because all of them cut corners and make compromises in their research designs in the interests of both economy and speed' and 'the effect of these compromises on the data – the biases introduced and the effect on the sampling error – is just not known.'

For example, if we were to try to decide which of the services measuring the Toronto TV market is the 'best' or 'most reliable' we should have to compare:–
(a) *The Nielsen Panel*, with its initial non-response, its short half-life, small size, and dubious estimating procedures.
(b) *The Elliott-Haynes* telephone survey, with its high non-coverage, poor selection procedure, biased estimating formula and lack of quality control.

(c) *The ISL Panel,* with its non-probability aspect, and high non-response.

(d) *The McDonald-BBM* surveys, with their non-coverage, biased selection procedure, low response and poor quality of response.

Since we have no data on the quantitative impact of these different sets of defects, such a comparison becomes essentially subjective and non-scientific.[41]

Shortly before leaving BBM in 1961, Duncan Grant wrote that 'there has never been any serious criticism of the validity of BBM research.'[42] But Purdye was certainly critical of BBM's methodology, and BBM came under strong criticism as well from advertisers and private broadcasters for the lack of validation of its research procedures and the low response rate in its diary-based surveys. As a result, a planning committee composed of the Association of Canadian Advertisers, the Canadian Association of Advertising Agencies, and the Canadian Association of Broadcasters asked for an independent evaluation of BBM's research methods. The advertisers and their agencies were also unhappy with the slow delivery of BBM reports, while the broadcasters were dissatisfied with the fact that even though they paid most of BBM's costs, the advertisers controlled BBM policy. In addition, some of the broadcast members wanted more surveys* as well as measurement of out-of-home tuning and were threatening to turn to other ratings services. Following a stormy meeting in Hamilton on 30 October 1961, the membership agreed (by a vote of 148 to 92) to a somewhat more equitable distribution of fees. But the advertisers and agencies retained six of the board of director's nine seats, on the grounds that BBM surveys would thus have more credibility, and broadcasters remained ineligible to serve as chair.

By 1962 there was a real danger that BBM – which was some $5,000 in debt – might collapse. Under temporary director and long-time board member Bill Hawkins of CFOS Owen Sound, however, BBM began to put its house in order. Hawkins managed to eliminate the debt and persuaded Bill Byram, who was still at CFTO, to serve as BBM president. One of Byram's first acts was to hire professor Douglas Dale, chairman of the Department of Mathematics at Carleton University

---

* In a poll of member stations in western Canada in April 1960, thirteen stations felt that two surveys a year were adequate, seventeen wanted the number of surveys increased, and five had no comment. In contrast, of eleven stations surveyed at the same time in Atlantic Canada, only one wanted the number of surveys increased.[43]

and one of the foremost statisticians in Canada, to conduct a thorough reassessment of BBM's survey techniques. During the fall of 1961, BBM's research and development committee had considered hiring the Alfred Politz organization in New York to conduct an evaluation of its procedures, but baulked at the estimated cost of $125,000 or more. There were also objections to using a firm that was both commercial and American. The committee subsequently decided to approach the Canadian Advertising Research Foundation to see whether it might conduct or arrange for an evaluation.[44] But nothing had come of this plan, so Byram retained Dale as a technical research consultant and commissioned him to undertake a series of studies to determine, among other things, whether the listening habits of respondents differed from those of non-respondents and how the response rate might be improved. Dale found no significant differences between the two groups, except that small households were underrepresented in the respondent sample, which was easily remedied.

While Dale was completing his studies, BBM took a number of independent steps to improve its operations. In 1964 it became the first ratings service in the world to introduce computerized sample selection, and it later developed computer programs for reach and frequency studies, quintile and profile analyses, and time block averages. In 1964 it also took over the publication of telephone coincidental surveys from Elliott-Haynes and increased its diary-based surveys from two a year to four a year, though eventually it had to drop back to three a year for reasons of cost. And in 1966 it dropped the telephone surveys, increased the fees for advertising agencies (which raised their contribution from 7 to 12 per cent of revenues), and changed its name to BBM Bureau of Measurement. It also revised its constitution so as to provide for two additional directors for the broadcast sector – bringing the membership of its board to nine broadcasters, seven advertisers, and seven representatives from the advertising agencies. Broadcasters were also allowed to chair the board for the first time, although it was not until 1972 that a broadcaster was elected as chair.

In 1966, following Dale's studies, BBM redesigned the bilingual household diary and changed the accompanying incentive. Over the years, BBM had experimented with a variety of incentives. The minutes of the research and development committee in 1953 report that:

A number of premiums were examined and their costs considered. Those that appeared practicable were:

1. Orange Peeler with loose card 3¢ – with card attached 3½¢.
2. Tape Measure 6¼¢ – folding would be extra at 65¢–70¢ per hour.
3. Pack of 10 assorted Needles 2.9¢.
4. Pack of 16 assorted gold-tipped Needles (with cellophane window) – less than 5¢.
5. Curlmaster Comb in assorted colours 3.35¢.
6. Pocket Comb – less than 1¢.
7. 'Dog' 12-Needle Pack 3½¢.
8. 'Dog' 6-Needle & 1 Threader Pack 3¾¢.

Before selecting one of the above it was suggested that a test should be made to determine the pulling power, ease of mailing, and cost of postage for each.[45]

It was decided that the 10-needle pack (2.9¢ each) would be used for the 1954 survey. During the 1960s, the premium consisted of a card of safety pins. Dale experimented with a whole range of incentives, including dollar bills, cheques, coupons, and sweepstake prize offers of $100. But he found that the most effective incentive turned out to be a 50-cent piece; this had the effect of increasing the response rate for mailed diaries (rather than at the telephone enumeration stage) from less than 20 per cent to 40 per cent. BBM became the Canadian Mint's main customer for these coins, which were seldom used in everyday transactions. On occasions when the Mint was unable to supply enough of the coins, BBM had to use two quarters instead, with a resultant drop in the response rate. The 50-cent coin was apparently a tempting target in bulk; in 1971, for example, the theft of some mailbags caused the loss of one week's diaries in several cities.[46]

BBM'S SWITCH TO DUAL-MEDIA PERSONAL DIARIES

The problem still remained, however, that one member of participating households – usually the harried home-maker – still tended to keep the diary for the entire family. This meant supplying basic demographic data and recording all listening and viewing by half-hour periods between 6:00 a.m. and 1:00 a.m. for an entire week. Whether one person could – or would – do so accurately was highly questionable. On 1 December 1966, therefore, following simultaneous tests in twenty areas the previous October, BBM held a special general meeting to consider whether to replace its household diaries with dual-media individual or personal diaries. The membership decided, almost unanimously, to make the switch, and the new system was introduced in

1967. Diaries for recording both listening and viewing were now sent to selected members of households – including children, although their diaries were to be filled out by an adult. This change increased the response rate for mailed diaries to almost 50 per cent and facilitated the acquisition of demographic data. But it also increased survey costs. In 1967 BBM lost $71,000 – despite the fact that its annual revenues had increased from $448,000 in 1963 to $690,000 in 1967.[47]

As a result of these measures, BBM created greater confidence in its data and improved its overall image. Talk of bringing in competitive services subsided, and within a few years BBM became the only audience measurement service for radio in Canada, while in television the competition was reduced to Nielsen. Elliott-Haynes, ISL, Penn McLeod, McDonald Research, and Pulse all fell by the wayside. Between 1963 and 1968, BBM's membership increased from 357 to 534 or about 90 per cent of the broadcasting industry, including the CBC. Altogether it was a remarkable transformation. Byram's remark to the membership in 1968, 'we have no desire to make BBM a monopoly, nor a monster,'[48] would have been inconceivable even a few years earlier.

Even before BBM switched to personal diaries, the CBC began to change its tune. Following Laird's appointment, it ended its boycott of BBM and began purchasing its radio ratings, though still relying primarily on Nielsen in the case of television. In 1964 Laird recommended that the CBC also subscribe to BBM's television service,[49] but the suggestion was not immediately acted upon because of lack of funds. Of the $200,000 or so spent by the CBC for ratings in 1965–6, only $25,000 went to BBM. In 1965, however, Laird became a BBM director (a capacity in which he served until 1977) and began to forge a closer relationship between the CBC and BBM, especially after BBM adopted personal diaries. In the spring of 1968, for example, he wrote an enthusiastic memo to management about how the personal diary system was facilitating sales and had produced 'a pretty good yield from the investment made.'[50]

Although Nielsen also used diaries, it was not feasible for it to switch from household to personal diaries. In the United States, where it earned most of its profits, household diaries were used in conjunction with the audimeter, which measured household tuning. While the audimeter was not in use in Canada, it was not practical to use a different kind of diary in the two countries. Nielsen thus tried to show that household diaries for a single medium were superior to personal diaries that measured two media. In a presentation to the CBC research department in March 1969, George Ralph, the executive vice-president of A.C. Nielsen of Canada, claimed that recent company tests showed that measuring radio and television in one diary deflated viewing figures.

At the same time, however, Ralph pointed out that measuring random persons (like BBM) rather than sets (like Nielsen) inflated television-viewing figures. This prompted Ken Purdye to ask whether these two factors would simply cancel each other out, making Nielsen's estimates comparable to those of BBM, and, if not, which effect was stronger. Purdye also questioned the logic of concluding that radio-listening and television-viewing levels are understated when both media are measured in the same diary. 'Is it not equally plausible to conclude that television viewing and radio listening are *overstated* when each is measured in its own diary?'[51]

In 1969–70 the CBC still paid more for Nielsen's television ratings ($197,000) than for BBM radio and television ratings ($149,000). But following another formal review of the television ratings services in 1969–70 (the first since 1964), Laird recommended that the CBC terminate its contracts with Nielsen and rely on BBM exclusively. While believing that 'there appears little to choose' between BBM and Nielsen in terms of reliability, Laird liked the fact that BBM's methods and procedures were 'fully open to inspection,' whereas Nielsen had become 'increasingly reluctant to provide information of this kind.' As well, Nielsen charged twice as much as BBM for its television ratings, even though these were 'much more limited in scope.'[52]

Laird acknowledged that without the support of the CBC, Nielsen would probably withdraw from Canada, leaving BBM with a monopoly. But he argued that 'CBC has a strong voice in BBM management and has various ways of exerting special pressure on BBM should the need arise.'[53] For example, the director of TV sales (English) and the director of research were on the BBM board of directors; the director of research was a member of the board's executive committee; the director of statistics was chair of the BBM cells committee; and other senior members of the CBC's research and sales staff were on other BBM committees and special study groups.[54] 'Moreover, unlike Nielsen,' Laird argued, 'BBM is itself an association of members whose individual interests are now so varied that this is also unlikely to result in any sluggishness of action or lack of initiative often associated with monopoly concerns.'[55]

Laird's case for going with BBM exclusively was not accepted by management, and the CBC continued to subscribe to both Nielsen and BBM. Ironically, therefore, the CBC – which existed in part to ensure a Canadian-made product on the airwaves – supported the production of audience data by an American branch plant. In retrospect, this probably seemed justified in terms of securing reliable service as the CBC's research department generally found the quality of Nielsen's data to be superior to that of BBM's.[56] However, unlike in the 1950s, the benefits of competition were limited to television, where the CBC actually had its own system of measuring audiences (see chapter 10). And by dividing the resources available for audience measurement between two services, the Canadian broadcasting industry ensured that the methodological compromises which had plagued the ratings field from its inception would continue to be a significant factor in the years ahead.

8

The CBC and the Ratings Maze, 1971–1993: From Personal Diaries to People Meters

I believe that the diary is dead as a means of measuring TV audiences.

Doug Newell, 1989[1]

In his final presidential address to the BBM membership in 1973, B.K. Byram reported: 'without any direct attempt on our part, our competitors fizzled out and have left BBM virtually in sole possession of the broadcast ratings' field in Canada.'[2] Byram mentioned two factors in this success: BBM's association with O.E. McIntyre and the computer selection of its sample; and the computer programs designed for it by Cybernauts through which it was able to produce large amounts of data in a short time. But he also thought 'the time has come for BBM to examine some of its old concepts,' and within a few years, BBM actually began to contemplate the possibility of using a meter-based measurement system for television. In the short run, it settled for making further changes in its diary format, but the shortcomings of any diary system became increasingly apparent as the number of radio and television stations continued to grow. With the arrival of people meters in the mid-1980s, BBM tried to work out an arrangement with Nielsen for the joint operation of a national television ratings system using the new technology. But the divergent interests of the various parties involved proved impossible to overcome. BBM tried to go it alone with a people meter of its own, but lacked the resources and support to do so successfully. In the end, it was forced to rally around its diary method once again and pin its hopes on some form of passive meter technology.

BBM'S SWITCH TO SEPARATE DIARIES FOR RADIO AND TV

In theory, the most reliable diary is neither the single-medium household diary (adopted by BBM in 1956) nor the dual-media personal diary (introduced by BBM in 1967), but rather the single-medium personal diary. Indeed, as the number of radio and television stations increased, it became more and more difficult to keep an accurate diary even for one medium. BBM diary-keeepers were expected to provide demographic data (age, sex, languages spoken, occupation, and later education); keep a record of listening and viewing for each fifteen-minute period of the broadcast day; and indicate whether their tuning was 'at-home' or 'out-of-home.' They were told to carry their diary 'all the time in your pocket or handbag so that you can remember to enter *ALL* your listening and viewing.' 'All your tuning,' the instructions emphasized, 'includes listening or viewing done while you are away from home (out-of-home) such as at a friend's house, in a cottage, in a car, in a restaurant, or hotel, or barber shop, etc. – even on a holiday or business trip.'

By the early 1970s, BBM was being pressured by two contradictory demands. On the one hand, a number of members (largely in radio) wanted separate surveys for radio and television, though more for financial reasons than to improve accuracy. Radio broadcasters such as Stuart Brandy of CKEY felt that radio was subsidizing television under the existing format, since it contributed twice as much revenue to BBM as television but received only the same benefits.[3] On the other hand, a somewhat smaller group wanted multimedia studies covering radio, television, and print which would better enable them to determine advertising effectiveness. Both approaches entailed substantially greater costs than the dual-media personal diary, which had already strained BBM finances. BBM's research and development committee estimated that it would cost an extra $731,000 to conduct separate surveys for radio and television – or about 50 per cent more.[4]

To help sort out these demands, the research and development committee conducted a series of tests between 1972 and 1974 in consultation with Douglas Dale. The first of these, a $40,000 quality-control study in Toronto in March 1972, was actually the first validation study of BBM's personal diary technique. The standard used was the coincidental telephone method, which had been employed in similar studies in the past because it is relatively free of cooperator bias.[5] The study tried to determine whether diary-keepers are consistent in their recording throughout the week; whether they record their actual tuning accurately; and whether those who return diaries differ in terms of tuning from those who do not. It produced a 'strong suspicion' that the use of diaries inflates recorded tuning at the beginning of the week and deflates it at the end. It also found that respondents tended to have different tuning habits than non-respondents. In the case of radio, those who returned diaries tended to be heavier listeners than non-respondents, but also tended to underreport their listening. In the case of television, respondents watched slightly less than non-respondents, but also slightly overreported their viewing. Overall, the dual-media diary yielded tuning levels about seven per cent higher than those of the telephone coincidental.[6]

In November 1973 BBM conducted a second study comparing various diary formats. It found that a radio-only diary produced a higher response rate and higher levels of tuning than a dual-media diary.[7] However, because it did not use a telephone coincidental survey as a benchmark, there was no direct way of telling whether the radio-only levels were too high or the regular diary levels were too low (or whether perhaps both were the case to some degree). To be sure, the quality-control study found that the dual-media diary yielded higher levels of tuning than the telephone coincidental. But a further study in January 1974, which again used a telephone coincidental, found virtually no difference in tuning levels for radio-only and dual-media respondents, though both were still higher than for the coincidental telephone survey. And it found only a modest difference in the case of non-respondents, with dual-media non-respondents actually further below the telephone coincidental norm than radio-only non-respondents. As a result, there was no solid evidence, especially in the case of radio, that dual-media diaries are more accurate than separate diaries. The only clear result was that any kind of diary involves a substantial cooperator bias.[8]

Given these inconclusive findings, BBM hired statistical consultant Allan Paull of the University of Toronto to appraise their validity and recommend a course of action. Paull described the quality-control test as 'well designed, professionally implemented, and competently analysed' and supported the use of a telephone coincidental survey as a benchmark. On the question of diary formats, he concluded that the use of the radio-only diary was 'insupportable without further extensive research,' largely because of its apparently greater degree of cooperator bias.[9]

At its annual general meeting in March 1974, the BBM membership discussed the question of using separate diaries at length. A motion was made by Peter Jones, who had replaced Bill Byram as BBM president, to conduct still further tests – to the annoyance of some radio members. 'What do we want to know?' one member asked. 'The last tests were either right or wrong.' But Jones stated that BBM had to find out for sure which diary format was best, and the motion was carried with the added provision that the question would be put before the membership at the 1975 annual meeting.[10]

Jones pointed out that the choice of a particular diary format did not simply revolve around the question of accuracy. Dual-media diaries are more economical and can provide information on the relationship between radio and television. But they are also less capable of meeting the special information requirements of business for each medium.

On the one hand Television is characterized by program loyalty rather than station loyalty, it is subject to a wide variety of fare on each station with seasonal changes both in programming and audience viewing habits. On a national basis it is more of a mass medium with its programming capturing all demographic population groupings. Radio by distinction tends toward consistency in programming with seasonality being more the reflection of the changes in the community, and there is greater audience loyalty than we find in Television. With exceptions, radio tends to be more local in its appeal. From a physical standpoint, daily pattern changes result in perceptible audience shifts upon daylight hours in the dates surveyed.[11]

In addition, television requires smaller samples than radio.

Following a testing program from May to November 1974 at a cost of about $140,000, BBM's technical committee recommended the introduction of separate diaries and the use of different samples and survey dates for each medium. These recommendations were approved by the BBM board on 28 May 1975 and sanctioned by the membership at its annual meeting on 26 June.[12] The new diary instructions, which favoured casual over concentrated listening or viewing, still called for considerable diligence on the part of diary-keepers. 'It counts as listening so long as you were paying some attention to what was being broadcast,' they read, and 'it counts even if you were listening for just a few minutes.' Following a study of response rates in April 1975, BBM decided to discontinue measuring listening for children between the ages of two and six, but to continue measuring their viewing.[13]

FIRST BBM METER COMMITTEE

BBM had scarcely implemented its single-medium personal diaries when it began contemplating a much more radical move – the use of some form of electronic measurement for television. The main reason was the growing complexity of the broadcasting environment, especially in the case of television, which made the use of diaries increasingly problematic. As the research and development committee told the BBM membership in 1978, 'cable penetration is now at 68 percent;* converter ownership is growing; cable substitution is prevalent; pay TV may well be on the horizon. All of these developments are putting pressure on BBM's time period diary, which requests respondents to record, quarter hour by quarter hour, the call letters of the stations they were watching.'[14] In addition, BBM continued to be plagued by mail disruptions. In 1968 and again in 1970, it had to cancel its summer survey because of a postal strike. Another strike in 1975 resulted in the cancellation of the spring survey and a financial loss of $175,000.[15] And although it carried out a contingency survey during a strike in 1979, the results were not considered satisfactory and were not released.

Moreover, both postal and printing costs were on the rise, making it increasingly expensive to conduct surveys by mail. In 1977–8, BBM suffered a deficit of $40,000 and projected a loss of $340,000 for the following year, unless fees were increased.[16] Aggravating the situation was a deteriorating participation rate. 'Without being able to quantify a change in public attitude,' Peter Jones observed in 1979, 'we're seeing people being more and more reluctant to participate in research. Even though it is only a little worse each year, it does add cost as we have to compensate with higher mail out.'[17]

In 1975 BBM began investigating electronic measurement systems in other countries, and the following year it set up a special committee to develop a proposal for a meter-based system for television. In July 1977 it signed a $75,000 contract with Torpey Controls Ltd. to build a prototype unit using existing circuitry and the vertical blanking interval.[18] During 1978 and 1979, the prototype was tested in Ontario, Quebec, and British Columbia and the results were considered satisfactory. However, the estimated cost of switching from diaries to meters was considered prohibitive, especially since diaries would still be required for radio and to supplement the data gathered for television.[19] Torpey was later hired to investigate the possibility of refining the meter by incorporating some of the technology used by the Closed Captioning Institute, but nothing came of his investigation.[20]

* Although the use of cable was growing rapidly, this statement is inaccurate. Between 1970 and 1979, the proportion of Canadian households with cable increased from 16 to 52 per cent (as of 1991 it stood at 71 per cent).

SATURATION SAMPLING AND GROWING SCEPTICISM ABOUT DIARIES

In the spring of 1983, after a series of field tests and evaluations, BBM implemented what is called household flooding or saturation sampling for its radio surveys; that is, each member of a sample household (aged seven and over) now received a listening diary. A few years later, BBM also adopted household flooding for its television surveys. In the case of television, however, each *set* in a household was allocated a diary, as had been Nielsen's practice all along. BBM's resort to household flooding was largely the result of falling response rates, but it reduced effective sample size and increased sample error. Although the new methodology was accompanied by an increase in sample size, it is questionable whether the problem was adequately addressed by either BBM or Nielsen. Both camouflaged it to some degree by referring to sample size in their published reports in terms of the number of persons or sets surveyed, rather than the number of households.[21]

In 1984 a major revision of BBM sampling error estimates was completed by Martin Frankel, a professor at the City University of New York and a BBM statistical consultant; Oleh Iwanyshyn, a CBC research officer; Nort Parry, the director of radio research for All Canada Radio and TV; and Ken Purdye, BBM's vice-president of research and development. They recommended that more detailed information on sample sizes be published in BBM reports so that users would know the degree of accuracy they were getting for their money. They also called for further examination of BBM's weighting system and the requirement to produce a county-by-county reach report with each survey. But they avoided saying whether sample sizes were adequate or not on the grounds that this depended on how data were used. They also ignored the question of whether all members of a household could be expected to be equally diligent in maintaining a diary.[22]

Faced with growing scepticism once again about the accuracy of ratings, both broadcasters and advertisers began to look seriously at other forms of audience measurement. Even before the introduction of household saturation sampling, the CBC research department had come to the conclusion that the diary method was no longer acceptable, and it was not alone in this belief. 'It is now time,' said CTV's vice-president of marketing in the mid-1980s, 'to get our audience measurement techniques out of the dark ages.'[23]

Canadian broadcasters were not alone in being concerned about the reliability of diary-based audience measurement. In the United States, the cable industry believed that diaries did not give full credit to cable viewing. In 1981 the Cable Advertising Bureau asked Nielsen to undertake a study of the diary method. Nielsen, not surprisingly, concluded that diaries were ineffectual in measuring cable, though so too was the audimeter. As NBC's vice-president for research explained in 1984, 'the traditional ratings services, Nielsen and Arbitron, do not provide meaningful measurements for ... individual cable systems. There are 7,700 individual cable systems and close to 40 cable networks in this country. The combination of relatively low penetration plus the multiplicity of signals yields a small audience base for measurement.'[24]

INTRODUCTION OF THE PEOPLE METER

The situation was thus ripe for a new service using a new measurement technique. In the late 1970s, word came out of Germany that the research company GFK was working on a different type of meter. Nielsen was also known to be experimenting with a meter that would measure viewing rather than tuning. But the first company to put into operation a new meter-based system of measurement for television was the British ratings giant Audits of Great Britain (AGB), which introduced its 'people meter' in 1982. It was, in effect, an electronic diary rather than an unobtrusive and independent or 'passive' meter. It had the advantage of capturing viewing and demographics simultaneously and did so at a lower cost than for other methods. It could also track audience flow more precisely and determine audiences for much smaller time segments. But it still required viewer involvement; instead of a printed diary, viewers used an electronic keypad to register their choices. This reduced, but did not eliminate, the task of recording one's viewing.

Funded by the American networks, which were unhappy with Nielsen's monopoly in the meter field, AGB began testing its system in Boston during the summer of 1985. It eventually deployed its people meters in Ireland, Thailand, and the Philippines, but was unable to dislodge Nielsen from the American ratings market. Shortly after AGB made its initial overtures, Nielsen unveiled its own people meter, consisting of a small computerized mechanism wired into a television set and connected to a central computer. In the case of the Nielsen meter, when a set is turned on, red lights flash on the meter until members of the household press their preassigned buttons on a numerical keypad. (Visitors select an unoccupied button and enter their sex and age.)

Unlike the audimeter, the Nielsen people meter automatically records the demographic data for each viewer. It is not, however, a passive meter and is thus vulnerable to button-pushing fatigue. Whenever a new program is selected or the set remains on the same channel for some time, viewers must confirm their presence; if anyone leaves, they have to record their departure.

In July 1987 both CBS and ABC cancelled their contracts with Nielsen, and CBS went so far as to sign a $2 million one-year deal with AGB.[25] But Nielsen remained undeterred and launched its own National People Meter service in September of that year. It took a year for Nielsen to reach its goal of 4,000 households, and its initial people meter data did little to win the confidence of the networks. According to an analysis conducted by Lawrence W. Hyams, ABC's director of Audience Analysis, during the first six weeks of the fall season the networks lost 10 per cent of their prime time audience from the year before.[26] In January 1988 executives from the three networks claimed that they had collectively lost as much as $58 million in advertising revenues as a result of Nielsen's figures. But AGB's figures were not much more consoling, and by the end of the 1987–8 season, the ratings drop for each network, according to Nielsen, turned out to be only a few percentage points. In the end, therefore, the networks decided to stick with Nielsen. AGB fled the country, reportedly having lost in the neighbourhood of $75 million.

THE ON-AGAIN OFF-AGAIN MARRIAGE OF NIELSEN AND BBM

Barry Kiefl recalls visiting Nielsen's US headquarters in 1982 and being shown a people meter system that had been installed in fifty test homes in Tampa Bay. And later that year, Nielsen made a proposal to CBC to begin operating a people meter system in Canada. Nothing came of it immediately, but in August 1984 Nielsen made a demonstration of its system to the CBC research department in Ottawa. Although the CBC still made no formal commitment, Nielsen felt that it had enough support to announce its intention to launch a people meter service in Canada.

BBM naturally reacted with great alarm and demanded to know why it was not being given an opportunity to compete. It decided to turn to AGB for help, and the two parties quickly reached a tentative agreement whereby AGB would develop a people meter system for network television in Canada (local markets would still be measured by diaries) as a subcontractor to BBM. To approve and oversee the AGB contract, BBM set up a new meter committee chaired by Peter Swain, owner of Media Buying Services, and composed of representatives from CBC, CTV, TVA, Global, and the advertisers and their agencies, most of whom were also Nielsen clients. In a surprising turn of events, however, the BBM meter committee voted in favour of a tendering system and decided to develop the necessary technical specifications itself.

Kiefl represented the CBC on the BBM meter committee. His main concern was to avoid a situation in which BBM would end up competing with Nielsen in providing people meter service, which he thought would be unnecessarily wasteful. In January 1985 he advised his assistants in Montreal and Toronto to 'be careful with AGB. The CBC is going to be in a difficult position when it comes to a choice between AGB, Nielsen's or others and we must remain detached and objective.'[27] Four organizations were eventually invited to make bids: AGB, Nielsen, Arbitron/PEAC, and a French company called Secodip. Each had a pilot people meter system in operation, but none had as yet completed tests in North America. Arbitron/PEAC, a joint venture of the American ratings company and a Toronto-based media research firm, had developed an 'on screen' (rather than a button) type of people meter called Scan-Canada which could also be used to measure the consumption of household products. Secodip's system still had technical bugs and no software for data analysis; in the end it did not make a formal bid.

Following presentations by AGB, Nielsen, and Arbitron/PEAC in mid-May, the BBM meter committee found itself split three ways. BBM staff still supported AGB; the advertisers favoured Arbitron/PEAC; and the CBC and a number of other broadcasters leaned towards Nielsen. The advertisers liked Arbitron/PEAC because it promised to correlate the viewing of commercials with product sales. However, Kiefl was 'skeptical of a system which would not only ask people to push buttons indicating their TV viewing but also wave a laser-wand over all household product purchases.' 'The implications,' he informed management, 'are too important to allow us to use such a system without extensive testing of such factors as respondent fatigue and co-operation and the potential bias on TV viewing data.'[28] In addition, neither AGB nor Arbitron/PEAC had Nielsen's knowledge of Canadian broadcasting. (Scan-America closed down in 1992 and is reported to have cost Arbitron upwards of $200 million.)

The Association of Canadian Advertisers, which favoured Arbitron/ PEAC, advised the BBM meter committee to delay making a decision until the results of current tests in the United States were available.[29] Frustrated by this delay, Nielsen launched a test of fifty homes in Toronto and suggested that it would go ahead with a national meter system with or without BBM. In November 1985, after more than a year's deliberation, BBM awarded the meter contract to Nielsen, but only after a strange series of votes. The BBM meter committee recommended, by a vote of 6 to 2, that a contract be offered to Arbitron/PEAC with its Scan-Canada system, the two votes against coming from Kiefl and the CTV representative, both of whom favoured Nielsen. But when the BBM board of directors met to consider this recommendation, only five of its twelve members voted, and they decided 3 to 2 to accept Nielsen, with Kiefl this time being among the majority.[30]

'BBM has been criticized for taking fourteen months to arrive at this decision,' BBM chairman Gary L. Miles told the membership a month later. 'I contend that this is BBM, the organization, operating at its finest. Here was a decision which in most companies ... would have been made within the first month and that would have been the end of it. Because BBM ... wishes to reflect the concerns and air the views of all its divisions, the process became truly democratic.'[31] A truly democratic process, however, would probably have resulted in the selection of Arbitron/PEAC and might well have saved BBM considerable aggravation. For confusion then reigned over which party was to draw up a final contract. BBM set about to do this, but before it was able to complete a draft, Nielsen submitted one of its own, which BBM found unacceptable. BBM's Peter Swain suggested that the agreement be broken into smaller segments for negotiation, beginning with the questions of ownership and reporting. But this approach was not adopted; instead, a full draft was prepared and submitted to Nielsen for comment.

The BBM draft agreement called for a test in 260 homes in metropolitan Toronto, for which it was to be paid $175,000. If the test was determined to be successful, Nielsen would proceed to install meters in 1,800 households by a three-stage process. The full system was projected to cost about $5 million annually, though by the fall of 1986 the figure had been revised to $6.6 million. The operation was to be overseen by an audit committee nominated by BBM. It would appoint an independent statistician, who would be given full access to Nielsen's records and allowed to test the system. The data would be owned by

BBM, which could market it as it saw fit, and Nielsen would give up its local contracts with individual television stations.

In Nielsen's view, BBM's draft agreement differed substantially from its original proposals on such matters as pricing, payment schedules, and the relationship between Nielsen and BBM. In March 1986 Nielsen's David Tattle met with BBM representatives to try to sort things out. Although Swain thought that BBM should retain control over and provide the documentary basis for contract negotiation, it was agreed that Nielsen would redraft the agreement for BBM's perusal, and in June a meeting was held to consider Nielsen's new draft.

Among those supporting Nielsen's position was CTV president Murray Chercover, who wrote to Kiefl: 'CTV is not interested in people meters service from BBM or any other source which restricts Nielsen, for example, to data collection only. We believe that report production, servicing, analysis, etc., should be available from BBM and/or from Nielsen but certainly from more than one source.' Chercover had several other concerns which he thought might 'preclude CTV's involvement with BBM.' First, he did not think that CTV should have to help pay for testing the system, since 'we did not ask Nielsen to participate in our program development costs.' Second, he thought it 'extraordinary' that the advertisers and their agencies would bear only 10 per cent of the costs, with the rest falling on broadcasters (especially CTV and CBC). He anticipated that Nielsen would decide to undertake a people meter service on its own and that many of CTV's affiliates would commit to Nielsen.[32]

Complicating matters was the fact that some stations felt that they fared worse in BBM's local surveys than in Nielsen's. CFTO-TV advised Nielsen that it would be a customer if it decided to go it alone.[33] Ironically, Nielsen was ready to sign the contract, but CTV wanted to redesign Nielsen's relationship with BBM to allow it a full servicing and marketing role, and the BBM board of directors was not willing to go along with this wish. As a way out of this impasse, Kiefl suggested in November 1986 that the CBC act as an 'underwriter' for the system in return for reduced fees in the future. Though nothing came of it, the proposal called for the creation of a new company called Meters Inc. funded by BBM members. BBM would sign the meter contract with Nielsen and then assign its rights to the new company.[34]

During the next six months, negotiations between BBM and Nielsen remained at a standstill. But in July 1987 the two parties finally announced the signing of an agreement to introduce people meters into Canada. Broadcasters were expected to cover 75 per cent of annual costs, now projected at $7.3 million and rising steadily, with advertisers and their agencies paying the rest. The CBC made a commitment of $2 million on the condition that BBM raise two-thirds of the broadcasters' share by 30 April 1988. But CTV, which was expected to pay more than $1 million, refused to come on board. It thought that the proposed fee structure, which involved higher rates for broadcasters with larger audiences, was inequitable. There was also a concern among other broadcasters that there would not be enough meters outside Ontario and Quebec to constitute a representative sample of the national audience.[35] As a result, the agreement between BBM and Nielsen fell through. Nielsen blamed BBM, but the industry cooperative argued that the broadcasters simply wanted to see how the situation developed in the United States. Although BBM indicated that it would keep the door open, Nielsen said the relationship between them was finished.[36]

Both parties decided to push ahead on their own, with Nielsen – which had to date invested $3 million on people meters in Canada – taking an early lead. Nielsen had already installed 250 meters in Toronto and during the next year made another 950 installations across Canada. On 18 September 1989, Nielsen launched a people meter service for network television in Canada. Families were given a single $50 payment for agreeing to participate for three years. In addition to the CBC, Nielsen's subscribers included CTV, TSN, the CRTC, Media Buying Services, and various advertising agencies. Its reports contained the most extensive information to date about the viewing habits of different demographic groups. But once again, some of the early data proved disconcerting as certain audience levels dropped below previous estimates. 'CBC Brass in Shock as New Poll Cancels One-half Its Viewers' read one headline.[37] This greatly exaggerated the situation. But a comparison of BBM and Nielsen figures after some of the bugs had been worked out of the new meter found that Nielsen gave consistently lower estimates of per capita viewing for all age groups except men aged eighteen to thirty-four, even though it gave higher estimates of viewing in non-cable households and to pay television and specialty channels.[38]

In the fall of 1988 BBM approached Les Entreprises Vidéoway Ltée, which had developed an interactive cable television system, to see if its technology could be adapted for use as a people meter. A subsidiary of the Montreal-based Groupe Vidéotron Ltée (which owned the second-largest cable operation in Canada), Vidéoway made a proposal to BBM in February 1989 to develop both the hardware and software for a television audience meter or TAM system. BBM awarded a contract to Vidéoway, set up a new meter committee, and proceeded to seek financial support from public and private broadcasters to develop and test the TAM system. Following a meeting in April 1989, a group of broadcasters pledged almost $1 million in support of the project, or about half of what was needed. Later that year, BBM decided that more extensive changes in its meters were necessary to ensure that there was no possibility of patent infringment; these were made between November 1989 and May 1990, when the first production model TAM was delivered to BBM. But despite this precaution, PEAC Media Research brought a $49 million lawsuit against BBM and Vidéoway during the summer of 1990, claiming that they had infringed on its patents.

In July 1990, BBM gave a demonstration of the TAM system at an Association of Broadcast Communicators seminar in Vancouver. By the fall, TAMs had been installed in 400 households and tests were being undertaken in Toronto and Montreal. The goal was to have meters in 7,400 households across Canada by the spring of 1992. But the tests were conducted on a shoestring budget and the results proved to be a major disappointment for supporters of the TAM system. Participants in the tests, it seemed, did not want to push the buttons.[39] It is doubtful whether all members of BBM were upset by this outcome, however, since the estimated annual cost for the TAM system was about $12 million or twice the cost of BBM's diary-based service. Following BBM's failed test, talks were resumed with Nielsen for a joint venture to extend people meters from the national network level to local and regional broadcasting. But in late January 1991 a proposed deal fell apart because of the concerns of local and regional broadcasters about costs and various technical matters. Although pressure from advertisers got the negotiations going again a few days later,[40] nothing came of them and BBM continued to use the diary method for both radio and television.

In a promotional document for its TAM system, BBM had outlined four basic limitations of the diary method:

First, since the diary is divided into (15-minute) timeblocks throughout the day, participants can record their viewing of just one station for each quarter hour. Yet we know that most people now view multiple stations during that time frame. Second, the length of time between the ratings period and the release of the reports is too long. Currently, it takes 3 to 6 weeks from the end of a survey to the release of the reports. This is because the diaries have to be mailed back to BBM and the data has to be input. Third, the accuracy of the television diary is under question. With the proliferation of signals available today, and the fact that cable companies are required to substitute the Canadian broadcast of U.S. simulcast programs, respondents are often confused as to which station they are viewing. The diary methodology relies on respondents to remember what program they have watched and on which channel it was aired. Finally, response rates have dropped in recent years. This has not only affected data reliability but also made conducting surveys more expensive.[41]

To improve response rates, BBM raised the incentive to $1.00 and redesigned its diaries. And in a paper presented at the Worldwide Broadcast Audience Research Symposium in Toronto in June 1992, Ken Purdye and Gerard Malo drew from data in the failed BBM meter test to argue that viewers do not, in fact, change channels nearly as often as supposed. 'Contrary to conventional wisdom, most sets stay tuned to one channel during a quarter hour period. Those tuned to more than one, stay with a principal channel during the great majority of the quarter hour, sampling another channel or two for just short periods of time. For most viewers there does appear to be one identifiable channel for most of the quarter hour, as assumed by the paper diary.'[42] But they admitted that this finding did not mean that the diary is a valid methodology. It only shows that 'the extent of actual channel changing as shown by live meter data does not necessarily rule out the diary a priori.'[43] And the problem of producing fresh and accurate data in a multi-station environment still remained.

THE PASSIVE PEOPLE METER

Although the diary's days are probably numbered, especially for television, it is not clear whether the people meter will dominate audience measurement for the foreseeable future. Upset by the early people meter data, the American networks joined forces in 1988 to commission a major investigation of the new technology. Acting together as the Committee on National Television Audience Measurement (CONTAM), which had been created after the 1963 congressional hearings, they hired Statistical Research to carry out yet another study. CONTAM's multivolumed report,[44] completed late in 1989, confirmed many of the networks' suspicions. It found that the amount of recorded viewing in people meter households declined over time, especially for certain demographic groups. In a survey of participants, a third reported getting tired of using the meter, half of these said that their accuracy suffered as a result, and over 10 per cent said that they hardly ever logged out when they finished watching a show. The report was also critical of the way in which Nielsen recruited its sample and concluded that the rate of cooperation was below government or even industry standards.

'At some point,' the CONTAM report said, '... a totally different measurement approach will have to be considered.'[45] This will probably involve some form of passive people meter; that is, one that will register listening or viewing behaviour automatically without any direct input from the audience. The possibility of developing such a device has long been contemplated. 'To eliminate all biases,' an article in the CBC's *Audience Research Bulletin* observed in 1958, 'apparatus would be required which would record on film the number of persons listening or viewing a set and the degree of their attentiveness as shown by their activities, facial expressions and exclamations.'[46] The author of the article thought that 'this technique would not only be impractical on the grounds of expense but would be repugnant to most people as an unwarranted invasion of the privacy of their homes.' But this assessment would now seem to have been premature.

Until recently, passive meter technologies were, in fact, quite impractical. The dynascope which Charles L. Allen, a professor at Oklahoma State University, unveiled in the 1960s was a cumbersome device consisting of mirrors and a stop-action movie camera. In the 1980s David Kiewit, who became Nielsen's director of engineering after working on military surveillance and targeting systems, invented an infrared sensor that could scan a room for 'hot bodies.' But unfortunately it could not differentiate between people and their pets, or even between people and light-bulbs. He later developed a wall-mounted sonar set, but it too encountered problems in identifying viewers.

By the late 1980s, however, a solution to these problems seemed in sight. In 1988 Nielsen began a national test in 200 households of an infrared device that required no activation by viewers. The following year, the French company Télémétric deployed a form of passive meter called Motivac and began to challenge the television ratings monopoly of Médiamétrie. About the same time, Arbitron funded an effort at the MIT Media Lab to develop a passive meter and also began testing the French system. Although scanning devices only look for the presence of a face, and have no way of knowing what that face is doing, they still seem quite intrusive. But even in this regard, a solution may be close at hand. 'If the key problem with measuring "people" is that they move around too much,' NBC's vice-president for research noted in 1984, 'perhaps one solution is to devise a meter that moves with the people. The concept for such a meter already exists: a battery-operated wristwatch meter to accompany the wearer everywhere.'[47]

Although passive people meters may be too expensive initially to measure audiences in small markets, it is safe to assume that the long-standing problem of accuracy in audience measurement is susceptible to a technological solution. But even if it is, the public will not necessarily be better served by audience measurement. In this regard, it is worth recalling that one of the proposals of BBM and Nielsen for a jointly run people meter system in Canada called for the measurement of audiences for commercials only.

9

Audience Power versus Public Needs: Five Arguments against Ratings

The differences between the commodity audience and the public viewership, between manufacturing the commodity audience through ratings and measuring the public taste through social research, cannot be overemphasized.

Eileen Meehan, 1990[1]

Most of the arguments made against the ratings system over the years fall into two categories: reasons for the questionable accuracy of ratings, many of which have been demonstrated in the previous two chapters; and ways in which ratings have been misused by broadcasters. Both apply more to programming than to advertising, since the ratings produced by any particular method are treated by advertisers mainly as a currency of negotiation. The purpose of this chapter is not to reiterate these arguments, but rather to show that even if it were possible to produce accurate ratings and eliminate their abuse, the result would still not be cultural democracy in broadcasting. 'Ratings,' the rhetoric goes, '... are but polls of the people to find out what they want from television. In fact, ratings are a way of empowering the people to have the final say on television programming. The networks seek to do nothing other than accurately mirror the state of popular tastes.'[2] But this view ignores the fact that other kinds of information are necessary to know what the public wants from broadcasters, and it overlooks the extent to which ratings themselves are undemocratic.

Program rating and audience share figures – and the raw data from which they are derived – can, of course, be reanalysed in various ways to help broadcasters serve the public. As Arthur Laird reminded his fellow broadcasters in 1964, ratings provide valuable information for programmers as well as advertisers.

[I]t is strange how the notion has arisen that ratings are only of value to broadcasters as a selling tool. On the contrary, given reasonably sound basic information, and provided you analyse it properly, ratings can be valuable for a variety of purposes – for detecting weak spots in schedules, for examining the effects of lead-in programming, for indicating how programs of different types share audiences when they run against each other, for showing up differences in audience habits in different parts of the country, and so on. All this can be extremely useful in showing where program or schedule adjustments may be needed and, more generally, for relating a station or network's overall objectives to its actual achievements.[3]

It is only through audience measurement data that broadcasters can trace patterns of listening and viewing behaviour for different seasons, days, and times of the day; determine levels of listening or viewing for different types of programming, including Canadian-produced programs; and assess the performance of individual stations and networks.

It is not primarily for these reasons that a ratings *industry* exists, however. Rather it exists because of the need of advertisers to know which programs will enable them to reach the desired audience in terms of size and composition. This is the main reason why tens of millions of dollars are spent every year in North America on audience measurement. And it is the requirements of advertisers – rather than those of program planners in public broadcasting organizations such as the CBC – that determine the nature and form of ratings data. 'It is apparent,' Irwin Shulman wrote to Laird in 1964, 'that all commercial audience-measurement data ... is designed to serve relatively uniformly the needs of stations, sponsors, time-buyers, agencies and salesmen, and only secondarily the specialized requirements of research practitioners.'[4] And as Laird himself admitted on one occasion, 'these various commercial ratings services for which the Corporation is paying fairly large sums of money, while reasonably adequate for purposes of time-selling[,] are becoming increasingly inadequate and indeed often grossly misleading for program purposes.'[5] Laird thought at the time that the 'gaps in our information about audiences' could be reduced if 'considerable additional budget sums are made available.' But it could be argued that programmers have even less need of detailed ratings data than advertisers do, except in so far as programming is designed simply to achieve the largest audiences possible.

Meehan has pointed out that the ratings industry is governed as much by its own internal economics as by the needs of advertisers or broadcasters. Thus, 'ratings per se must no longer be treated as reports of human behavior, but rather as products – as commodities shaped by business exigencies and corporate strategies.'[6] This way of looking at ratings is borne out by the history of ratings services in Canada, although in the case of BBM, for example, advertisers would seem to have exerted more influence than broadcasters. And the implication is that, even if the CBC was to press its programming-based audience information requirements more effectively, ratings would still have to be manufactured in such a way as to ensure 'cost effectiveness, productivity, and profitability.'

THE CONVENTIONAL WISDOM

'In view of the centrality of ratings in broadcasting,' Donald Hurwitz has observed, 'it is surprising to discover how little serious intellectual scrutiny they have received.'[7] This lack of scrutiny can be seen in the way that ratings have been uncircumspectly linked to the concept of cultural democracy. 'Radio audiences,' wrote Gleason Archer in *Big Business and Radio* (1939), '... control the program trends of the industry. Program directors may and frequently do offer new features to the radio public, yet the listener really sits in the driver's seat. Listener response, not necessarily by mail or by telephone, determines the development or discontinuance of any type of program.'[8] Through radio-audience measurement, C.E. Hooper and Matthew N. Chappell asserted in *Radio Audience Measurement* (1944), 'the radio industry seeks to furnish people with the programs they prefer, and not with programs which some advertiser or company executive *believes* they prefer, nor yet with those which some reformer asserts they *ought* to prefer. The determination of the public's radio program preferences and desires is the basic function served by radio audience measurement.'[9]

In a separate preface, Chappell suggested that audience measurement was 'the beginning of a great branch of science – the science of human behaviour in the mass.' It was, however, beyond the capacity of universities 'to contribute in any great measure' to this new science. Instead, 'the responsibility for its development must rest with business.' While business was still in the 'embryonic stage' of 'designing and perfecting the methods for measuring specific instances of public response to stimuli,' it would eventually be possible to abstract general principles or laws which would 'make the more wasteful measurement of specific instances unnecessary.'[10] This vision of a new science of mass behaviour might conceivably have been linked to a totalitarian dream of social control. But Chappell presented it as a means of ensuring that broadcasting fulfilled the wishes of the American people.

This argument has been reiterated on numerous occasions since Chappell's day. 'The "mass of consumers" does not decide, in the sense that it initiates programs,' CBS president Frank Stanton wrote in 1959, 'but it does respond to our decisions. A mass medium survives when it maintains a satisfactory batting average on affirmative responses, and it goes down when negative responses are too numerous or too frequent.'[11] 'If Not the People ... Who?' Arthur C. Nielsen asked rhetorically in the title of an address delivered to the Oklahoma City Advertising Club on 20 June 1966. 'Nothing in American life,' wrote Martin Mayer in 1979, '... is so democratic, so permeated with egalitarianism, as the use of television ratings to influence program decisions. Whatever the failings of Nielsen ratings, they do assert the equality of souls.'[12] Or as H.M. Beville, one of the founders of American ratings, put the matter in 1985, 'ratings ... are democracy in action.'[13]

That mechanisms such as box office receipts and radio and television ratings provide an adequate indication of what the public wants has generally been taken for granted by critics and supporters of cultural democracy alike. In recent years, however, some of those who would defend cultural democracy in principle have argued that traditional means of public input are not capable of realizing it in practice. In other words, the cultural products characteristic of modern democratic societies may not necessarily be a true reflection of public wants or values.

At the general level, for example, David Nord has argued that 'producers of popular culture sometimes exert strong control over the market and use this control to their own advantage.' In particular, they seek to maximize profits and avoid unnecessary risks through the use of standardized products or formulas, which offer people what they will accept, but not necessarily what they want. According to Nord, these formulas are 'largely the creation of producers rather than audiences,' as is shown by the fact that 'the greater the market power a producer has (the greater the opportunity to control risk), the tighter and more standardized will be the formulas.'[14] Nord finds ample evidence in support of this hypothesis in the history of American book publishing, magazines, films, popular songs, comic strips, and radio and television programs. From this perspective, audience measurement is not used primarily to assess what the public wants, but to determine which formulas are still working and to help generate new formulas when the old ones begin to fail.

Nord's analysis suggests that the problem with ratings is how they are used. But ratings suffer from several inherent weaknesses as an instrument of cultural democracy. First, in the ongoing battle between ratings producers, victory has usually gone to those companies whose methods of measurement have either had a bias towards the so-called commodity audience or else have been primarily designed to generate the demographic data desired by advertisers. Second, ratings give heavy listeners or viewers a greater say over programming than lighter listeners and viewers. Third, comparisons of programs in terms of their ratings tend to imply that all things are equal, which is seldom the case. Fourth, even if comparisons are only made between programs in equivalent situations, the program with the largest audience for individual broadcasts may not necessarily have the widest appeal as measured by its audience reach over a period of time. And finally, audience size, share, and reach are not perfectly correlated with audience enjoyment or appreciation; it is often the case that a program with a large audience is enjoyed less than one with a small audience. Given their complexity, it is worth examining each of these arguments more closely.

THE BIAS TOWARDS THE COMMODITY AUDIENCE

It is well known that advertisers are now less interested in large audiences per se than in reaching that segment of the population most likely to purchase their products. This segment, which is sometimes referred to as the 'commodity audience,' varies from one product or service to another, but in general consists of members of the urban middle classes between eighteen and forty-nine years of age. Meehan has drawn attention to the way in which various audience measurement techniques used in the United States have had a built-in bias towards this group; that is, by their very nature, they have favoured the use of samples of listeners or viewers with a disproportionate number of urban middle-class households. This was the case, for example, with telephone-based measurement methods during the period when telephone ownership was largely restricted to the upper and middle classes in major cities. The result, according to Meehan, is that ratings disenfranchise minority groups such as intellectuals and the elderly.

Meehan advances the general thesis that 'forms of [audience] measurement are selected on the basis of economic goals, not according to the rules of social science.'[15] She claims that ratings companies seek in various ways to balance the natural preference of broadcasters for a method of measurement that would tend to overestimate audiences (and thus facilitate increases in advertising rates) with the opposing desire of advertisers for one that would underestimate them. A balance might be achieved, for example, by using a technique to gather data that inflates listening or viewing, while at the same time overrepresenting the commodity audience in the chosen samples. However, Meehan does not provide any direct proof of her claim; there is no concrete evidence of conscious decision-making along the lines indicated. She only shows that most methods have had a bias towards the commodity audience.

Ratings firms have not been oblivious to the special needs of broadcasters and advertisers. But Meehan overlooks several considerations that would suggest a modification of her thesis. First of all, there was probably no practical alternative in the early years to using audience measurement techniques which favoured the commodity audience. Second, as measurement techniques became more refined and the clientele for audience data grew, advertisers were able to secure ample demographic breakdowns without having to rely on a biased methodology. Moreover, in Canada at least, the existence of organizations such as the BBM Bureau of Measurement has provided a countervailing force against the economic goals that Meehan associates with American ratings firms, partly because these organizations have always been interested in having the CBC as one of their customers.

THE BIAS AGAINST LIGHTER USERS

Even if ratings were to be based on samples that are fairly representative in terms of age, gender, and socio-economic status, however, they would still not reflect the listening and viewing preferences of all members of the public equally. For the main problem with ratings in terms of representation is not, as Meehan implies, that they underrepresent certain demographic groups. It is rather that they represent people in

TABLE 1
Radio quintiles in Canada, 1990

Quintile	Percentage of listening	Hours per week
#1 (Lightest listeners)	2.6	0–6.3
#2	8.7	6.3–12.8
#3	15.3	12.8–21.0
#4	25.4	21.0–35.8
#5 (Heaviest listeners)	47.9	35.8–123.8
	100.0	

Source: BBM Bureau of Measurement, *1990–1991 Radio Data Book,* 20.
The analysis is for all persons twelve years of age and over.

direct proportion to their amount of listening and viewing. The idea of broadcasting as a cultural democracy in which programs succeed or fail through a public vote ignores the fact that ratings effectively give some people more votes than others, for the simple reason that some people spend much more time listening or viewing than do other people.

The disproportionate amount of time people devote to radio and television can be illustrated in various ways. One way is to divide listeners or viewers into three equal groups according to how much they listen to or watch in a week. In the case of television, a British study (of London housewives in 1971) found that a typical distribution was:

Heaviest third – 30 hours TV on average per week
Medium third – 20 hours TV on average per week
Lightest third – 10 hours TV on average per week[16]

Another way is to divide the population into five equally sized groups or quintiles, ranging from the lightest listeners or viewers (quintile 1) to the heaviest listeners or viewers (quintile 5). For radio, the situation according to 1990 BBM data is indicated in Table 1.

The proportion of total listening or viewing accounted for by each quintile has remained remarkably constant over the years. BBM data indicate that in the case of television, there has been virtually no change between 1969 and 1989 (see Table 2). The differences between quintiles in terms of viewing per week are substantial. In 1989 the average hours of weekly viewing for each quintile were: quintile 1 (4.8

TABLE 2
Television quintiles in Canada for 1969 and 1989

	Percentage of viewing	
Quintile	1969	1989
#1 (Lightest viewers)	4	4
#2	12	11
#3	18	17
#4	25	25
#5 (Heaviest viewers)	41	43
	100	100

Sources: CBC Research, 'The Relative Appeal of Different Radio Stations to Light Viewers of Television' (July 1969), 2 [CBCRD]; BBM Bureau of Measurement, *1989–1990 Television Data Book*, 42 [BBM Files]. The data for the CBC study were derived from BBM; the 1989 BBM data are for all persons two years of age and over.

hours), quintile 2 (12.4), quintile 3 (19.8), quintile 4 (28.9), and quintile 5 (48.4).

If the listening and viewing habits of all quintiles were essentially the same, their disproportionate use of radio and television would not matter from the standpoint of using ratings to determine what kind of programming the public wants. If, however, these habits are significantly different, then the ratings give the heaviest quintile ten times as many 'votes' as the lightest quintile in the case of television and almost twenty times as many in the case of radio. Also, the heaviest quintile (whether for listeners or viewers) has more impact than the three lightest quintiles combined.

There are a number of possible arguments against the view that everyone should have an equal say in programming. First, it could be argued that those who use radio and television the most deserve the most input. But this would be like saying that heavy users of medical services should have a greater say in the nature of the health care system. One reason – though by no means the only one – that people may use a service less is because it does not adequately serve their needs. To give them less say into its operation for this reason would create a situation in which those who are the most dissatisfied have the least say about how things should be changed.

Second, it could be argued that this situation – where heavy users have more 'votes' – effectively operates in other cultural industries, such as film, music, and publishing. Films are made in large measure in response to box office receipts, so that frequent film-goers get to see more films of the type they like than others do. The difference, however, is that the commercial film industry in Canada is not supported by taxpayers' dollars. Of course, individual taxpaying Canadians do not contribute to the CBC equally. But in so far as the tax system is equitable, they all support the CBC in accordance with their ability to do so. Moreover, their different levels of support are not the result of different levels of need, even though actual programming-related needs may vary considerably from one group to another. Similarly, the broadcasting-related needs of those who make greater use of CBC radio and television are not necessarily greater – and certainly not more deserving of attention – than those of lighter users, given that all users contribute to the CBC equitably. In this regard, it should be kept in mind that even 'normal' users (those occupying quintiles 3 and 4) have substantially less say than heavy users.

Third, it could be suggested that because light users are generally younger, better educated, and better off financially, they have more alternatives to radio and television than do heavy users. They participate more in activities outside the home and are better able to articulate their needs. Why, then, should they be given more say? But why, by the same token, should they be given less? If ratings help to decide the relative balance of programming, including the proportion of education-information programming, should not all citizens in a democracy have an equal say in the outcome? The obvious response, of course, is that commercial broadcasters could not be expected to let the public decide such things as how much informational programming there should be – which is to say that ratings are not used to determine programming balance but only which programs within predetermined categories will continue to be aired.

Finally, it could be pointed out that the preceding data on listening and viewing quintiles apply to all broadcast outlets, not just to the CBC. It is conceivable that lighter listeners and viewers might devote proportionately more time to CBC programming than to non-CBC programming. Goodhardt and his colleagues found that heavy viewers of television watched more ITV, with its greater emphasis on light entertainment, than BBC programming.[17] If this were also true for the CBC, then arguably lighter users would have a disproportionate impact on CBC programming, at least in so far as the CBC is influenced by ratings. However, various CBC studies have found that heavy users

TABLE 3
Distribution of television viewing in Britain, 1985

Category	Percentage of viewing time	
Entertainment	55	
Light entertainment		17
Light drama		21
Films		8
Sport		9
Demanding programming	38	
Drama, arts, etc		7
Information		20
News		11
Other (children's, etc)	5	

Source: A.S.C. Ehrenberg, *Advertisers or Viewers Paying?*
(1986), 8.

of radio, and especially of television, are just as likely to choose the CBC as other programming outlets. As a result, light users are still less able to register their programming preferences for the CBC than are heavy users.

The question remains, therefore, as to whether heavy users have significantly different listening and viewing habits than light users. According to what might be called the constancy hypothesis, the way in which people distribute their listening and viewing among different types of programming does *not* vary substantially between heavy and light users. In other words, light users are not any more selective than heavy users. For example, Goodhardt, Ehrenberg, and Collins concluded that light viewers do not concentrate on minority programs with a cultural or specialist appeal rather than popular entertainment programs. 'If anything,' they wrote somewhat incongruously, 'light viewers tend to watch the popular programmes – that is one reason these programmes have high ratings.'[18] Nor are light viewers more selective in the sense of being more regular viewers.[19] In the final analysis, they maintained, we all watch similar kinds of programs. More recently, Ehrenberg calculated that the British population divides its viewing time as indicated in Table 3. According to Ehrenberg, these percentages vary only slightly between different social classes for any particular programming category and the same is true for 'younger and older, heavier and lighter viewers, and so on.'[20]

This analysis does not explain why heavy viewers in Britain traditionally preferred ITV to the BBC, and it has, in fact, been challenged by Michael Svennevig and David Morrison. While admitting that 'it is true that all broad genres of television programmes are watched by all classes of people,' they point out that 'what is often overlooked are the differences in viewing between specific types of programmes within the same genre of programmes.'[21] In other words, different segments of the population may have different *tastes*, even though they have the same general *desires*. As a simple illustration of this distinction, Svennevig and Morrison cite Paul Lazarsfeld's discovery some years ago that the middle classes in Vienna preferred bitter chocolate, while the working classes liked theirs sweet.

Unfortunately, Svennevig and Morrison were not able to offer any statistical evidence in support of their hypothesis. As they pointed out, the services provided by the Broadcasters Audience Research Board are not designed specifically 'to chart the minutiae of taste, and therefore are imperfect tools for the task.'[22] The same situation exists in Canada with the BBM Bureau of Measurement. Its data do not indicate directly whether heavier consumers of radio and television have significantly different tastes than lighter consumers. This is not to say that the raw data to conduct the requisite analysis have not been collected, but rather that the analysis has never been carried out either by BBM or by the CBC, which receives the raw data from BBM in computerized form.

What BBM data have shown is that certain demographic characteristics differ between heavy and light users. Analysing BBM data in 1969, for example, the CBC research department found that light television viewers were concentrated in the younger age groups and had more formal education (see Table 4).

In a 1984 survey, the CBC also found that levels of viewing are linked to age and socio-economic status. Lighter users are more likely not only to be younger but also to have more education and to hold a managerial, executive, or professional position.[23] This finding can be substantiated by more recent BBM data (see Table 5).

It should be emphasized that this result does not, by itself, prove that the viewing habits of quintile 1 are necessarily different from those of quintile 5, even in terms of taste within program types. What is needed is either a synthesis of individual analyses of taste by demographic category or else a direct analysis of taste by quintile, and there is no BBM or CBC study that provides either of these directly. However, there is some indirect evidence that in the case of television, at least, heavy and light users perceive the medium differently and place differ-

TABLE 4
Demographic comparison of TV quintiles in Canada, 1969

Demographics	Light TV users (Quintile #1) %		Heavy TV users (Quintile #5) %	
	Men	Women	Men	Women
Age				
18–24	25	28	11	8
25–34	21	22	16	18
35–49	30	30	25	29
50+	24	20	48	45
Education				
None	5	–*	7	–
Grade school	22	–	36	–
High school	45	–	49	–
University	28	–	8	–

Source: CBC Research, 'The Relative Appeal of Different Radio Stations to Light Viewers of Television' (July 1969), 3, 6 [CBCRD].
*Educational levels for women were not measured.

TABLE 5
Demographic comparison of TV quintiles in Canada, 1989

Demographics	Light TV users (Quintile #1) %	Heavy TV users (Quintile #5) %
35+ years of age	38	66
Some university completed	23	8
Managerial/Executive/Professional	18	7

Source: BBM Bureau of Measurement, *1989–1990 Television Data Book,* 43 [BBM Files].

ent degrees of emphasis on its uses and gratifications. A national survey organized by the CBC in 1972, for example, found that those who place the greatest emphasis on television as a means of relaxation are also those who watch the most television.

The study showed that, while the average adult Canadian watched television for almost four hours a day, the distribution of viewing was very uneven. The heaviest 10 per cent of viewers accounted for 25 per

TABLE 6
Responses to 'What do you generally do when you want to relax?' in
1972 CBC national TV survey (percentages)

	Anglophones	Francophones
Watch television	46	51
Listen to music	6	6
Listen to radio	3	3
Read	34	16
Hobbies	13	7
Just rest (sleep, do nothing, sit around)	15	23
Other answers	12	8

Source: CBC Research, 'What the Canadian Public Thinks of Television and of the TV Services Provided by CBC' (February 1974), 11–12.

cent of all viewing; the heaviest 20 per cent accounted for 43 per cent; and the heaviest 50 per cent accounted for 77 per cent.[24] And it found that, two decades after its introduction in Canada, television had become the most prevalent form of in-home leisure in the narrow sense of relaxation, passivity, and escape. When participants were asked to explain what it was about any particular TV program that made it preferable to others, one of the most common responses was that it was relaxing. And the most prevalent answer to the question 'What do you generally do when you want to relax?' was simply 'watch television' (see Table 6). One-half of anglophones and a third of francophones even agreed (or 'tended' to agree) that television was 'only' or 'mainly' for relaxation or killing time. 'To watch television,' the study noted succinctly, 'is, for many people, to relax.'[25]

Among lighter viewers, however, there was substantially less emphasis on television as a means of relaxation (see Table 7). It might be argued that those who most often relax without television have no other uses for television. But such is not the case. In fact, most viewers in the 1972 survey indicated that they expected television to fulfil a variety of functions and did not simply regard it as an entertainment medium. When asked to complete the sentence 'The best thing about television is ...,' a somewhat larger percentage actually selected 'education-information-culture' rather than entertainment. Although the required analysis was not conducted, one could reasonably hypothesize that lighter viewers would either place more emphasis on non-

TABLE 7
Television versus reading as preferred means of relaxation by viewing quintile in 1972
CBC national TV survey (percentages)

	Lightest-viewing Quintile 1	Quintile 2	Quintile 3	Quintile 4	Heaviest-viewing Quintile 5
Anglophones					
Watch TV	25	45	51	48	66
Read	49	43	37	35	23
Francophones					
Watch TV	30	49	57	59	66
Read	31	18	17	14	7

Source: As for Table 6, p. 13.

entertainment programming than do heavy viewers or prefer different kinds of entertainment programming.

The underlying question in all of this is whether, taken overall, lighter users (say, quintiles 1–3) are more selective or discriminating than heavy users (quintiles 4–5) *in the specific sense* that they are less likely to listen to or watch a program that does not promise to be reasonably satisfying. In other words, the suggestion is that what distinguishes the discriminating from the undiscriminating listener or viewer is not the choice of particular programs or types of programming per se, but the reasons for listening or viewing. The undiscriminating user is the one who listens or watches for reasons such as filling in time, being present with someone else, or being too tired to do anything else. It is clear that there are many reasons why some people use radio and television more than others. The question is whether one of these reasons – and a significant one – is the fact that lighter users are more likely to listen to or watch a program in anticipation of some kind of positive experience from the program itself.

THE PROBLEM OF UNFAIR COMPARISONS

Even if the constancy hypothesis as applied to levels of use is borne out by some future study, other basic problems with ratings would still remain. For even in the case of heavy users, their views on programming are not represented fairly by ratings. The reason is not simply that ratings reduce the question 'Should a particular program be retained?' to the question 'How large is the audience for the program in question?' All public opinion polling involves a reduction of the public mind – although in this case no account is taken of the fact that people might favour keeping a program even though they personally do not watch it and have little interest in doing so. As Jacques Ellul once observed, public opinion analysis necessarily 'effects a separation of what is measurable from what is not. Whatever cannot be expressed numerically is to be eliminated from the ensemble, either because it eludes enumeration or because it is quantitatively negligible.'[26]

Nonetheless, when people are polled about their preferences, all of the choices are normally placed on an equal footing. (After developing an appreciation index for programs, the BBC discouraged its staff from making comparisons across genres.) Surveys of audiences for radio and television programs differ from the norm, however. Although each program may ultimately be compared with all of the others, its ranking is based upon how it has fared in competition with a much smaller number of programs; namely, those shown at the same time and in the same area. These smaller competitions are affected not only by the kinds of programs involved but also by the amount of publicity devoted to each, the popularity of the programs preceding and following them, and even the networks or stations on which they are broadcast.

During the 1930s, ratings were known to advertisers as 'relative program popularity ratings.' But as C.E. Hooper admitted in 1939, these were

not truly a measurement of the popularity of any one program as compared with all others. If things *were* different and all radio programs were broadcast at the *same* time – and every program *could* be heard on every radio set – the per cent listening to each could be measured during that single period of broadcast time. The percentages listening to each could be computed, could be arranged in order of rank and the advertising man would have before him a true index of relative program popularity.[27]

Hooper suggested dropping the term entirely, and his advice was soon followed. But the practice of publishing lists of the most popular programs continued. As a critic of ratings observed a few years later, 'Fred Allen['s radio show] was never in the Top Ten until he moved to a different spot on a different network – a better time and following a better program. He joined the elite although his program hardly varied from what it had previously been.'[28]

The most obvious factor affecting the rating of a program is, of course, the nature of the programs against which it is competing. There are countless examples, but one of the more graphic ones in the case of the CBC is from the fall of 1956, when the two CBC television stations in the metropolitan Toronto area (CBLT and CHCH) switched from eastern daylight to eastern standard time one month earlier than the nearby Buffalo stations (WBEN and WGR). This created a situation in which the main competition for 'CBC Television Theatre,' which was shown on Sunday evenings from ten to eleven, switched from news and a sportscast on both of the Buffalo stations to two game shows, '$64,000 Challenge' and 'What's My Line,' on WBEN. Against the news and sports, 'CBC Television Theatre' captured an estimated 75 per cent of the metropolitan Toronto audience; but against the game shows, its share of audience dropped to less than 25 per cent.[29] Compared with all other programs, 'CBC Television Theatre' would have been close to the top of the list on the basis of the first competition, but near the bottom on the basis of the second.

Radio and television commentators have continued to use ratings reports to compile lists of the top ten or top twenty shows. For example, in a December 1970 story lamenting that Canadians 'still prefer U.S. programs and showy circuses rather than mental nourishment,' Blaik Kirby of the *Globe and Mail* listed the top ten programs as:

 1. World of Disney (CBC)
 2. Saturday NHL Hockey (CBC)
 3. The Partridge Family (CBC)
 4. Wednesday NHL Hockey (CTV)
 5. Ed Sullivan (CBC)
 6. Bill Cosby (CBC)
 7. Adventures in Rainbow Country (CBC)
 8. Room 222 (CTV)
 9. Carol Burnett Show (CTV)
10. Friday Night Movie (CTV).[30]

No explanation was given of how these rankings were determined, but it can safely be assumed that none of these programs was broadcast at the same time as another on the list; otherwise, both would no doubt have ended up much further down. The fact that 'not one news' show made the list was simply a reflection of the relatively even division of the audience between different newscasts, not of the popularity of news.

The rating for a program is in some respects less misleading than its share. A program with a large share in non-prime-time might still have a smaller rating than a program with a smaller share in prime-time. And in some cases, comparative analyses of ratings may prove useful. But more often than not the results are inconclusive. An early CBC research report attempting to determine whether there was a strong desire for religious programming concluded typically that, because conditions varied greatly from one program to another, it was 'very difficult ... to *sum up* a general situation in a particular program field in terms of ratings, or in numerical terms of any kind.'[31]

DIFFERENT MEASURES OF POPULARITY

The audience size of a radio or television program over a period of time constitutes a legitimate measure of its popularity and provides one indication of the degree to which it fulfils public needs and wants. But measurements of audience size and share have become so common that it is virtually forgotten that they are not the only way of measuring program popularity. For example, a program such as 'CBC Television Theatre' might conceivably have reached a larger proportion of potential Canadian viewers over a period of time than an American game show, even though it had a smaller audience for any particular broadcast. That is, it might be the case that people who like game shows watch them quite frequently, whereas those who enjoy high-quality drama partake of it with less regularity. In such a situation, which is the most 'popular' program – the one with more frequent viewing or the one with more widespread viewing? Clearly, it is a matter of definition, and the definition preferred by advertisers may not necessarily be the most appropriate one in terms of cultural democracy.

That this kind of situation does occur can be seen from a study conducted by the CBC research department in 1965 (the only one of its kind, to my knowledge) while developing television panels (see chapter 11). The study used a variety of measures to assess both the audience and the enjoyment level for three music and variety programs ('Ed Sullivan,' 'Danny Kaye,' and 'Juliette') and three country music

TABLE 8
Audience rankings for six CBC programs broadcast 29 January to 18 March 1965
(rankings supplied by author)*

Category	Don Messer's Jubilee	Country Hoedown	Red River Jamboree	Danny Kaye	Ed Sullivan	Juliette
Average audience size	2.5	4	5	2.5	1	6
Total population reach	4	2	5	3	1	6
Average number of viewings per viewer	2.5	4	5	2.5	1	6
Average enjoyment index	1	4	3	2	6	5
Overall enjoyment evaluation	2	3	4	1	5	6
Best liked/ least liked comparison	2	3	5	1	4	6

Source: CBC Research, 'An Appraisal of Three Country Music Shows' (June 1965), 5–8.
*It should be noted that the figures on which the rankings are based were very close in some cases.

shows ('Don Messer's Jubilee,' 'Country Hoedown,' and 'Red River Jamboree') over a seven-week period.[32] The audience was assessed on the basis of each program's average audience size, its total (undupli-cated) audience reach over the period in question, and the average number of programs watched by each viewer. Enjoyment was assessed in terms of each program's average weekly enjoyment index, its enjoy-ment index when considered overall, and its ranking on a best liked/least liked scale (see Table 8). While the effects of using different criteria are even more apparent in the case of audience enjoyment, there are also significant differences in the popularity ranking depending on the criteria used. For example, 'Don Messer' placed second on the basis of average audience size, but only fourth in terms of total audience reach. The difference was accounted for by its very loyal and appreciative following of older viewers.

AUDIENCE SIZE VERSUS ENJOYMENT

What Table 8 also makes clear is that the most-watched programs are not necessarily the ones which are enjoyed the most, regardless of how one measures audience size or enjoyment. For example, 'Ed Sullivan' ranked first in terms of various audience measures, but fourth, fifth, and sixth on the basis of different enjoyment measures. The variation was probably because it tried to provide something for everyone, which generated large audiences but resulted in lower levels of enjoyment, especially for individual programs. It is significant that when viewers were asked to indicate their enjoyment for the various series overall or in comparison with other series, it fared somewhat better.[33]

Peter Menneer, the head of the BBC's Broadcasting Research Department, has argued recently that 'there is (close to) *no relationship*' between audience appreciation and audience size. 'Some high audience programmes are not highly thought of by their viewers. Many low audience programmes are high performers in terms of audience appreciation.'[34] While this overstates the case against ratings as a guide to programming performance, it does not require much reflection to realize that measurements of audience size provide very little information about the precise nature and causes of audience reactions to different programs, stations, and networks.

The main value of audience measures from a programming standpoint is as a guide to how programs are developing in terms of their own particular objectives, rather than as a basis for comparing one program with another. To serve this end, ratings must be plotted over a substantial period of time and the results interpreted with care and discretion. Even then, however, ratings remain a partial guide to what Canadians want and need from their broadcasting system.

From the beginning, the CBC research department has recognized the limitations of ratings. 'Perhaps the most important point to remember,' observed an early report, 'is that, at best, *program ratings can only be approximations* and that they consider *only one aspect* of a program's total impact – audience size.' It added that 'it would be of great interest for the Corporation to know far more than it does at present about what people think of the programs.'[35] With this point in mind, the department developed various other tools for assessing audience reactions. But it remained enamoured of ratings. Though embracing qualitative research techniques, it might well have taken as its motto a dictum of Kelvin's that was quoted in Nielsen brochures in the 1950s: 'If you can measure that of which you speak, and can express it by a number, you know something of your subject. If you cannot measure it, your knowledge is meagre and unsatisfactory.'

10

Towards More Meaningful Public Input: From the Schwerin Technique to Image Studies

The people of Canada are shareholders in a $90,000,000 business. They have a right to say how the business is run.

Kate Aitken, 25 August 1959[1]

One of the reasons why Austin Weir advocated the creation of a separate research department was to enable the CBC to engage in qualitative audience research. 'In the field of qualitative research or programme analysis as carried on by the BBC,' he wrote to Donald Manson in 1952, 'nothing whatever has yet been done in Canada.' While admitting that 'qualitative analysis cannot replace quantitative audience measurement,' he felt that 'the former can have a profound effect upon the latter and at this moment there is a demand such as never existed before for qualitative information.'[2] Neil Morrison also thought that there was a pressing need for qualitative studies. 'While audience size and composition information gives some indication or guidance about the popularity of programs and the preferences of audiences,' he observed a few years later, 'there are so many other factors aside from program quality which determine audience size that this information has distinct limitations entirely aside from the question of its statistical reliability. Other methods need to be used which are more fruitful in judging program effectiveness and in improving quality.'[3]

By qualitative audience research, Weir had primarily the pretesting of programs in mind. But Morrison expanded its scope considerably to include a variety of survey techniques. These provided useful insights into things like the scheduling of particular programs and reactions to new programming formats. But they did not deal for the most part with larger programming issues such as the use of advertising, the amount of Canadian content, and the relative emphasis on different kinds of programming. They did not give an overall picture of what the public wanted from the CBC. In a working paper prepared in February 1959 for a proposed study of the CBC's image in Toronto, Soucy Gagné wrote that 'it would not perhaps be out of place to consider also whether it would not be of prime interest to investigate just what aims and standards the public would like the CBC to have.'[4] But this suggestion was not acted upon. Instead, the study in question concentrated on what the public knew and thought about the CBC. About the same time as Gagné's paper appeared, however, Kate Aitken, a member of the CBC board of directors, had the audacity to organize an audience survey of her own that did, in fact, ask Canadians what kind of programming they wanted from the CBC. Aitken was given a rough ride before she was finished, but her project seems to have hastened the development of new forms of qualitative audience research.

A FRAMEWORK FOR EXAMINING QUALITATIVE AUDIENCE RESEARCH

As mentioned in chapter 1, there are four basic criteria that need to be satisfied for genuine public participation in the determination of programming: representativeness, equality, regularity, and meaningfulness. In principle, if not always in practice, ratings or quantitative measurements of audience size satisfy the criteria of representativeness and regularity. But within the representative samples employed, heavier listeners or viewers have proportionately more input than lighter listeners or viewers. And for both groups, input is restricted to whether or not they listened to or watched a particular program. Ratings thus fall down in terms of equality and meaningfulness, and it is these shortcomings that qualitative audience research seeks to address.

Although the term 'qualitative audience research' is widely used, its meaning needs to be clarified. Within the social sciences, quantitative and qualitative studies are usually distinguished in terms of their methodology rather than by what they undertake to study. Put most simply, quantitative research examines relations between variables with the aid of statistical analysis, while qualitative research employs a variety of methods, including history, political economy, ethnomethodology,

Audience research techniques and public participation

	Representativeness	Equality	Regularity	Meaningfulness
Ratings	High	Low	High	Moderate
Program testing, focus groups	Low	High	Low	High
Surveys, image studies	High	High	Low	High
Panels	High	Moderate	High	Moderate

and textual analysis. Within audience research, however, there is a different basis to the distinction. Quantitative audience research is based on ratings and thus considers audience reactions to different programs, stations, and networks solely from the standpoint of audience *size* and *share* and related measures. Qualitative audience research is also concerned with audience reactions and, unlike qualitative research in the social sciences, often makes substantial use of statistics. But unlike quantitative audience research, it focuses on such things as audience enjoyment and appreciation. It is interested in what people think about programming and program services in subjective terms, including their reasons for liking or disliking specific programs or aspects of programming, when they would like certain programs scheduled, and how they feel about the overall programmming balance.

There are three basic categories of qualitative audience research techniques: program testing, including both pretesting and focus groups; one-time surveys, including large-scale image studies; and permanent audience panels. A preliminary assessment of these categories in terms of the four criteria of public participation is set forth in the table.

This chapter will examine qualitative audience research techniques that are employed on an irregular basis (program testing and special surveys), and the next chapter will look at the CBC's continuing network television panels. Although the panels come the closest to obtaining public input that is representative, equal, regular, and meaningful, it is only through a combination of quantitative and qualitative techniques that these criteria can be satisfied fully. The results of various research methods need to be systematically integrated to produce a useful and reliable picture of what the public wants from the CBC.

THE USES AND LIMITATIONS OF PROGRAM TESTING

When the CBC research department was formed, there were three main systems of program testing in use: the CBS Program Analyzer, Teldox, and the Schwerin technique. The CBS Program Analyzer, developed by Stanton and Lazarsfeld, required small groups of participants to indicate their reactions to programs and program segments by pushing various buttons in specially designed seats. It also used follow-up sessions to probe into the reasons for various responses. Teldox, invented by Albert E. Sindlinger, was essentially a refined version of the CBS Program Analyzer. Instead of pressing coloured buttons, participants drew flowing curves of their likes and dislikes. Sindlinger also developed a wire-recording apparatus called Recordox, which took down the remembered likes and dislikes of Teldox panels a month later. The third technique, developed by Horace Schwerin immediately after the war, was to have listener and viewer juries, as they were called, mark questionnaires at specified intervals during a pilot broadcast. Though considerably larger than the CBS Program Analyzer groups, Schwerin's juries were also questioned afterwards about the reasons for their reactions.

In 1960 CBS became the first network to test new television programs when it began inviting passers-by into its New York headquarters to see pilots of shows. ABC and NBC later used Preview House, a screening room in Los Angeles, to test new shows.[5] Program testing has also been carried out by companies such as ASI (Audience Studies Incorporated). Founded in 1960 by Pierre Marquis and Ralph Wells as an internal research department for Columbia-Screen Gems, ASI was purchased by a California service conglomerate in 1972 and became a privately owned company five years later with offices in Los Angeles, Chicago, New York, Frankfurt, Tokyo, and Hong Kong. In the tests, participants viewing a program, commercial, or feature film register their reactions by turning a dial to 'very dull,' 'dull,' 'fair,' 'good,' or 'very good,' as the case may be. Ushers cruise the aisles to make sure that the dials are turned and derelict viewers are electronically removed from the audience. Questionnaires are conducted to elicit other kinds of reactions, follow-up discussions are tracked by voice-activated cameras, and a modified lie detector is used in conjunction with some forms of evaluation.[6]

Program testing of this kind is not without its critics. In *The Great Audience* (1951), for example, Gilbert Seldes found somewhat ridiculous its application to the minutiae of program production. Schwerin, he noted facetiously, 'has data to prove that so small a point as shifting the relative positions of a gay and sentimental song may affect the holding power of a program by as much as ten per cent.' Sindlinger had claimed that pretesting was a way for creative artists to escape the pressure of studio executives. But 'with pretesting,' Seldes argued, 'the manufacturers of the popular arts find justification for repeating their formulas, and an independent creative mind will have little chance unless a Sindlinger test group gives him a vote of confidence.'[7]

Weir thought that program testing (whether for pilots or on-air programs) could, however, help to improve the quality of programs, especially during the experimental period of television development. The question was not whether to engage in program testing, but which system to adopt. In his view, the CBS Program Analyzer was preferable because it was easy to set up and operate and provided the best means of obtaining information about the reasons for various reactions. 'The value of any program analyzing technique lies in its ability to attach reasons to the "like" and "dislike" program profiles,' he explained to the general manager. 'A "dislike" reaction at any minute, for example, can mean "disliking" the voice of the announcer, "disliking" the subject matter of the program, "disliking" the background music, etc.'[8] Weir thought that participants would be more hesitant to give reasons for liking or disliking a program in an audience of several hundred than in a group of ten or fifteen. In making this argument, he seems to have been influenced by Victor Gruneau, who had proposed that his own company conduct program evaluation studies for the CBC using the CBS system.[9]

While agreeing on the need for program testing, Manson wanted more information about the different systems. 'I do not think we can make a decision to adopt the CBS program analyser until we have seen it demonstrated and have discussed its methods a little more,' he wrote to Weir. 'Here too, I think you could do some work on costs.'[10] Although Weir had estimated that the CBS system would cost the CBC between $1,000 and $1,500 (for either the stationary or portable version) and about $1,000 for each program test, the general manager wanted to know how much it would cost over a year or two. In response, Weir merely reaffirmed that the CBS system was 'the most practical and economical means of program testing presently in existence.'[11]

In the meantime, Schwerin got the jump on the competition by entering into a partnership with Canadian Facts to offer his service in Canada. He had originally approached Gruneau Research in 1951, but when Gruneau expressed no interest, he turned to Canadian Facts and worked out an arrangement the following year. Despite Weir's arguments on behalf of the CBS Program Analyzer, Morrison decided to hire Canadian Facts to conduct some experimental program tests using the Schwerin technique. The testing began in the spring of 1955 and continued for a number of years thereafter.

One of the first tests using the Schwerin technique involved the English television version of 'La Famille Plouffe,' one of the few CBC programs that gave English-speaking Canadians a glimpse into the society and culture of Quebec. (Whether this was an accurate view is another question; critics later argued that it depicted a Quebec untouched by the Quiet Revolution.) During its first season on English television, the program had been subjected to so much criticism that its sponsor had decided to drop it. Before abandoning the program, however, the CBC decided to remake one episode using anglophone actors rather than the original francophone cast, who had done the program in both French and English. Both versions would then be tested using the Schwerin technique. The results suggested that an anglicized version would probably not increase the audience substantially and would likely alienate some of those who already enjoyed the program. They also confirmed that, although the audience for the program was not large, it had a substantial core of interested and loyal viewers. As a result, the idea of using an anglophone cast was dropped in favour of making a number of minor changes which the testing had indicated might help to increase the program's appeal.[12]

The potential value of this kind of adjustment was overlooked by Seldes in his blanket criticism of program testing. For example, a 1956 telephone survey of reactions to the 'Plouffe Family' in the prairie region revealed that part of the problem with the program was that it was not fully intelligible to anglophone Canadians. 'Unfamiliarity with the roles and actions portrayed, lack of knowledge about the meaning of cultural symbols, social customs and the absence of equivalent experiences for people in Regina result in the program being labelled as "foreign" and "nonsensical" by some viewers.'[13] (Among those who indicated that they did not want the program on the air again, only six of sixty-eight said that it was because they 'don't like French-Canadians, foreign programs etc.')

Program testing thus serves a legitimate and valuable function in so far as it helps producers to make programs more intelligible to their intended audience. But the danger still exists that it will simply be used to make programs more pleasing or enjoyable to the majority and could thus compromise the artistic and creative integrity of producers. Moreover, the Schwerin technique did not make use of representative samples, so that its findings were of questionable generalizability.

Among those to benefit from a positive Schwerin test was Robert Goulet. But after Schwerin discontinued his operation in Canada in 1967, the CBC seems to have largely abandoned the pretesting of programs. In 1979 Brian Stewart, head of the Toronto research office, told a media commentator that the CBC had neither the money nor the staff to test concepts, and that 'we would steer away from asking the public what's acceptable *before* the event. It strikes us as much too limiting. We prefer to test reactions to programs already on the air, not just the numbers of viewers but their feelings about a show.'[14]

RECENT USE OF FOCUS GROUPS

American production companies now test all their new shows using focus groups, which are usually made up of eight to twelve people who fit a certain profile, such as liking sit-coms or being avid watchers of news. The group's discussion is recorded for subsequent analysis and its response to the program is sometimes filmed as well. In recent years, the CBC has also used focus groups to obtain feedback on programs. It was through a focus group, for example, that it learned that the otherwise superb drama 'North of 60' was striking a false note because of the absence of dogs. And after some puzzling fluctuations in the size of the audience for 'The National,' the CBC decided to run a focus group test. In this case, there were sixty participants (thirty men and thirty women), all of whom were regular news viewers. After completing a short questionnaire and watching an edition of 'The National,' they were divided into eight groups of six to ten members each (segregated according to age but not by gender) for two-hour discussions. The sessions were recorded on audiotape and observed through one-way mirrors; this was done with the participants' knowledge, although they were not told that the testing was being done for the CBC. Group leaders asked the participants what they wanted in a national newscast, what kinds of stories they wanted to see, and in what order the stories should be placed. In general, they liked lighter human-interest stories and those with an element of human drama, reports on environmental issues, and the fact that there are no commercials; they disliked repetition, lengthy reports on politics, and scenes of violence and bloodshed.[15]

Focus groups provide broadcasters with the most concrete and potentially meaningful responses to programming of any available research technique. But they are fairly expensive to run, costing about $2,500 on a per unit basis. And because of their small size and the way in which they are constituted, they cannot be assumed to be representative. As Barry Kiefl has explained:

Focus groups are the most subjective, bluntest instrument in our research arsenal. Because of the extremely small sample size, the results are rarely generalizable to a population, and because of the normal recruiting practices of most research firms, one is never very sure of the reliability of the data provided by respondents. Most research firms don't recruit using random, scientific techniques. Instead, they or their sub-contractors compile lists of people who have participated in groups before. Thus, one usually ends up with 'professional' respondents.[16]

Before the specific points raised in focus groups can be regarded as representative, it must be shown that they can be subsumed under broader generalizations based on scientifically conducted surveys.

WEAKNESSES OF EARLY CBC SURVEYS

From the beginning, the CBC research department organized a variety of surveys on programming matters (see chapter 12). These were used to determine appropriate times for programs, assess reactions to new programming concepts and formats, and learn more about the programming interests of different groups. In many cases, they pursued a combination of such goals. For example, when audiences for the 'Farm Forum' broadcasts on radio began to decline, the department conducted a survey to determine whether television might be a more appropriate medium. It concluded that although television might increase attentiveness and comprehension, it would probably not revitalize the farm forum movement, which was becoming more of a vehicle for social interaction than for study, discussion, and group action. A few years later, another survey found that listeners still liked the regionally produced drama segments on the CBC's noonday farm broadcasts, which were thought by some to have outlived their usefulness.

Most of the department's early surveys were based on unrepresenta-
tive samples, however. 'In view of the methods employed in this spot
survey,' a 1956 report on audience reaction to 'The Plouffe Family'
explained, 'the findings cannot be considered anything but preliminary.'[17] 'The sample on which the study was based was small, and limited to University educated parents,' a 1958 report on 'Nursery School
Time' observed, 'so the results have no general statistical reliability.
However, it is hoped they will serve as a useful basis for a discussion of
the program.'[18] 'The respondents are not necessarily typical of CBUT's
total daily audience,' a 1959 report warned, 'nor are they representative of the Vancouver viewing audience in general.'[19]

Moreover, none of the early surveys – or even a combination of them
– provided a general view of what the public wanted from the CBC.
They seldom asked participants about their general programming
desires and thus produced few significant ideas about how the CBC
might serve Canadians better. Partly for this reason Kate Aitken
decided shortly after her appointment to the CBC board of directors to
take matters into her own hands. Though described (many years later)
by the CBC's first director of research as a 'mole for the private broadcasters,' Aitken was probably sincere in her desire to make the CBC
more responsive to the public in the formulation of program policy.

AITKEN'S NATIONAL RADIO-TV SURVEY

A well-known writer, lecturer, and broadcaster, 'Mrs. A.' was appointed to the CBC board of directors in December 1958. In February
1959 she suggested that a national listener-viewer survey be undertaken to find out what Canadians thought about the CBC's radio and
television programming.* Not only that, but she offered to organize the
survey herself as head of the board's subcommittee on programs and
finance. Much to her surprise, the author of nine cookbooks soon
found herself embroiled in controversy as critics charged that she had
produced a plan for 'cooked research.'

Aitken proposed that some 500 mayors, service-club officials, and
other community leaders each nominate fifteen 'responsible and

---

* According to Aitken's undated six-page 'Report on National Radio-Television Study'
  (CBCCR, AR3-1-20), her proposal was discussed at a board meeting on 1 February.
  However, the minutes for the board meeting in Ottawa on 2–5 February (at which Aitken was appointed to the program committee) make no mention of it. Conceivably, it
  was discussed either casually beforehand or else at a meeting of the board's executive
  committee.

responsive' citizens for membership on the panel. She anticipated that of the 7,000 nominees, between 2,000 and 3,000 would agree to serve as members. Her original idea seems to have been that each participant would simply listen to or watch CBC programs at will and, over the course of a year, write letters to CBC headquarters with comments and suggestions. She would then prepare a synopsis of the responses for the board's consideration. However, this plan was soon modified in several respects – the reporting period was shortened to fourteen selected days (spread over a two-month period), participants were asked to choose one of nine designated areas of programming on which to offer criticism, forms were provided to help participants organize their comments, and staff in the audience relations division edited and summarized the results. In return for participating, each panelist received a two-dollar subscription to *CBC Times*, a weekly publication which included program schedules.

After further discussion at the committee level, Aitken's proposal was approved by the board's executive committee at some point during the summer.[20]* But Aitken was asked to work in conjunction with Charles Jennings of the program committee and Jack Trainor and Raymond Lewis from the research department. She agreed to do so, and the persons who were to select the panel members were chosen and contacted by mail. At this point, however, the research department began to have second thoughts about the study, especially since it was expected to administer it but had no hand in its design. On 24 July, Trainor and Lewis 'expressed department disapproval of the project and suggested that it be abandoned.'[22] Two weeks later, the department set forth its objections in a report to the president entitled 'An Appraisal of Mrs. Aitken's Panel Study.' But having secured the authorization of the board (or its executive committee), Aitken was determined to proceed.

The research department had good reason to object to Aitken's project. In the first place, it was not the function of board members to organize audience research, even with the department's assistance. The board was responsible for overall policy and could request certain kinds of research, but it was a different matter entirely for one of its

---

* According to Aitken's notes, the board gave its unanimous approval on 25 June. But the board meeting in Toronto was on 20–24 June and the minutes do not record approval of her project. The only mention of it is in conjunction with a discussion on advisory committees, where it is implied that it is almost complete. According to one journalist, she first presented her idea in April and won the board's approval in early August.[21]

members to take charge of an actual project and made the research department vulnerable to the following criticism:

Typical of the many little unnecessary 'empires' ... within the C.B.C. are its news-gathering service ... its film-processing laboratories ... and its audience survey department. Last year the C.B.C. spent hundreds of thousands of dollars to find out whether you preferred its programs to Buffalo, Bellingham and your record player. But so inadequate are the reports by the 37 members of its audience survey staff in Ottawa, the 8 in Montreal and the 7 in Toronto, as well as the reports purchased from outside sources, that Mrs. Kate Aitken ... is now enlisting hundreds of voluntary audience surveyors. If Canada needs Kate's Kibitzers, why does the C.B.C. pay out so much money – out of your pocket – to build up this new and evidently useless little empire in its head office?[23]

Aitken correctly perceived that the research department had failed to provide the CBC with a clear picture of the kind of programming that Canadians wanted from it. But she did not appreciate the extent to which the department was working in this direction. Nor did she realize the difficulty of developing a scientifically acceptable method of providing meaningful public input into programming. Her own approach was so blatantly unscientific that it was rightly dismissed by professional survey researchers like Walter Elliott and Victor Gruneau. Elliott pointed out that participants were not likely to choose a category of programming they did not like. And Gruneau noted that the method of selecting the panel ignored basic sampling requirements. 'What makes Mrs. Aitken think mayors and reeves are representative of the Canadian people?' he asked. 'If she's going to use this data to make decisions about what Canadian people like and dislike, she's going to be way off base.'[24]

The front-page story in the *Toronto Star* in which these assessments were offered was later described by Aitken as 'inaccurate, untrue and malicious.'[25] But the only possible basis for this extreme reaction was the fact that she was quoted as saying that the results of her survey would 'definitely' bring program changes, that programs would be expanded, shortened, or dropped altogether on the basis of what her 'army of critics' said they liked or disliked. (This statement probably exaggerated her real intentions, though it does not mean that she was quoted incorrectly.)

The criticisms of her method made in the *Star* were essentially valid and were reiterated by other survey researchers in subsequent newspaper articles. 'This is not research in any proper sense of the word,' A.G. Hetherington of Hetherington Associates Motivation Research told the *Toronto Telegram*. 'It is an interesting promotion. The chances of getting a representative group are pretty well nil. If you want to cook research – then this is the way to do it.' 'As a very old and dear friend of Kate's and one who admires her tremendously,' Charles C. Hoffman of BBM, conceded, 'this could not, would not, work in any way in any country in any type of survey. The bias created in selecting the type of person will make the results such that they could not be used for specific purposes or comparisons.'[26]

Criticism of Aitken's study was not confined to methodological considerations. It was also argued that the board was abdicating its responsibility by allowing a panel of listeners and viewers to guide CBC programming. 'The really disturbing thing,' *Maclean's* editorialized in late September, 'is that such a featherhead project was actually approved, without audible protest, by the CBC board of directors and the CBC management.' While reassuring its readers that Aitken's 'well-meant folly' would probably be 'quietly dropped' after a couple of months, *Maclean's* took pains to point out that her scheme 'repudiates the whole philosophy and purpose of the CBC.' Whereas 'the CBC was created to give Canadians something different,' the panel responses would either cancel each other out or else reduce CBC programming to 'the lowest common denominator of unanimous acquiescence.'[27] 'If Mrs. Aitken's idea is that the CBC should be directed by the prejudices and inexpert opinions of 2,500 people,' the *Star* asked a month or so later, 'why did she accept a directorship on the new CBC board at all? Why not let them direct, and throw the CBC to the winds?'[28]

These reactions were reflected in a number of letters to the CBC. A statistician from the head office of the Toronto Dominion Bank expressed concern that 'programmes of classical music and serious talks and plays ... may be sacrificed to whatever the bulk of Canadians, as represented by the panel of critics now contemplated, may prefer.' He suggested that some of the participants be nominated by the presidents of Canadian universities. Another 'taxpayer & constant watcher & listener' of CBC from Highland Creek, Ontario, wrote that 'surveys can be lethal if their limitations are not realized' and should not be used to guide policy. At the same time, however, it was acknowledged that they could be helpful to program planners, provided that they are not used 'to cut out some types of programs already being presented,' but only 'to ascertain if there are other types of programs which should be presented so that the CBC can more nearly reach the goal of presenting something for everyone.'[29]

It is interesting to observe that Aitken used very similar language in her reply to the Toronto statistician (to whom she offered a place on the panel). 'The purpose of the study,' she wrote, 'was not criticism of CBC programmes but rather an intelligent effort to discover if the programmes were sufficiently varied to interest all groups of viewers and listeners.'[30] Aitken was not, however, perfectly devoted to this purpose; she was not prepared to await the completion of her study before deciding what kind of changes needed to be made to CBC programming. Instead of keeping a completely open mind, she told the *Star* in late August 1959 that the CBC needed to do a better job of selling Canada to Canadians, give more impetus to children's programs, provide more programs on Sunday for working wives and husbands, broadcast fewer westerns, and play less highbrow and rock 'n' roll music and more light classical, 'which is what people want.'[31] These may have been desirable objectives, but by announcing them when she did, Aitken left herself open to the charge that she was organizing a study merely to support her own views.

Despite continuing criticism,[32] the survey-portion of Aitken's study was carried out between mid-November 1959 and mid-January 1960. Of the 517 'selectors' contacted by the CBC, only 174 (or 34 per cent) submitted names of 'selectees.' And although 1,739 of the 2,306 persons nominated initially agreed to participate, only 1,104 actually contributed comments, a far cry from Aitken's original expectation.[33] Scarcely had they completed their task than Aitken released some 'preliminary results' while attending a board meeting in Winnipeg, despite a previous decision by the program committee that there should be no publicity until it had considered the findings. Viewers, Aitken revealed, liked westerns largely because of the horses ('boy, do they love those horses'), were lukewarm about chorus lines ('producers love dancing girls, but the viewer isn't so mad about them'), and wanted different commentators for NHL broadcasts as well as something 'completely divorced from hockey' between periods.[34]

At the board's meeting on 27 January 1960, 'regret was expressed' – presumably by Aitken – 'at the premature publicity which the Study had received.' It was agreed that 'when the report on the study was complete, a copy should be forwarded to Mrs. Aitken by Management for study. Mrs. Aitken would then forward her comments to the Secretary who would distribute them, along with the report, to members of the Program Committee in advance of the next meeting.' The newspapers, which were now clamouring for more details, would be advised that no further information would be released until the board had considered the final report.[35]

On 22 April the board informed the press that the report was complete but, because of the personal nature of participants' comments, would not be made public. Instead, it would simply be turned over to senior program people for study. (This was the only official statement on the study.) 'The results are in from the CBC's do-it-yourself program criticism by citizen volunteers,' the *Ottawa Citizen* reported, 'but the CBC is keeping the verdict for itself.'[36] The real reason for the board's decision to keep the report secret, however, was not the personal nature of volunteers' comments; it was the fact that it contained a thoroughly damning critique by the CBC's own research department of the study's methodology. While acknowledging that a tremendous amount of material had been amassed, the department pointed out that 'the sheer bulk and variety of the information obtained is no guarantee of its value and potential usefulness.' In fact, because of the way in which the study had been conducted, it revealed 'almost nothing at all about the true or even approximate nature of audience reactions to CBC programs,' and its use 'might well result in a deterioration rather than an improvement in audience acceptance of CBC services and in public goodwill toward the Corporation.'[37]

As professional pollsters had warned, neither the 'selectors' nor the 'selectees' were representative of Canadian audiences. For example, 62 per cent of the participants were professional, business, or managerial workers, whereas less than 20 per cent of the Canadian workforce fell into these categories. An abnormally high proportion of the participants were between thirty-six and fifty years of age and there was almost no one under twenty. And in comparison with the 1,009 persons who contributed comments on English network programs, only 95 reported on French-language programs. The result of these and other biases, according to the research department, was 'to produce a final group of respondents much more favourably disposed toward the Corporation and its programs than are its normal audiences.'[38]

In addition, the open-ended nature of the questionnaire meant that the information gathered was so sparse, diverse, and ambiguous that most of it could not be interpreted in any useful or meaningful way.

With only just over 1,100 respondents spread over 9 separate categories of radio and TV programs, in two separate language networks, with many respondents within the same category choosing different programs to comment on, and with those who did discuss the same program often dealing with quite different aspects of it, the outcome was inevitable. Almost no individual program commented on was treated sufficiently thoroughly by a sufficiently large number of people to allow any generalizations to be made from the results.[39]

For example, there were seventeen miscellaneous and often vague comments about the 'Fighting Words' broadcast on 22 November, which had an estimated audience of 425,000.

The research department could be forgiven if it wanted to make Aitken's study an object-lesson in the folly of allowing unqualified persons to engage in audience research. Certainly, it was very concerned and felt that far too much attention was being paid to unsolicited or unscientifically gathered comments from the public. 'We would earnestly recommend,' it concluded, '... the advantages of utilizing to the full, whenever possible, the technical advice, experience, and skill of a Research Division eager at all times to be of assistance on any problem.'[40] Arthur Laird has recently recalled that 'CBC top management never did officially accept that potentially embarrassing Research report that helped kill the Aitken project. As we left his office after the presentation, President Ouimet carefully lifted the document from his desk and handed it back, officially unread!'[41] Yet although its critique was sound, the report overlooked the possibility that some of the material generated by Aitken's study might have been used to flesh out and give greater meaning to generalizations derived by scientific sampling. It also ignored the fact that audience research had as yet failed to produce very many substantive generalizations about audience needs and desires by which to guide programming policy.

PLOTTING THE IMAGE OF THE CBC

During the 1950s, there was a great deal of hostility towards the CBC in the press, in the business world, and among politicians. The corporation still had many supporters, but they tended to keep a lower profile. The extent of public approval was not really known, even internally, and this served to undermine morale. The press and information division was so desperate for positive material that it asked the research department to analyse 900 or so letters about Canadian television written for a contest in 1956 run by *New Liberty* magazine. The department complied even though the letters did not constitute a representative sample or even indicate the true views of their authors, since each contestant was required to explain both 'why I like Canadian television' and 'why I dislike Canadian television.'[42]

At a management meeting in 1957, Ronald Fraser, the CBC's director of public relations, lamented that his staff spent 'perhaps 90 percent or more' of their time responding to attacks from outside. Fraser called this negative public relations and hoped that the CBC might 'finally start moving in the realm of ... positive public relations' where the initiative would come from the CBC. To do so, he thought it 'essential that we be as familiar as possible with the various images of the Corporation held by our various publics.' Before public relations could begin improving the CBC's image, it needed to know to what extent and in what manner that image had been affected by anti-CBC propaganda.[43]

The next year, Fraser asked Morrison to 'provide us with the assistance we so badly need in laying the foundation for an intelligent public relations program – either short or long range.' He suggested that audience research might 'carry out or ... have carried out a number of surveys which would give us some idea of the image held of the Corporation by those not familiar with its workings in any way other than as viewers or listeners.'[44] This request was bolstered by a memo from Ouimet in November 1958 asking that plans be developed 'for an annual or semi-annual audience survey in all regions of the country on the basis of a carefully chosen statistical sample.' He was 'not suggesting,' he said, 'that the CBC is prepared to change its basic character in an effort to become all things to all men. All we want to do is to see ourselves as others see us.' But he added that 'if our surveys of public reaction indicate that we display unattractive characteristics which are not essential to our role, we will have a firm ground on which to base corrective action.'[45]

Ouimet was concerned about the impact of CBC announcers on the corporation's image. He proposed turning the supervisor of broadcast language into a supervisor of announcers; revising the hiring specifications for announcers 'with increased emphasis upon the candidate's naturalness and warmth of personality and on his potential in blending the common touch with the educational qualifications and interests we require'; and arranging for 'seminars or indoctrination sessions ... with announcers in an effort to get across to them initially that approach and attitude to the public and to their jobs which we would like them to have.'[46] He also instructed Dan McArthur, the former head of news and currently the director of special program projects, to examine the impression created by CBC announcers. McArthur then asked Morrison whether his department could do a study on announcers. Morrison said that the department was tied up with other commitments, but promised to try to get some information through the image study which was being undertaken.[47]

The project was first discussed by the research department's planning committee early in 1959, and members of the department were invited to submit working papers. At the end of March, the committee decided to conduct image studies in Montreal and Toronto using personal interviews. The studies were to include questions on attitudes towards each of the local radio stations, the technical quality of television signals, and the way in which radio and television were being used. The committee also considered estimates for fieldwork, which had been received from Nation Wide Interviewing and Pilot Research, and decided to accept the bid by Nation Wide. It was considered essential to conduct the studies without the participants being aware that the information they provided was being sought by the CBC. The interviews began with general questions about radio and television, and the interviewers were not informed of the CBC's involvement.

In May it was decided that the project should be restricted to Toronto and then followed up with a national survey in the fall. But the idea of doing an image study in Montreal was revived a year later in conjunction with a comprehensive survey of listening and viewing in Quebec. For the Toronto study, personal interviews were conducted with 736 heads of households (male and female) between 10 June and 17 July 1959. It was in some respects an inopportune time to conduct a study of the CBC's image. A bitter strike by CBC producers in Montreal the previous winter had tarnished the reputation of the corporation, especially in Quebec. A vigorous parliamentary investigation of CBC operations was just winding up. On 13 June Premier Leslie Frost accused the CBC of biased coverage in reporting the results of the Ontario election on 11 June. And on 15 June Joyce Davidson's frank comments on Queen Elizabeth's visit became headline news in Toronto.

The final report described the study as a 'pilot' and 'exploratory' inquiry and emphasized that many of the techniques used had 'as yet only tentative reliability and validity.' The CBC image, which was defined as 'the sum total of perceptions and feelings around which an individual reacts to the CBC,' was addressed in terms of programming, management, and corporate structure. It was found that a large segment of those surveyed were not very aware of or concerned about the CBC. Almost a third could think of no specific difference between the CBC and other broadcasting companies, although 70 per cent were aware that the CBC receives funding from Parliament. While only a small percentage thought of the CBC in terms of preserving Canadian culture, further questioning revealed that this attitude was based largely on impressions about CBC television. Despite identifying the CBC quite strongly with information programming, the CBC was not considered to be highbrow by most of the sample; only 24 per cent agreed that 'CBC programs are usually above the head of the ordinary person,' while 63 per cent disagreed (the rest had no opinion).[48]

In 1962 Laird asked Constance McFarlane to carry out the first national image study. The questionnaire was tested extensively in the field beforehand to ensure that it was easily understood, unambiguous, and as free as possible from any inadvertent bias. Canadian Facts was hired to conduct lengthy personal interviews with nearly 4,400 adults about their feelings about the CBC and other aspects of Canadian broadcasting. The study was intended to 'substitut[e] fact for conjecture' and 'exorcize some of the fictions and fallacies that are so often mistaken for public opinion.'[49]

'What Canadians Think of the CBC' (1963) was the largest study of Canadian media undertaken up to that time and provided a much-needed boost to the CBC's morale. Far more respondents said that the CBC was doing 'well' or 'very well' in terms of its mandate than thought it was doing 'badly' or 'very badly.' While news was considered to be the CBC's strongest area, the study emphasized that 'there is certainly no indication ... as has sometimes been charged, [that] it is in the field of entertainment that CBC has failed to attain the level of performance that is expected of it.' 'The Corporation,' it asserted, 'is felt to be doing almost as good a job in entertaining as in educating the public.'[50]

Other major image studies were undertaken by the CBC research department in 1972 and 1984. In the 1972 study, which involved a representative national sample of 4,939 adults, participants were first interviewed in their homes by Market Facts of Canada; they then recorded their viewing for a week in diaries; and finally they were interviewed on the telephone by Adcom Research about the CBC as a corporate entity.[51] For the 1984 image study, the department used a representative national sample of 2,900.[52]

By the late 1980s, demand for up-to-date empirical data on public opinion about the CBC's performance had grown dramatically. In 1987, therefore, CBC Research created a comprehensive once-yearly survey called the Annual Media Survey (AMS). It was initially restricted to anglophone Canadians, but in 1990 began to include francophone Canadians as well. English data are based on a representative national sample of 1,358 anglophone respondents aged twelve and over; French data are based on a representative sample of 719 francophone respondents aged twelve and over in Quebec, parts of Ontario, and New Brunswick. The sampling, fieldwork, coding, and data entry for the CBC-designed Annual Media Survey were initially carried out by Market Facts of Canada, while data analysis, interpretation of results, and preparation of reports were done by Erin Research. AMS provides information on program likes and dislikes, leisure habits, feelings about new programs, concerns about CBC funding, views on program fairness and balance, and so forth.

In times of economic restraint, the cost of conducting large-scale surveys has become a major consideration. Reliable national and regional data on both the radio and television services of the CBC would require a sample of 4,500 to 5,000 respondents; otherwise, there would not be a sufficient number of regular or even occasional CBC radio listeners. But to survey a group this size, whether through telephone interviews or mailed and self-administered questionnaires, would cost in the neighbourhood of $300,000. As a result, the other major qualitative tool in the CBC research department's arsenal – the network television panels – will probably assume increasing importance in the coming years.

11

Beyond the Ratings Mentality?
The CBC Network Television Panels

To give thousands of dollars to our program people and entrust them with entertaining, stimulating or otherwise satisfying the public, and then not to spend a few extra dollars to find out if in fact they have done so, would seem almost criminal.

Arthur Laird, 29 January 1965[1]

When the CBC research department began to engage in qualitative audience studies, it ruled out initially the panel technique developed by the BBC (its so-called listening or viewing thermometer) as too expensive and difficult to implement in a country as large as Canada. At the time, moreover, panels were subject to considerable methodological criticism, most of which was quite warranted. The department did not close the door on this approach entirely, stressing in its criticism of Aitken's ill-fated panel project that 'none of the remarks made in this evaluation are intended to refer to audience panels in general. They refer only to this particular exercise.'[2] But it was not until the board of directors endorsed the idea that the department began to reconsider the use of panels. Even then, it required further prodding from management before panels were established for the English and French television networks.

When the department did proceed under Laird's direction to set up panels, however, it went to great lengths to overcome the methodological weaknesses in other panel operations. As a result, the panels became one the CBC's most useful and reliable gauges of public reactions to programming and even became a model for the BBC panel. They provided various kinds of information for use by producers, program and schedule planners, public relations personnel, sales staff, senior network and corporate managers, and several outside agencies. They temporarily reduced reliance on externally produced ratings, lessened the need for costly and time-consuming surveys on reactions and attitudes to programming, and provided a basis for relating stated preferences to actual behaviour. Following much discussion with program people, the early panel questionnaires concentrated on eliciting reactions to what *had* been broadcast. But they also probed viewers' perceptions of gaps and inadequacies in program menus and sought ideas on topics that might interest them. And in recent years, there has been increased emphasis on using the panels to explore what the public wants to see on CBC television. Of the various research techniques used by the department, the panels come the closest to fulfilling – in and of themselves – the criteria of regularity, representativeness, equality, and meaningfulness. Combined with special surveys, focus groups, and ratings, they give the CBC a potentially powerful set of tools for learning what Canadians desire from national public broadcasting.

LUMSDEN'S VOLUNTARY PANEL PROPOSAL

During the spring of 1959, the French network of the CBC was trying to re-establish its television service after a disastrous strike by its Montreal producers. In its haste to resume operations, it scheduled several programs which came under heavy criticism in the press and elsewhere for their alleged lack of moral standards. The most disturbing of these for the moral guardians of French culture was 'La plus belle de céans,' a racy drama aired on 3 May about Mother Margaret d'Youville, founder of the Grey Nuns. Horrified religious groups complained bitterly to the CBC and their members of Parliament, and on 7 May Rémi Paul (Berthier-Maskinonge-Delanaudière) asked George Nowlan, the minister of national revenue, whether the CBC intended to apologize to the Grey Nuns for this 'nauseating ... insult to Catholics and French Canadians.' Agreeing that the program was indeed offensive, Nowlan said that the CBC was conducting an inquiry into how it could have originated and would take 'appropriate disciplinary action ... against those who were responsible.'[3]

The following month, the general question of offensive programming on the French network was raised at a meeting of the Special Committee on Broadcasting. On 16 June, Noël Dorion (PC, Bellechasse) asked Marcel Ouimet, the CBC's deputy controller of broadcasting, whether the French network had any facility for dealing with criticism of its programming. After Ouimet explained the role of the CBC's press and information service, Dorion asked acting president Ernie Bushnell: 'Do you not think that it would be a good policy for the C.B.C. to have an advisory board [on programming] made up of persons from outside who would have nothing to do with C.B.C. organization matters?'[4]

The broadcasting act of 1936 permitted, but did not compel, the CBC to 'make such bylaws as may be necessary ... to provide for the appointment of advisory councils to advise it as to programmes.' But as mentioned in an earlier chapter, the CBC was never enthusiastic about the idea and no councils lasted for very long. Concerned that the CBC was not doing enough to publicize itself, the Massey commission recommended that regional advisory councils be re-established in accordance with 'existing official policy.' It thought that in addition to 'keeping the CBC aware of the needs and wishes of the public,' advisory councils would facilitate 'keeping the public informed of the plans of the C.B.C.'[5] It also favoured the creation of national advisory councils on talks, though less for their advice on program policy than as a source of 'information on programme material.' However, the CBC still took no action to re-establish advisory councils of any kind. As a result, a number of groups continued to press for their creation; indeed, the Fowler commission reported in 1957 that 'an astonishing number of organizations suggested that advisory groups of one kind or another should be established to help the CBC in designing its programming.' Despite this pressure, the commission thought that 'it would be not only impractical but wrong in principle to set up a whole series of advisory groups.' It would, it said, 'to a large extent ... usurp one of the important functions which the board of governors has been established to discharge, and that is to represent the people of Canada.'[6]

The matter seemed thus to be settled once and for all. But Dorion's question raised it again and Bushnell made the surprising reply:

Mr. Dorion, I was asked a question the other day about advisory committees. I indicated that our experience in the past, a number of years ago, had not been a happy one. May I say however that we have been giving very active consideration to the appointment of a committee, particularly in the province of Quebec, such as you suggest. As a matter of fact, I will be perfectly frank with you and tell you if it had not been for the absence of the President that this matter probably would have been proceeded with before now. As you can see, I am somewhat reluctant to take a major step of that kind without his full agreement or at least without his knowledge. The matter has been held in abeyance. I would like to say, however, as far as I am concerned, and as far as some of the members of the Board of Directors are concerned, we think the idea is an excellent one.[7]

Contradicting committee chairman G.E. Halpenny's comment that 'everybody seems to be in agreement,' Liberal member J.W. Pickersgill asked Bushnell how an advisory committee could be set up without clashing with both the board of directors and the Board of Broadcast Governors, 'who, it seems, were set up for precisely this purpose.' Bushnell responded that there would not necessarily be any clash because the advisory committee would be working with CBC programming people, and it would be 'very helpful' to have a 'wide variety of views coming from the outside.' Despite his earlier comment about the CBC's unhappy experience with advisory committees, he added: 'I think we can work in complete harmony.' Progressive Conservative member Egan Chambers asked whether the Massey and Fowler commissions had recommended advisory committees. Bushnell said that they had, though this was true only of the Massey commission.[8]

Undeterred by Pickersgill's objection, Bushnell placed the creation of a Quebec advisory committee on the agenda for the board of directors' meeting in Toronto on 22–24 June and had a draft press release prepared announcing its appointment. He reminded the board of the volume of criticism of French network programming and argued that an advisory committee on programming was a practical way to bring morality into line with public wishes and stem criticism of the CBC in Quebec. To his surprise, however, several members of the board – Raymond Dupuis, Alixe Carter, C.B. Lumsden, and William L. Morton – disagreed. Dupuis remarked that if an advisory committee found that its advice was not accepted, the situation for the CBC might be worse than before. Carter pointed out that the creation of an advisory committee in Quebec might lead to similar demands in other provinces. And Lumsden and Morton thought that the CBC should respond to public criticism through its own efforts. Reliance on an external committee would be an abdication of responsibility. If the CBC could not control and balance its own output, Morton said, it should go out of business.[9]

As an alternative to a program advisory committee in Quebec, Lumsden then raised the possibility of setting up listener and viewer panels. These would provide comments on programming but would have no formal advisory responsibility. Concerned primarily to find some means of placating the critics of French network programming, Bushnell quickly dropped his own proposal and latched on to Lumsden's idea. He suggested that the CBC might say that it was studying the alternative idea of setting up voluntary program appraisal panels as a possible solution to the problem of maintaining high moral standards. In the same vein, Lumsden recommended that the CBC explain that it favoured panels over advisory committees because their use would not constitute an abdication of the corporation's own responsibilities.[10]

FIRST STEPS TOWARDS AN AUDIENCE PANEL

The casual manner in which the board endorsed the idea of program appraisal panels belied the difficulties involved in their operation. The CBC research department had been deterred by methodological as well as financial and administrative considerations from setting up panels similar to those of the BBC. In a memo drafted on 14 July 1959, Sy Yasin, a research officer in Ottawa, reiterated the view that it would be 'both expensive and inefficient to start with a full-blown national panel.' He proposed that the panel be segmented and developed in stages, beginning with panels in Montreal, Ottawa, and Toronto. During this time, the CBC could conduct experiments to see whether volunteer panelists – which the BBC preferred – differ from recruited panelists. Yasin saw no need to rush things, if only because 'the idea behind building a panel operation is as much, if not more, for PR purposes as for information.' In this respect, he thought that 'it would be useful to ascertain the extent to which being a panel member generates good will towards the Corporation. This implies that some instrument or scale should be developed which would measure the general attitude of an individual towards the CBC. Naturally, the instrument would have to be such that its purpose is not too obvious to the respondent.'[11]

However, as Earl Kliman, a research officer in Toronto, observed a few days later, 'the Board of Directors resolution has resulted in a complete change of outlook with regard to this problem. They want a national panel to be in operation by fall.' He admitted that 'the report of the discussion and the resolution itself are vague and undefined, and fail to explain what purpose is to be served by such a panel.'[12] Nevertheless, Raymond Lewis telexed a request on 16 July to Robert

Silvey, the head of BBC Audience Research, for a 'complete kit of materials now being used in your panel operations.' He had, he said, an 'urgent need primarily for recruiting techniques, instruction forms, questionnaires and processing procedures.'[13]

The board's timetable proved to be impractical. Kliman, who had submitted a preliminary set of recommendations in his July memorandum, wrote to Morrison in October that 'subsequent evidence and a felt need to reorganize our thinking in this regard caused me to suspend work on it before having submitted it for discussion or approval or having worked out costs.' As a result of rethinking the matter, Kliman now recommended a pilot project in Toronto. He thought that the panel should have about 400 to 500 members (drawn from a sample of about 2,000) and operate for a year before having its members replaced. He also felt that participation should be voluntary, even though 'this does not provide a truly representative sample of opinion.'[14]

Kliman's proposal seems to have fallen victim to the 'pressure of more urgent work' within the department.[15] But it was not, in any event, an adequate basis even for an exploratory panel operation. It overestimated the length of time that panelists could serve effectively and required the use of a questionnaire that was much too complex for practical purposes. Moreover, the department had not really decided, in its own mind, whether panels would be of sufficient value to the CBC to justify their cost. While the idea of panels was not dropped entirely, it was placed on the back burner for several years.

ORGANIZATION OF NETWORK TELEVISION PANELS

In late February 1962, Eugene Hallman, the CBC's vice-president of programming, met with Arthur Laird, by then the acting director of research, to convey management's objectives with regard to audience research. Hallman explained that management wanted more effective and rapid means of measuring audience reactions to controversial programs. 'There is a special interest,' he reiterated in a memo the following day, 'in knowing whether or not certain of our programs which provoke strong public reaction and produce public controversy indicate a failure on the Corporation's part to assess accurately in advance the likes and dislikes of our audiences.' 'At the present time,' he added, '... we have to rely almost exclusively on telephone calls, letters, and the reviews of newspaper columnists to measure public reaction to specific shows.'* Although allowing that use of the diary method would yield more complete information, Hallman favoured a telephone survey panel because it would provide data more quickly. He assumed that two panels would be necessary, one for English programs and the other for French, and envisaged that the research department would require at most 'several days notice' to organize a telephone survey of reactions to a specific program. He thought that the results would mainly be used 'either in replying to criticisms contained in letters or in general answers to public discussion about CBC's activities.'[16]

Although Hallman asked for a response by early March, Laird took no immediate steps to act upon his request 'to establish what would be involved in creating a panel.' In the spring of 1963 he informed the department that he 'would like to revive this whole matter of panels and alternatives at an early staff meeting.'[17] But it was not until the summer of 1964 that he contacted McDonald Research to begin working out plans for a panel operation.

Laird did not at this stage rule out the telephone survey technique favoured by Hallman. But it was soon decided that there were two major problems with it. First, as McDonald Research pointed out in a report to Laird in October, its costs 'would probably be inconsistent with the utility of the resulting data.' McDonald estimated that it would cost almost $5,000 a week to survey twenty programs. And second, it was difficult to use in rural areas. A working committee composed of Laird, Ken Purdye, and Constance McFarlane set about, therefore, to design a panel operation using diaries. Together they spent hundreds of hours conceptualizing the panel and designing its methodology, including the sample and questionnaire. As part of this process, McDonald was hired to conduct a study to determine whether a self-completion diary could yield comparable program evaluation data at an acceptable cost and within a reasonable time frame ('not more than 10 days to 2 weeks after the programme week').[18]

During the first three months of 1965, McDonald Research ran an ex-

---

* The views of vocal minorities were, by then, known to be quite untypical of audience response. According to Constance McFarlane, an unsuccessful attempt was made to establish a generalizable relationship between unsolicited comments and representative opinions. One hypothesis was that if 90 per cent of telephone calls are critical, this represents 5 to 10 per cent of the audience. But it soon became clear that there is no hard and fast rule in this regard.

perimental fourteen-week panel operation under the guidance of Purdye and McFarlane. It included a special survey to see to what extent panels could be used to investigate other types of problems. The survey concluded that 'a questionnaire inserted with the regular panel diary will prove to be an excellent vehicle for studying subjects of current interest to the Corporation.'[19] As a result of its success, a regular panel for English television network programming (CBC and CTV) was instituted in the fall of 1965. And in April 1967 Hallman wrote to Laird that 'the Board and Management have assigned *highest priority* to the implementation this Fall of our plans for a French Network panel comparable to the service now provided for the English Network TV Service.'[20]

In January 1965, as the first returns began to come in, Laird sent Hallman a lengthy memo on the 'scope, cost, and immediate future' of the English television network panel. Its main purpose, he wrote, 'is to "go beyond the ratings" and to obtain information on what those who see our programs actually think of them.' Up to this time, the research department had conducted numerous special surveys on reactions to particular programs and types of programming, but it had not been able to produce continuous qualitative data on a wide variety of programs. With this kind of data, Laird argued, the CBC would 'no longer have to accept the patently false assumption that audiences to big-audience programs necessarily get more enjoyment or satisfaction from them than do audiences to small-audience programs.'[21]

Laird also suggested that the panels would have 'considerable implications ... for sales.' The Fowler committee on broadcasting was shortly to call on the CBC to derive more of its revenues from commercial sources, and Laird observed that:

Not only will we be able to provide them [sales] with much more specific information than they have ever had before concerning the age, sex, educational, and occupational composition of the audiences that our network programs and CTV network programs are reaching but, in due course, given the funds, this is an ideal type of operation in which to establish, periodically, the actual purchasing habits of those who watch different types of programs ... The advantages to our network sales people could be very great indeed because of course it would put them in a position of offering certain network programs as vehicles for delivering not merely big audiences of particular kinds of potential customers for nationally advertised products. I see this as a definite prospect for the future.[22]

In Laird's view, gathering information on viewers' purchasing habits was a legitimate extension of the conventional demographics of audience composition. He saw no conflict of interest between using such information to attract advertisers and remaining faithful to the principles of public service broadcasting.

Laird disagreed with Hallman, however, about the efficacy of using the panels to deflect criticism of the CBC. He acknowledged that one of their principal benefits would be to 'put the Corporation in the position of feeling that, come hell or high water, come Braithwaite or Bushnell, no one who purports to tell us what the public thinks of our programs can possibly know as much about this as we know ourselves.' This, he said, 'could perhaps be a landmark in the Corporation's development.' But he emphasized that he was 'not suggesting that consideration should be given to using such information regularly to refute public criticism.' Like the BBC, he suggested, the CBC 'would do well not to seek such publicity – unless special circumstances require it.'[23]

Laird stressed that 'none of this will supersede, or nullify the value of, commercially-purchased ratings information.' Indeed, the panel was designed not only to elicit reactions to on-air programs but also to measure audience size on a weekly basis.[24] The panel's audience-size data filled an important need since BBM and Nielsen still only measured network television audiences three or four times a year. The panel thus provided the first continuing data on television audience size in Canada. Since the late 1970s, panel-based estimates of television audience size have not been used by the CBC because they are considered to be less reliable than BBM and Nielsen measurements.* However, audience-size data are still collected through the panel to facilitate analyses of audience composition, especially in relation to reactions to programming.

---

* It was observed over time that the panel's estimates were consistently higher than those of BBM and Nielsen. Although it was not really known why this was so, it was thought to follow from the hypothesis that if respondents are given diaries ahead of time, it tends to increase their viewing (or reported viewing). In this regard, the CBC's panel diary goes one step further than the diaries of BBM and Nielsen in that it lists the names of a limited number of programs (mainly CBC) by day. In other words, it is basically a TV guide. See discussion below.

The main value of the panels lies in the qualitative information which they generate. This takes two main forms: an enjoyment index for a variety of programs and some of their components; and responses to supplementary questions (both specific and open-ended) on one program each day. The latter are based on discussions with producers and the anticipation of possible audience reactions. Special questionnaires are also periodically inserted in the diaries.

OPERATION OF THE PANELS

The initial panel operation was undertaken on a shoestring budget. Its weekly budget was about $2,600 – or $65 a program for each of the forty CBC shows covered. '[M]y whole approach to this thing,' Laird said, 'has been that we simply had to get some kind of continuous research operation going, even a fairly humble project to start with that could be paid for out of our present budget, since it was clear that if we were to wait until really adequate funds were available it might be like waiting for Godot.'[25]

Members of the panels were recruited for a period of twelve weeks and given a premium if they returned a specified number of diaries. Originally, the English network panel had about 2,000 members, though the number fluctuated considerably during the early years. The panel was selected on a probability basis to be representative of all persons over the age of twelve living in television-equipped homes where English was the main language. This system, as Laird took pains to point out to Hallman, was in contrast to that used in previous panel operations. 'No volunteering, no Kate-Aitken type special recruitment of friends and buddies, no recourse even to the kind of procedure adopted by the BBC in recruiting panelists by making periodic announcements on air and in the press. This is a strict probability sample operation, panel members being selected in such a way that any bias resulting from the selection has been reduced to a minimum.'[26]

Within a couple of years, the English network panel was increased slightly to 2,200 members, but this number still proved inadequate for certain purposes. For example, as Laird pointed out in 1966, 'it frequently does not provide enough viewers of afternoon programs to indicate anything more than how many people are watching.'[27] During the next few years, the English panel was increased to about 2,500, but without solving the problem, and to expand the panel beyond this number was not economically feasible. To acquire even this many required an initial selection of about 12,500 names since the yield was only about 20 per cent. About 40 per cent of those contacted would initially agree to cooperate, another 40 per cent would refuse to cooperate, and the remaining 20 per cent could not be contacted even after three telephone calls. Of those agreeing to cooperate, about half would actually return a diary in any given week.[28]

To eliminate any pro- or anti-CBC bias that might affect recruitment or influence panelists' reactions, the panel was administered by an independent field company, although the coding, key punching, and data processing were originally done by the CBC for reasons of economy. The first company to run the panel was McDonald Research, but when it ran into difficulties, the operation was taken over by Complan. There is reason to believe that some panelists were aware of the CBC's involvement, however. In the first place, there were a number of newspaper stories on the panel.[29] In addition, the preponderance of CBC programs in the early diaries* led some participants to suspect that the panels were intended for the use of the CBC. In late 1967 Earl Kliman, who had left CBC to work at Complan, passed on to Laird a letter from a Vancouver panelist. 'It has been interesting guessing your biases during the question period,' it read. 'I would say you are slanted toward the CBC; – you do not ask questions about CTV programs, nor do you even list all CTV programs.'[30]

The diaries sent to panelists tried to discourage them from 'duty viewing.' But from the beginning, it was observed that levels of recorded viewing tended to be very high during the first week of participation on the panel. Recorded viewing levels would then decline until the fourth week and remain fairly stable thereafter. This tendency did not necessarily mean that data for the first three weeks were inflated as a result of initial enthusiasm for the project; there was also the possibility that data for the final nine weeks were deflated as enthusiasm for keeping a precise record of viewing declined.[31] However, a study con-

---

* The first questionnaire had 26 CBC and 14 CTV programs. Two years later, there was about the same division. For example, the diary for the week of 24–30 March 1967 listed 107 programs. Of these, 50 were broadcast on the full CBC network, 24 were 'CBC-available,' 7 were CBC limited-network programs, and only 26 were CTV programs. In his memo to Hallman on 29 January 1965, Laird said that the inclusion of CTV programs was 'done, first, for certain purposes of comparison, but also to obscure further the fact that it is the CBC who is running this panel. So far as the panelists are concerned it is a McDonald Research operation, but if the only programs included had been CBC programs some of the panelists would probably have smelled a rat, and their answers might have been biased as a result.'

ducted for the CBC by McDonald Research in 1965 provided fairly strong evidence that the first few weeks of data produced inflated estimates of audience size. It compared audience estimates obtained from the panel members in weeks two and eleven with estimates obtained using day-after telephone calls.[32] As a result, the research department subsequently discarded the first three weeks of information obtained from panelists in calculating audience-size estimates.[33] At the same time, to minimize the possible effects of respondent conditioning, the membership of the panel was periodically rotated.

The audience-size data produced by the panels were not directly comparable to the ratings produced by the syndicated services. In the first place, the panels measured the cumulative audience for a program (that is, the audience to any part of it), whereas BBM and Nielsen measured the average quarter-hour audience. In addition, the panels covered different geographical areas, used different definitions of 'adult' and 'teenager,' and employed different sampling techniques. The panels were also concerned with individual viewing, whereas the ratings services were oriented towards set-usage.

Nonetheless, some consistent differences in audience-size estimates soon became apparent. On the one hand, the panel tended to provide higher estimates than the ratings services for certain American entertainment programs, such as 'Beverly Hillbillies,' 'Bob Hope Theatre,' 'Red Skelton,' and 'Green Acres.' On the other hand, the ratings services tended to give much higher estimates for other types of programs, especially CBC productions with more serious content, such as 'Nation's Business,' 'Provincial Affairs,' 'Newsmagazine,' 'Festival,' and 'Telescope,' and CBC programs following 'Saturday Night Hockey,' such as 'Juliette,' 'World of Music,' and 'In Person.' Overall, viewing levels were generally higher in the ratings services than in the panel.[34]

Some of these discrepancies could be explained by the fact that programs such as 'Nation's Business' and 'Juliette' did not have neat quarter-hour time slots, so that their audience was measured by the ratings services in conjunction with other programs. However, there was also the possibility that those who served on the CBC panels were somehow different in terms of program preferences than those who participated in BBM and Nielsen surveys. One indication of this possibility was the fact that the level of response for the CBC panels was lower than for BBM surveys, although this difference in response rates could also be explained by the different premiums awarded. Another indication was that the format of the diary used by the CBC panels was different from that of BBM and Nielsen diaries – in particular, the CBC diary named individual programs. To determine whether – and to what extent – the format of the CBC panel diary was responsible for differences in audience-size estimates, Ken Purdye suggested that an experiment be conducted using former CBC panel members.

Purdye proposed that four subsamples of 400 to 500 previous panel members (the use of previous panel members throughout eliminated the possibility that different levels of recorded viewing were the result of differences in the types of person recruited) record their viewing using four different types of diary: i) a standard CBC panel diary requiring panelists to check programs viewed from a selected list and indicate their degree of enjoyment for each; ii) an 'open-ended' diary containing no program names and requiring panelists to write down the names of programs viewed and answer a question on enjoyment for each; iii) a standard CBC panel diary except for the removal of the section on enjoyment; and iv) a typical syndicated ratings service diary requiring participants to record listening and viewing on a time-period basis. It was hoped that by comparing the results, light would be shed on three questions: What is the effect of listing program names in a diary? What is the effect of asking viewers of a program to answer a question on their enjoyment of it? And what is the effect of using a program-oriented diary rather than a time-period-oriented diary?

The study, which was conducted during the last week of March 1967, found that the inclusion of a question on the enjoyment of programs in the CBC panel diary did *not* have any effect on measures of audience size. Thus use of the panel to measure levels of audience enjoyment did not in itself undermine its ability to provide audience-size data. At the same time, however, it was also found that the regular CBC panel diary yielded significantly higher levels of general viewing than did both the open-ended diary and the type of diary used by the ratings services. Moreover, it was concluded that most of the differences between the panel audience estimates and those of the ratings services stemmed from their different questionnaires rather than differences in response rates or sampling procedures.[35]

THE ENJOYMENT INDEX AND PROGRAM PRODUCTION

The most distinguishing feature of the panels is their 'enjoyment index' for particular programs and program segments. It is based on a synthesis of viewer responses to a five-point scale of enjoyment ('I enjoy it very much,' 'I enjoy it quite a bit,' 'it's all right, not bad,' 'I don't enjoy it too much,' 'I don't enjoy it at all'). For some reason, which is no longer clear, the department used a discontinuous rather than a natural or equal-interval scale.* It also stretched the raw data from a 0–5 scale to a 0–100 scale, which (in conjunction with the discontinuous scale) tended to make changes in enjoyment ratings seem more dramatic (e.g. from 70 to 74 rather than, say, from 4.1 to 4.2). This practice probably encouraged the tendency to forget that the enjoyment index for a particular program had no absolute value and was only intended to facilitate certain comparisons. 'I have noticed,' Ken Purdye wrote to Laird, 'that these weekly reports treat the audience panel data on enjoyment as though they were stock market quotations, with significance attributed to very small fluctuations. We should not forget that audience panel information is collected via a sampling operation; the usual rules of statistical inference apply.'[38]

A telex to Toronto producer Len Starmer (whose shows included 'Wayne and Shuster') on 7 November 1966 provides an example of what Purdye may have had in mind.

Enjoyment index for October 22 World of Music was 63 – a considerable drop from previous week's index of 70.

Special guest Josh White did not go over too well. This contrasts sharply with warm reception given to Ginny Tiu Revue, guests on October 15 broadcast.

Audience reaction to Malka and Joso about the same as previous week. They were enjoyed slightly more than Josh White but not enjoyed as much as the Tijuana Brass number or the Filipino Dancers. Of the three songs which they sang Michelle was by far the most enjoyed.

---

* According to an early department report, enjoyment figures were calculated as follows. 'Respondents who say they "enjoy it very much" are multiplied by 5, those who "enjoy it quite a bit" are multiplied by 3, and those who say "it is all right/not bad", "don't enjoy it too much", or "don't enjoy it all" are multiplied by 2, 1, and 0 respectively. The numerical total for all replies is then divided by the total number of viewers who made the evaluation and the resulting figure divided by 5 and multiplied by 100 to produce the final index, which must be between 0 and 100.'[36] One problem with this system is that anomalies occur when statistical tests (e.g. t-tests, correlations, analysis of variance) are performed on discontinuous interval data. In 1987 the department asked Erin Research to assess different methods of weighting responses to its five-point scale. George Spears of Erin recommended switching to a natural scale ('the best from a statistical perspective'), even though this would necessitate 'a break with tradition.'[37]

A number of comments from viewers suggest that an occasional explanation of the subject matter of foreign songs might add to their understanding and enjoyment.[39]

A week later, the news got worse:

Enjoyment index for October 29 World of Music was 59 – lowest yet since show settled into its regular format on October 15.

Audience size this week at 13 per cent level indicating that audience has grown somewhat since start of hockey.

No number in this broadcast was received with enthusiasm. Malka and Joso's three songs drew only lukewarm praise. Two numbers by Los Indios Tabajaras enjoyed to about same extent as Malka and Joso. The singing of Margot Lefebvre was enjoyed even less than other numbers in show.[40]

These do not appear to be isolated examples from the early days of the panels. 'Note that the 74 Enjoyment Index was below the season-to-date average of 78,' the weekly panel report observed typically of the 'Fifth Estate' program for 16 November 1976. 'The "Quebec Elections" audience reported an Enjoyment Index of 66,' the same report noted approvingly, '14 points higher than the Enjoyment Index for the "U.S. Presidential Elections"!'[41]

More recent reports include enjoyment indices (EIs) not only for programs as a whole but also for individual characters and specific program elements, such as story line, dialogue, acting, pace, settings, photography, and even humour. For example, a report for the 'Complex Offer' episode of 'Street Legal,' which was broadcast on 17 November 1989, summarizes the results for characters as follows:

EIs ... are between 3 and 6 points higher than the season-to-date averages. Leon's EI of 84 is his highest ever, and Chuck's EI of 77 moves him into the upper 70s range for the first time. While Carrie's EI of 84 is generally consistent with her high average of 81, Olivia's EI of 80 shows a marked increase from her average EI of 75 this season. Dillon's EI of 76 and the 75 by Nick are higher than their single previous ratings, and Alana's EI of 71 and Gloria's 72 are quite respectable first-time figures.[42]

Even individual sub-plots are rated according to enjoyment (the drunk-driving segment was given the highest score of 81, while the vagrancy and prostitution cases had scores about ten points lower).

The question is not simply whether the differences cited in these examples are statistically significant (e.g. 'World of Music''s drop from 63 to 59); when the enjoyment index was instituted, measures of statistical significance were extremely difficult to compute (especially given the questionable use of a discontinuous scale). It also needs to be asked whether an enjoyment index is a fair basis for assessing performance, especially for individual program components. A future star might not be an immediate hit on a variety show; one performer or character might suffer from the way other characters are assessed; or a character with a low enjoyment figure might still be essential to the structure of a story. In fairness, enjoyment figures are usually part of a package of information about how programs and program components are received. And they may well serve as a way of protecting performers against the politics of production. But the potential for abuse still remains, especially if comparisons are made across genres. To the extent that program content is adjusted on the basis of enjoyment figures, there is a loss of creative integrity and a return to the mentality that goes along with ratings generally. Creativity does not consist of shifting plots and performers around on the basis of an enjoyment index. In some cases, poor enjoyment figures might suggest programming problems, but they seldom point to long-term solutions.

Certainly, there may be problems in using the same enjoyment scale for all types of programs. During a review of the panel's first year of operation, Laird raised the possibility of using a different rating scale for newscasts, such as one based on interest, on the grounds that 'enjoyment' did not properly or fully characterize reactions to newscasts.[43] But the decision was deferred, and it was subsequently decided that there would be 'no special questions' for the news.[44]* One reason may have been that when parallel questions on interest and enjoyment

---

* A memo, probably from Laird (the source is not indicated on the extant copy), to the head of CBC News in October 1966 suggests otherwise. It reads: 'Incidentally, we're not asking people how much they "enjoy" the News this year. It's the wrong term. We're taking a rather different approach which should tell us more about how valuable, worthwhile, interesting etc. they feel the News to be.'[45] However, a 1967 study noted that 'it has always been evident that the CBC panel question on enjoyment is, to say the least, ambiguous in its application to the two programs CBC News and CTV News.' In fact, 10 to 15 per cent of viewers of these programs did not answer the question, compared to 2 to 5 per cent non-response for other types of programs. For this reason, no interpretation was made in the panel reports of respondents' answers to the enjoyment question for news, although the question was retained in the diary 'since its conspicuous omission would raise other problems.'[46]

were used for information programs (e.g. 'This Hour Has Seven Days'), little difference was found in the two measures.

The enjoyment index was nonetheless considered to be inadequate for newscasts, and in the early 1970s further consideration was given to the possibility of using a number of scales to take account of the different expectations that audiences have for various types of programming. The idea was that if, for example, audiences watch a program expecting it to be informative, then they could be asked to assess it from that angle.

During the previous three and a half decades, the CBC had continually analysed the composition of its programming. Although various classifications had been used, they had all been devised from the standpoint of the broadcaster. In order to measure audience reactions in a more refined way, it was now proposed that programming be classified on the basis of the expectations of viewers. To determine what these were, the research department contracted K.M. Vagg Associates in 1972 to conduct a series of interviews in which, by card sorting of program names, respondents indicated their perceptions of similarities and differences in terms of seven factors.[47] The results were used to construct 'repertory grid' analyses in which 108 television programs were organized into 16 clusters (e.g. comedy, sports, news, westerns). Previously, a program like 'Man Alive' would have been classified under public affairs. But on the basis of viewer perceptions, it was found that:

The strongest linkage for 'Man Alive' (although even this is weak) is to the medical social dramas. 'Man Alive' is neither relaxing nor demanding, is very educational and involves you through having to concentrate or think about it. 'Man Alive's' linkage with other traditional information programs is very weak. It is not exciting, thought-provoking or unpredictable enough to have strong links with the nature programs. It is too involving (through concentration) and scores too low on surveillance to have strong links with the more traditional public affairs programs. It is more soft-core public affairs.[48]

The intention of the study was to develop scales to measure the different dimensions of each program and then incorporate these scales into the regular panel diary. But it was not practicable to do so for two reasons. First, the more complicated the questionnaire becomes, the more difficult it is to have it completed satisfactorily. Second, increasing the size of the questionnaire ran the risk of incurring greater postal costs for distribution and collection. As a memo to Laird in 1968 explained:

Our present mail-out with a covering letter and a special 'Way It Is' questionnaire weighs just under two ounces while the diary itself weighs just under one ounce. If we were to increase the size of the diary even slightly, we would most certainly be required to pay the additional 4 [cents] on both the mail-out and the return. Based on the present weekly average mail-out and return, this would in effect increase our weekly panel costs by approximately $220.[49]

In subsequent years, Brian Stewart, head of the Toronto research office, worked on a simpler relaxing/demanding scale, and these dimensions were incorporated into the questionnaire. This eventually led to attempts to type respondents according to whether they prefer relaxing or demanding programs, but it was found that most people like both equally.

RECENT INNOVATIONS

Despite periodic reassessments, the operation of the CBC panels has remained relatively unchanged over the years. In 1976 senior research staff concluded that 'the panels, in modified form, must continue, and that the qualitative information derived therefrom is essential.' Although suggesting that an 'overhaul' was in order, they took no steps to change the basic way in which the panels functioned.[50] A decade later, a committee of senior researchers from the Ottawa, Montreal, and Toronto offices headed by Constance McFarlane concluded that the panel was still a valuable and cost-efficient research tool.[51]

There have, however, been a number of innovations in recent years. One of these has been to ask panel members to watch a program and respond to a list of questions about it, thereby getting the views of those who do not normally watch as well as those who do. This method is sometimes used to elicit reactions involving adjectives other than enjoyment. For example, the diary for 18–24 January 1988 asked panelists whether they agreed or disagreed with fourteen descriptions of an episode of 'Danger Bay' (e.g. informative, too educational, childish, slow-paced). The diaries are also used to ask other media-related questions (e.g. opinions on sex and violence on television, whether panelists would allow people meters into their homes) or even broader questions on things like the environment or the use of nuclear energy.

Another recent innovation has been the creation of the Annual Media Survey, which uses the first 'wave' of the panel each year to track the CBC's image and examine attitudes towards broadcasting generally. However, the information gathered in this manner seems to be increasingly redundant, and the time has perhaps come for the research department to shift attention from what the public thinks about the CBC to what it wants from it in terms of new approaches to programming.

The panels have not eliminated the need for other research tools. In 1977, when the CRTC questioned whether the panels provided 'a really adequate relationship with the public,' the following response was prepared by a senior research officer:

The purpose of the panels is not to provide a complete relationship with the public, but to provide measures of the audiences to programs and the audience reactions to the programs. These measures and reactions are used in the evaluation of programs which have been broadcast; that is, they provide an audience reaction to what *has been done*. But the planning of CBC programming and program policy involves the utilization of much more information than is contained in the panels.[52]

In fact, the panels now go further and elicit opinions about what *could* be done. For example, the diary for 4–11 October 1987 requested panelists to watch 'Degrassi Junior High' and then asked: 'What are the more serious issues that you would like to see covered on the program?' But as this example suggests, the panels focus on fairly narrow program matters rather than the general balance and philosophy of CBC programming. From one angle, the fact that they do so is their major strength. But it is important to keep in mind that the public should also have a say in larger programming issues.

12

Three Models of Audience Research and the Case of the CBC

... the impact of CBC will not be evaluated by conventional ratings alone, but more by our success in Canadian programs and by the importance the audience places on the programs we provide.

Barry Kiefl, 1990[1]

Two points have been implicit in the preceding chapters: first, that the CBC has adopted a different approach to audience research than that of commercial broadcasters; and second, that while its research department has gradually developed the necessary tools for regular, representative, equitable, and meaningful public input into program planning, it has not yet exploited these fully in the interests of democratic broadcasting. The purpose of this final chapter is to clarify these points by elaborating three models of audience research – what will be called the audience maximization model, the audience feedback model, and the public participation model – and locating CBC audience research in terms of them. The models are meant to apply to audience research as it occurs – or might occur – in broadcasting organizations, rather than to the kind of audience studies undertaken by university-based researchers. A sample of several hundred CBC research report titles (covering a larger number of separate reports) from 1954 to 1990 (more recent research is largely confidential) has been selected to illustrate the range of research within each model and the differences between them. For a partial guide to academic audience studies, the reader should consult the select bibliography at the end of this work.

As their labels suggest, there is a degree of overlap between the three models: the ratings data upon which the audience maximization model depends also constitute a form of audience feedback; and the various kinds of reactions to programming which characterize the audience feedback model are also a form of public participation. That the approach of any particular broadcasting organization, including the CBC, does not fit perfectly into a single model should not be surprising, given the varieties of audience research and the diverse motives for engaging in it. At the same time, however, it will be argued that there are substantial differences between the three models and that the way in which audience research has generally been used within the CBC is most consistent with the audience feedback model.

THE CONTROL THESIS RECONSIDERED

In *Desperately Seeking the Audience* (1991), Dutch scholar Ien Ang argues that audience research functions primarily to give broadcasters a sense of control over audiences about which there is a 'basic uncertainty.' This thesis is thought to apply to both commercial broadcasters, for whom the audience is a market to be won, and public (or what she calls public service) broadcasters, for whom the audience is a public to be served. '[W]hile the philosophical assumptions of commercial and public service broadcasting are indeed radically different,' she writes, 'there is also a fundamental commonality in the two.'

[I]n practice both kinds of institutions inevitably foster an instrumental view of the audience as object to be conquered. Whether the primary intention is to transfer meaningful messages or to gain and attract attention, in both cases the audience is structurally placed at the reception end of a linear, one-way process. In other words, in both systems the audience is inevitably viewed either from 'above' or from 'outside': from an institutional point of view which sees 'television' audience as an objectified category of others to be controlled.[2]

Another way of putting this would be to say that the public is treated as an audience rather than as a partner in a collective enterprise.

According to Ang, both commercial and public broadcasters treat the audience as an unproblematic, ontological given, which is 'taken-for-grantedly defined as an unknown but knowable set of people, not more, not less.' For commercial broadcasters, ratings have always been the basic measure of success. But public broadcasters, such as the BBC and the Dutch VARA, are also coming to rely upon factual audience measurement rather than normative judgment to assess their performance; they have been 'gradually pervaded by a massmarketing mentality to almost the same degree as in the United States.'[3] The problem with this development, in her view, is that it ignores 'the complexity of the multiple practices and experiences that television audiencehood involves.' Once these experiences are understood, she says, it will be realized that the (television) audience is 'an imaginary entity, an abstraction constructed from the vantage point of the institutions, in the interest of the institutions.'[4]

Although Ang's work is limited to European and American cases, some of her general observations apply to the CBC. She points out, for example, that 'research is often motivated and legitimized for its role in rationalizing managerial decision-making procedures' and that it is, 'more often than not, ... a tool for symbolic politics [rather] than rational decision-making.'[5] There are, however, several problems with her thesis, especially from the standpoint of the CBC.

First of all, understanding the complexity of everyday viewing experiences (or the 'social world of actual audiences'), while certainly of interest to broadcasters, is probably a more appropriate task for university-based researchers than for broadcasting research departments. According to Ang, academic research has been 'deeply complicit with the institutional point of view,'[6] but recent works, such as Robert Kubey and Mihaly Csikszentmihalyi's *Television and the Quality of Life: How Viewing Shapes Everyday Experience* (1990) and James Cull's *Inside Family Viewing: Etyhnographic Research on Television's Audiences* (1990), constitute a challenge to this assessment.

Second, Ang commits the very sin against which she preaches by aggregating all broadcasters together and ignoring individual differences in their approaches to audience research. Both commercial and public broadcasters are said to adopt the 'institutional point of view' when it comes to audience research. But Ang ignores the extent to which public broadcasters such as the CBC have made use of qualitative audience studies to assess their performance. In fact, the CBC's research department has conducted a number of studies of the kind Ang envisages. An early example is 'Behind the Radio Ratings – An Impressionistic Look into the Flavour and Quality of Radio Use' (October 1964), a study supervised by Constance McFarlane in which in-depth personal interviews were used to probe the everyday realities of radio listening. Other examples are 'Dimensions of Audience Response to Television Programs in Canada or What Canadian Viewers Expect from the Programs They Watch' (January 1975) and a series of reports on the process of program selection which the department prepared during Laird's final years as director, including:

3/78 The Dynamics of Television Viewing, Part I: What Lies under the 1/4-Hour Average
4/80 The Determinants of TV Viewing: A Quasi-model of Channel Selection
1/82 Choosing TV Programs: Is It Habit or an Active Choice?

Third, it is an oversimplification to say that audience research is simply motivated by a need to reduce uncertainty about who is listening and watching, even though this is certainly a legitimate reason for engaging in it. In the real world of audience research, there are other motives which make more sense of the actual studies which audience researchers have produced.

Following political criticism of the CBC's treatment of news about Quebec, for example, the research department prepared 'Content Analysis of Newscasts – French Radio and TV Networks' (November 1964). In 'An Analysis of Viewer Perceptions of "Fairness and Balance" of CBC and CTV Information Programmes' (December 1977), it tried to show that criticism of information programming by politicians is a poor guide to public opinion. And in 'Happy Medium – A Content Analysis of Network Television News' (1978), a 177-page study carried out by Barry Kiefl, it even examined CBC's political coverage in *anticipation* of close scrutiny following the election of the Parti-Québécois. The results turned out to provide a useful counterweight to a study conducted for the CRTC by Arthur Siegel of York University, which claimed that there was a consistent bias in CBC reporting.

The purpose of 'Canadians' Reactions to the 1960 US Election Night Telecast on TV' (January 1961) was to demonstrate that audience mail and telephone responses to programs can also be misleading. In this case, while most callers had been critical of the CBC's decision to carry American election-night coverage of the presidential contest between Nixon and Kennedy, a special telephone survey found that 85 per cent of viewers were glad to have had the opportunity to see the broadcast. Similarly, in 'Those Who Write and Those Who Listen' (February 1983), the department found (p. 15) that programmers at Radio Canada International 'would have been completely misled had they had to rely on the preferences expressed by ... letter-writers and mailing list contacts.' It suggested (p. 16) that if this was the only kind of feedback available, programmers 'would probably do best to ignore' it and 'rely instead on their own experience and personal judgment.' But many other studies have been motivated by a desire to show that even programming staff may be quite wide of the mark in their assessment of programming preferences and reactions.

Moreover, given the CBC's mandate to provide Canadians with Canadian-produced programming, the research department has naturally produced reports such as 'Are We Watching Less Canadian-Produced TV Programming? The Viewing Share of Canadian-Produced Programs on CBC-TV and Other English TV: 1960–1979' (April 1980) and 'Canadian-Produced Programming for Canadian TV Audiences: How Are We Doing?' (January 1990). In a similar vein, it has been interested in the impact of cable on station competition:

12/69 The Impact of Cable Television in Canada on the Audience to Canadian TV Stations
10/72 Cable TV and Audience Fragmentation: At Year-end 1971
 3/75 Increasing Fragmentation of TV Audiences to Canadian Stations
 6/77 Cable TV Penetration in Canada and Audience Fragmentation at Year-end 1976, with Trends 1968–76

Finally, Ang argues that the institutional point of view 'silences actual audiences.'[7] But it is difficult to see how the kind of research which she proposes could give the public a meaningful voice in programming. It is true that audience measurement is an instrument of control, especially in the sense implied by James Beniger in *The Control Revolution* (1986), which Ang cites with approval. Beniger argued that as social systems and institutions become increasingly complex, it requires increasing amounts of information to establish and maintain order within them. From this perspective, information is a countervailing force against entropy or the tendency for all systems to exhibit complete uniformity or disorder. But this is very different from the kind of social control theorized by Michel Foucault, from whom Ang also draws support. While audience research is necessary in any broadcasting organization for control in Beniger's sense of orderly planning, it is television itself that is the main instrument of control or class domination for Foucault. By blurring this distinction, Ang makes 'institutional' audience research seem like an instrument that can only be used against the public and never on its behalf.

NON-AUDIENCE-RELATED WORK OF CBC RESEARCH

The 'institutional point of view' could lead to three quite different models of audience research. These models, it should be kept in mind, do not do full justice to the contribution of the CBC's research department because they do not take into account the work which it does that is not directly concerned with audiences. Apart from providing assistance on some of the projects undertaken by other departments, the department has produced numerous reports that do not fall within the traditional boundaries of audience research. These encompass methodological studies, programming balance statistics, content analyses, and program-related surveys.

Most of the department's methodological work has actually been carried out in the context of specific audience studies. But CBC research staff have periodically prepared separate reports on methodological questions, most of which deal with problems of determining audience size and reactions. For example:

/60 The Validation of Memory Questions about Listening, Viewing, Reading, etc.

11/63 The Selection of Individuals within Households as Respondents in Telephone Surveys: Method and Rationale

2/65 Degree of Similarity between Answers on Age, Educational Level and Languages Spoken

8/88 Audience Ratings: The Degree of Reliability Associated with Estimates Obtained from Samples of Different Sizes

The department has also conducted critiques of other studies and reports, such as:

1/64 A CBC Research Critique of the Toronto Star Weekly's Publication: 'A Comparative Study: Television – Star Weekly'

6/84 Comments on and Summary of the Goldfarb Study, 'The Culture of Canada'

2/90 Critique of the Fraser Institute's 'On Balance' Newsletter of Feb. 1990: 'The Meech Lake Accord'

4/90 Methodological Problems in the UBC Study, 'Gender Role Portrayals on North American TV'

From the beginning, the department has gathered statistics on ownership of radio and television equipment, which provide an indirect indication of audience demand for services. For example:

1/56 Distribution of Radio and TV Homes in Canada
11/60 How Many FM Sets? Estimates of FM Radio Set Ownership in Toronto, Montreal and Ottawa
12/65 Transistor Radios
10/69 Extent of Use of Cable TV in Canada
12/69 Color TV Set Saturation in Canada

In recent years, ownership statistics have usually been included in more general reports on audience behaviour, but special reports are still prepared as the need arises. For example:

12/83 The CBC and Its Environment, I: New Electronic TV Facilities – Some Characteristics of Those Who Have Them
1/86 VCR's: The Canadian Story

The department has not, for the most part, engaged in general research on broadcasting, but during the early years it did prepare a number of reports on developments such as the impact of television on radio and the growth of FM radio:

5/55 Reorientation of Radio in the United States and Great Britain
1/56 New Approaches to Radio Programming in the United States
9/58 Preliminary Report on Frequency Modulation Radio in the United States
4/61 Some FM Developments in the United States

The department has also been involved in the compilation of statistics on programming balance (e.g. the proportion of information and entertainment; the percentage of broadcast time in particular program categories; the degree of local, regional, and national production; and the amount of Canadian programming). Information of this kind provides an essential benchmark for interpreting audience needs and is critical for program planning. Unfortunately, it is not widely known outside the CBC and has never been included in surveys asking the public whether it would like more programming of one type or another, even though its inclusion might produce more-meaningful responses.

The compilation of programming balance statistics was originally carried out by the station relations division of the CBC, but by the early

1950s had become quite onerous and costly. For the 1954–5 season, over 150,000 program entries had to be coded and processed. In 1955 Alphonse Ouimet asked Morrison to look into the possibility of preparing program statistics by sampling. In 'A Proposal to Use Sampling Methods for Collecting CBC Radio and Television Program Statistics' (December 1955), the department concluded that the degree of error associated with sampling might be less than the amount of coding error inherent in the current statistics and estimated that sampling would reduce costs from $10,000 to $600 a year. It also recommended that the compilation of programming statistics be shifted from station relations to itself and that a number of changes be made in programming categories.

With Ouimet's approval, the coders in station relations were transferred to the research department, a new classification scheme was developed, and a series of reports were issued:

56–58 Program Statistical Analysis Report (8 reports)
59–61 Program Analysis – Origin, Make-up and Content of Radio and TV Programs (7 reports)
62–63 Program Analysis – A Classification of the Origin of Production, Form, Content and Make-up of CBC Radio and Television Programs (2 reports)

Although the department subsequently relinquished the task of compiling programming balance statistics on a regular basis, it has periodically made comparative programming balance analyses:

10/61 The Content of FM Station Programming in Toronto, Ottawa and Montreal – A Comparison of CBC and Private Station FM Programs (also 7/62)
10/63 Program Content: CBOT and CJOH-TV
 9/79 Analyse de contenue de certaines stations de radio à Montréal – 6h à 9h
 3/85 The Balanced Television Schedule – Comparison of CBC-TV Prime-time with Other Broadcasters and the Evolution of CBC English Network TV Schedule

The department has also continued to conduct various content analyses of specific types and aspects of programming, such as news, Canadian content, and gender roles:

2/59 CBC TV News: Content Comparison of Network and Vancouver Newscasts

1/65 How Canadian Is Canadian English Language Television? Based on Viewing of English TV Programs in Evening

4/82 The Presence, Role and Image of Women in Prime-time on the English TV Network of the CBC

5/84 Sex-Role Portrayal in Canadian Television, Radio and Pay Television (also 8/84)

9/85 Evening News Choices in Toronto – A Content Analysis of Local Television News in Spring 1985 (also for Vancouver, 9/85, and Halifax, 9/86)

Finally, the CBC's research department has conducted numerous public opinion surveys on non-programming issues for use by programmers and management. As Arthur Laird noted in 1974, 'the networks now conform scrupulously to that policy which requires them to conduct program surveys only in full collaboration with Research – unlike those bad old days when Norman Depoe used to hire his own "researchers"!'[8] The same year, the department conducted two national surveys on the public's concern with various election issues and their voting intentions for use on a CBC program. When the federal Conservatives challenged the results and criticized the CBC for conducting the survey in the first place, Knowlton Nash asked the research department's Ken Purdye to appear on 'As It Happens' with a rebuttal.

Other program-related surveys have dealt with road safety knowledge (6/66), unemployment (2/71), the War Measures Act and FLQ crisis (11/71), the right to strike (5/72), Canadian abortion law (1/75), wage and price controls (12/75), the monarchy (7/77), the Quebec referendum (11/79), the Geneva Summit (12/85), and explicit sex in the media (5/86). In March 1988 the research department conducted a survey on whether the CBC should ask the public for donations.

CBC RESEARCH STUDIES ON AUDIENCE EFFECTS

Also excluded from the following analysis of audience research models are studies on audience effects. 'From a long term standpoint,' Neil Morrison wrote in 1957, 'it was hoped that research could produce findings about some of the effects of broadcasting on various aspects of Canadian life.'[9] But although members of the department were encouraged to collaborate with academics on research articles, their work contributed little in this regard. 'I wish I were able to tell you that we've been able to make original or fundamental contributions to psychological or sociological theory,' Irwin Shulman wrote to an official in the American Academy of Arts and Sciences in 1962, 'but the work has not been underway long enough.'[10] Yet the same assessment could be made today. The department's emphasis has always been on the description of media behaviour, not on its theory, and its studies have provided few insights into the impact of broadcasting on society.

During the early years, the department did conduct a number of studies on learning effects. For example:

4/58 The North York School Study: Television Viewing and Book Reading Patterns and the Impact of the Television Program 'Junior Magazine' among Children in Grades 4–6

9/59 Farm Forum Wingham Study 1958–59: A Report on the Effects of TV on Certain Farm Forum Activity – Farmers' Reactions to a Televised Series on 'This Business of Farming'

3/62 Classroom TV and the Learning Process – Based on a Study of a School Telecast for Grades 2–3

5/70 Measuring the Effects of Television Programs: Three CBC Case Studies

The 4/58 study tried to determine whether a children's television program could be used to stimulate the reading of certain books. The 9/59 study looked at whether television might be used to generate new interest in the declining farm forums. And the 3/62 study considered whether children's perceptions of Eskimo life were affected by a fifteen-minute broadcast 'The Igloo.' But the results were neither novel nor enlightening. Although the department later used its network television panels to examine the retention of ideas from public affairs programs (5/70), this kind of study has been left for the most part to academic researchers.

In recent years, the department's only concern with effects has been in terms of such things as the effectiveness of publicity campaigns or the impact of simulcast-substitution. For example:

6/74 How Do Viewers Find Out about TV Programs?

3/76 Audience Research Implications of a Proposal to Abandon CBC Station Call-Letters: A Report to CBC Corporate Relations

6/78 Effects of Program Pre-emptions on Audience Size

9/78 Some Effects (Known and Unknown) of Simulcast-Substitution on CBC-TV Audiences

2/81 American Programs as Lead-ins to Canadian: Before/After New Season's American Shows

6/82 Changing the 'National' to 10:00 – Effects of Publicity on Public Aware-
ness and Tuning
12/82 Analyse de la pénétration du slogan publicitaire de Radio-Canada pour
la saison 1982/83
2/87 Recall of Advertising for CBC AM/FM Radio – Results from Add-on Survey using CBC Panel
4/88 The Amount of Interest in Viewing Movies based on Descriptions with
and without Sexual, Violent or Comedic Elements

THE AUDIENCE MAXIMIZATION MODEL

The first model of audience research is that which governs most commercial broadcasting organizations, where, despite lip-service to certain social objectives, the primary institutional concern is with what
Dallas Smythe called the deliverance of audiences to advertisers.[11] In
this regard, success is determined not simply by audience size but also
by audience composition, since advertisers are increasingly interested
in the maximum audience with a particular demographic make-up.
For this model, the major form of audience research is the production
of ratings in the broad sense of the term. Measurements of audience
size are considered the only real indicator of relative success in the
production of audiences and are routinely used in the commercial
broadcasting field. As a BBM report observed in the early 1980s,
'important decisions are based on BBM radio survey reports. In 1982,
advertisers placed over $500 million dollars with Canadian radio sta-
tions. Much of the allocation of this amount was made according to
BBM [ratings]. Programs are cancelled and renewed, careers are made
or broken according to "The Book."'[12] And as Ang points out, 'even the
creative community ultimately has to submit, often grudgingly, to the
regime of truth established by audience measurement, the truth of
"shares" and "ratings", because it is this regime of truth that has the
final say over what counts as "success" or "failure."'[13]

As we have seen, commercial broadcasters have not normally produced ratings themselves; instead they have relied on independent ratings services or else formed a cooperative measurement service in
conjunction with advertisers. But after obtaining ratings reports (and
in some cases, raw data) from outside services, they have expended
considerable additional energy analysing their own performance from
a commercial standpoint, determining the listening and viewing habits and preferences of different demographic groups, assessing the

impact of scheduling changes on audience behaviour, and generally developing a strategy for winning the ratings war.

In addition to ratings or quantitative audience research, commercial broadcasters have also made some use of qualitative audience research, beginning with the Stanton-Lazarsfeld Program Analyzer developed at CBS. But the purpose of such research has always been closely related to the goal of audience maximization. The underlying reason for program testing is not to improve audience satisfaction, but rather to develop a way of predicting the success that a new program is likely to have in attracting a large audience with the desired demographics. As with ratings, the crucial consideration is not the form of audience research, but rather the uses to which it is put. It is revealing that when the Harris committee began its investigation of American ratings services in 1963, it was mainly interested in how the networks used audience measurement data; but the representatives of the ratings industry quickly deflected the committee's attention to the problem of accuracy, realizing no doubt that this was a methodological quagmire from which the committee was unlikely to emerge.

'One of the fears of people in the CBC,' Austin Weir wrote to Neil Morrison in 1954, '... is that the chief purpose of audience research is merely quantitative – to show that audiences are not large enough and, thereby, influence policy in the direction of popularizing programs.'[14] Weir assured Morrison that 'nothing could be further from the truth,' but the CBC has certainly never tried to do without ratings and has on occasion been accused of being preoccupied with them. 'Bondage to ratings is a symptom of its insecurity and lack of direction,' wrote Dennis Braithwaite in 1976, adding that 'it would be difficult to find a purer exercise in needless masochism than the CBC's practice of conducting its own audience surveys and circulating the results among its executives.' For, as Braithwaite explained, 'most of the shows that the CBC takes greatest pride in – Performance, Musicamera, The Diane Stapley Show, Newsmagazine, Peep Show, to name a few – place very low in the ratings, while the imported American shows are tops.'[15]

At first glance, moreover, the CBC research department appears to have been as concerned with data on audience size and share as are its commercial competitors. Perusing the more than two thousand reports stored in the department's Ottawa office, one initially gets the impression that its physical output is little different from what one might expect to find at one of the American commercial networks. A number of reports seem to have a clear commercial purpose. For example:

4/67 Public Attitudes and Reactions to Certain Aspects of Television Advertising with Particular Reference to Advertising of Personal and Intimate Products
12/71 The Demographic Characteristics of the Heavy, Medium and Light Users of Various Products
72–77 The Cost Efficiency of Spot Advertising on CBC-Owned English-Language TV Stations (10 reports)
8/83 A Summary of Four Focus Group Discussions on CBO (Ottawa) Commercials
4/88 Selected Consumer Buying Habits Limited to Preferences for Twenty CBC Programs and Nine Televised Sports

And there are hundreds of reports that deal primarily with the size and composition of radio and television audiences. These fall into five subcategories: i) individual and special broadcasts (e.g. 'The Irish Rovers' Silver Anniversary Special'; ii) continuing programs and program series (e.g. 'Man Alive,' 'Road to Avonlea'); iii) types of programming (e.g. news, sports); iv) individual stations, cities, and areas; and v) networks and overall service.

Reports on the audience size and composition for individual and special broadcasts include:

3/58 International Hockey: Audiences for the Canada-Russia Hockey Game
6/58 1958 Election Night Results: Radio and Television Audiences
5/59 Springhill Rescue: Nov. 1st, 1958 – Toronto Radio and Television Audiences
10/72 Team Canada Hockey CBC Radio: September 1972
3/74 Audiences for CBC TV Coverage of Xth Commonwealth Games
1/77 The Montreal Olympics and Its Television Audience
9/79 Audiences to Election Night Programming on Network Television
11/84 The 1984 Summer Olympics: Overall Viewing Levels
1/90 The Grey Cup, 1989
2/90 Brian Orser: Skating Free

In the case of the audience size and composition for continuing programs and series, there are both one-time and multiple reports. One-time reports, some of which deal with a number of programs, include:

5/55 Report on Audience Size for the Weekly English Network TV Programme: 'The Plouffe Family'

6/56 The Audience for 'Kindergarten of the Air'

2/57 Audiences for 'CBC Television Theatre'

11/58 English Television Network Program Ratings (also 3/59)

6/69 'Reach for the Top': 1969 – Estimates of Audiences Obtained by CBC-Owned and Affiliate Stations, 1961–1969

7/79 English Language TV Network Programs; 1978–79 Season – Program Histories, Audience Size and Share of All TV Viewing of English Language Stations

8/80 Regularly Scheduled Prime-time Programs and Their Audiences on the Full and Metronet TV Networks: Comparison between 1979–80 and 1978–79 with a Note on Total Network Performance (also for 1981–82 and 1980–81 in 8/82)

5/83 Audiences to Telecasts of the House of Commons Proceedings

6/88 The Performance of CBC Television Network Programs – A Comparison of Sept. to March 1987–88 with Similar Periods in the Two Preceding Broadcast Seasons

5/89 Recent Trends in the 'Journal''s Friday Night Audience

Multiple reports include:

66–70 Audiences to CBC English TV Network Programs (17 reports; also for CTV programs)

70–74 The Performance of CBC English TV Network Programs: Fall–Winter Season (5 reports, title varies)

74–88 Auditoire des émissions du réseau français de télévision de Radio-Canada (approx. 25 reports, title varies)

76–77 CBC English-Language TV – Assessment of Audiences to Prime-time Programs (3 reports, title varies)

/84 A Review of Audiences to Network and Local TV Programs (5 reports)

86–88 CBC TV Audience Report – English Language TV Network Programs (9 reports, title varies)

The department has prepared numerous reports (mostly one-time) dealing with the size and composition of audiences for particular types of programming, especially since it began using computers to reanalyse ratings data. For example:

7/56 Religious Programs: Audience Size Data

6/70 Information Programs Broadcast on the CBC English TV Network: Fall–
Winter 1969–70

5/76 Auditoire des émissions d'information réseau français de télévision de
Radio-Canada – Pour la saison 1975–76 et historique depuis la saison
1970–71

10/78 Emissions du services jeunesse: Evolution de l'auditoire

3/79 Evaluation de l'auditoire des émissions de variétés à Radio-Canada – de
1973/74 à l'automne 1978

1/82 Esquisse de portrait des auditoires des émissions dramatiques du réseau
français de télévision de Radio-Canada 1981–82, 1980–81, 1979/80

7/83 English Language TV Network Programs ... Special Report: Part 1, Specials – General (also 7/84 and /85)

7/83 English Language TV Network Programs ... Special Report: Part 2, Sports
Specials (also 7/84)

5/84 Audiences for Local Programs during Prime-time on CBC English
Owned and Operated TV Stations – Fall 1979–Spring 1984

2/85 Auditoire des émissions d'information à la radio AM de Radio-Canada –
automne 1982 à automne 1984

2/87 Sports Programming on English-Language Television in Canada: A
Review of the Past Three Years

3/87 CBC's Sunday Night Specials: Audience Assessment for 1986–87

6/87 The Performance of CBC Canadian Network Drama: A Review of the Last
Four TV Seasons

9/88 Audiences for Early Evening News on CBC and Competing TV Stations in
Various Markets (also 5/89)

5/89 The Audience to CBC and CTV's Late Night National News in Various
Locations across Canada

Hundreds of other reports deal with the size and composition of
audiences for particular stations, cities, or areas. One-time reports
include:

2/55 Some Facts on Listening and Viewing in the Montreal Area

8/56 Some New Evidence of CBA's Effectiveness in Nova Scotia

10/58 TV Competition in Vancouver-Victoria Area: A Comparison of Ratings
between CBUT and KVOS-TV

12/58 CBE Windsor: Audience Research Report

1/60 Impact of CJSS-TV, Cornwall on Circulation and Audiences for CBMT
and CBFT Montreal, CBOT and CBOFT Ottawa

3/63 CBC Radio: Station Performance of 13 CBC-Owned Stations

/67 CBC and Non-CBC Radio in Newfoundland

6/68 The Radio Audience Situation in Vancouver

1/71 Audiences to CBC-Owned English and French-Language Radio Stations – Their Main Dimensions

3/72 Audiences for CBC Radio Stations and Programs: November 1968– January 1972

1/74 The Impact on the CBO Early Morning Audience of the Commercial Changes Effected on June 4, 1973

5/81 Evolution de l'écoute de la télévision à Montréal de 1968–69 à 1979–80

12/84 Ecoute de la radio et de la télévision au Manitoba

7/85 Auditoire des stations de base des réseau français de radio de Radio-Canada

Multiple reports include:

65–66 The In-home Audience to CBC Radio in ... Canadian Cities – A Retabulation and Summary of BBM Data (6 reports)

65–74 Audiences to CBC English-Language Radio Stations in Selected Time Periods (33 reports, title varies)

/73 CBC and Non-CBC Radio and Television Audiences in Metro Ottawa-Hull ... with Special Emphasis on CBC, CBO-FM, CBOT, CBOFT (2 reports)

74–77 Audience to CBL/CBQ/CBU Transmitters and Their LPRT's (5 reports)

80–82 An Analysis of Audiences to CBC-Owned Television Stations in Key Time Blocks (3 reports)

83–88 Auditoire des stations de la TV de Radio-Canada et des autres stations télévisions (5 reports)

Finally, there are dozens of reports on the size and composition of network audiences for CBC radio and television. One-time reports include:

5/66 Households Tuned to the CBC (Eastern) FM Radio Network

3/69 The Audience to CBC Radio: An Overview

3/76 CBC Radio and CBC Television: Their Respective Shares of the Total Audience to Radio and to Television in Canada

1/80 The Overall Audience Performance of CBC English and French TV Network Programming

4/80 CBC Network Television: Are Its Audiences Decreasing?

1/81 CBC Radio and Its Audiences – Summary of Research Results from the Past Five Years

6/84 Audiences to CBC Radio and CBC Stereo with a Reference to All Canada
Tuning – A Comparison of Three Years

Multiple reports include:

73–79 CBC English-Language Radio: The Size and Composition of Its Audience
(6 reports)
/80 CBC English-Language Radio: The Size and Composition of Its Audience
(2 reports)
80–86 Auditoire des réseaux français de radio de Radio-Canada (9 reports, title
varies)
87–89 Radio Audiences (11 reports)

On the surface, therefore, the CBC research department seems to
produce the kind of quantitative audience analysis necessary for program planning based on the principle of audience maximization. It has
even made periodic attempts to develop a method of predicting future
audiences. For example:

3/73 TV Futures – An Exercise in Estimating the Audiences to CBC and Non-
CBC Television in 1976 and 1981
12/77 A Predictive Code for Television Programs

There are, however, two questions that need to be asked. First, is
audience maximization the only or even the primary purpose for
which the above reports have been used? And second, are these
reports representative of the overall research output of the CBC? In
both cases, the answer is 'no.'

THE AUDIENCE FEEDBACK MODEL

Some of the reports prepared by the CBC's research department over
the years have been made at the specific request of another department within the corporation. But one of the first things that strikes one
about many of the reports is that it is unclear for whom they were
intended. This vagueness is probably because they were designed to
serve a variety of interests, ranging from commercial sales to program
assessment to strategic planning. But as a result, it is difficult to pin-
point a single philosophy of audience research within the CBC.

By its very nature, the commercial sales component has always been mainly interested in ratings and has thus influenced the production of reports characteristic of the audience maximization model. But senior management and program producers and planners have also had an appetite for audience measurement data. In the case of management, it has often been necessary to resort to statistics on audiences to counter criticism of the CBC's performance and demonstrate that the CBC is needed and appreciated by Canadians. This was one of the reasons for the creation of the research department in the first place. And since ratings do provide one indication of the public's reaction to programming, they are likewise of interest and value to programmers, especially when plotted over time (as happens in many of the CBC research reports cited above). All things being equal, both management and programmers would always prefer large audiences to small ones.

This is not the whole story, however, and we should not conclude that CBC research fits best into the audience maximization model. On the contrary, the approach of the CBC has generally been to decide what kind of programming the public needs, to translate this into specific program formats, and then to use a variety of audience research findings, including ratings, to determine how well it is meeting its objectives and how it might adapt its programming to achieve them more successfully. While not eschewing programming with mass appeal, the CBC has always assumed that serving public needs also means providing certain programs which will probably never draw large audiences by conventional or commercial standards. But whether programs have large audiences or small ones, it is necessary to assess whether they are doing the job expected of them. It was for this reason that Weir wrote to Morrison in early 1954 suggesting that programming staff specify the objectives of particular programs so that audience research staff could evaluate them appropriately – an idea which Morrison applauded, but which never seems to have been acted upon.

The basic assumption of the audience feedback model is that it is the task of CBC programming staff to decide what should be broadcast. Morrison would have allowed special-interest groups like the Canadian Association for Adult Education to have input at this stage, but not the public; its role is to react to what it is given and signal the CBC whether a different approach might in some cases be needed to achieve its programming goals more effectively. As the Annan committee in Britain expounded in 1977:

in programmes where producers define their objectives, audience research can tell them how effective they are being in obtaining that objective. The producer's job is difficult. He has to try to communicate through his programmes with people whom he does not know and whose tastes, background, understanding, attitudes and opinions vary widely. Audience research cannot dictate what a programme should say, but it can tell the producer what people thought it was saying, and how they reacted to the programme. In this way it can help the producer by indicating which of his aims have been realised and, perhaps, why.[16]

In the audience feedback model, in other words, the function of audience research is to let listeners and viewers react to what they are given, but not to help set priorities in the first place.

Both Morrison and Laird accepted this approach without question. 'Essentially,' Morrison wrote in 1957, 'Audience Research provides a channel of communication from Canadian audiences back to their national broadcasting system. The findings constitute an evaluation and criticism of the CBC's program service.'[17] Or as Laird wrote in 1964, 'basically, what we are doing in CBC Research is studying the impact of CBC services ... on Canadian audiences, so that we can indicate where changes or improvements in these services may need to be made and, as necessary, recommend how these changes can best be effected.'[18]

It is significant that both of these quotations refer not simply to audiences rather than the public, but to audiences in the plural. It is taken for granted that broadcasters are addressing not one audience or public but many. 'There are as many different "publics" as there are kinds of broadcasts (and most listeners are members of several of them),' observed a BBC audience research reference book in the 1950s, 'and although it is extremely difficult, if not impossible, to express their respective sizes numerically, it is certain that they vary very widely.'[19] Or as CBC president Alphonse Ouimet put it in an even more extreme form in the early 1960s, 'each of 18,000,000 Canadians has his own separate and distinctive tastes. Each has a right to his freedom of taste, along with the other basic freedoms.'[20] Given this belief, it is easy to see why the public would be denied a role in program planning; it could not be expected to express a collective and coherent set of priorities, but only to register demand on behalf of each person's or group's individual desires. The responsibility for choosing among these desires, since they cannot all be satisfied, falls back on CBC programmers.

Within the commercial networks, audience research staff use ratings data not only to assess programming performance but also to determine general levels, patterns, and habits of listening and viewing. The CBC research department has also produced numerous reports on audience behaviour. For example:

12/56 A Review of Available Information about Daytime Viewing in Canada and the United States

2/57 Late Night Viewing in Montreal and Quebec

6/58 Seasonal Listening Patterns: Composition and Size of Summer and Winter Radio Audiences 1956–1957

5/61 The FM Audience – A Report on the Listening Habits and Characteristics of FM Owners in Toronto, Ottawa and Montreal

12/66 Trends in Radio Tuning, 1964–1966

4/67 The Extent to Which People Watch Television over Broad Time Periods and by Various Sub-groups of the Population

7/73 Patterns of Television Viewing in Canada

10/73 Audience Information on the Monday–Friday 4:00–6:00 pm Time Period

/74 Morning Radio Audiences (6:00–9:00 am)

6/78 Audience Flow and Ebb around the CBC Late Night News in Toronto and Vancouver

3/79 Distribution of Total Time Spent Watching TV – All Canada and All Provinces by Station and Category of Station: Nov. 1968 to Nov. 1978 (also 3/80; also for urban areas with population over 25,000)

4/79 The 70's – A Changing Society Changed Their Radio Habits: Overview of Trends in Radio Listening and Audience Characteristics in the Seventies

7/80 Television Viewing Audience Levels – 6:00 am–2:00 am Viewing on Weekdays, Saturday and Sunday, All Canada

8/81 Is TV Viewing on a Sunday Different from Other Days of the Week?

1/83 How People Use Radio – A Review of Radio Listening Habits

10/84 Ecoute de la radio FM la nuit

2/85 Listeners to Radio between 1:00 am and 5:00 am – A Selected Issue from an Attitudes/Lifestyles Study using the CBC Panel Survey

4/87 Radio Use between 4 pm and 6 pm on Weekdays

7/87 Current Trends in English Television Audiences – An Examination of Viewing Patterns and CBC's Performance in 1986–87 (also 7/88, title varies)

5/89 Audience Composition for CBC-TV Stations on Weekday Late Afternoons

/91 How People Use Television: A Review of TV Viewing Habits

Such reports could presumably aid the process of delivering audiences to advertisers. However, they are also consistent with the desire of the CBC to achieve its various programming objectives. The same is true of reports on the habits and preferences of specific audience groups. For example:

12/56 Programming for Teen-agers: A Study of the Listening and Viewing Habits of English-Speaking High-School Students in Ottawa

9/57 Television Viewing Habits of Children Attending English Schools in Montreal

1/59 Radio Listening and TV Viewing in an Ontario Farm Area: A Study of Farm Uses of the Broadcasting Media in the Wingham Area in the Winter of 1958

10/79 Entre deux saisons – Etude auprès de parents d'enfants âgés de 12 à 15 ans

9/81 La télévision et les adolescents de 14 à 18 ans – Etude exploratoire

9/84 The Native Audience for Radio and Television in Canada's Northwest Territories

The desire of the CBC to satisfy diverse public needs, and not simply to maximize audiences, is reflected in its concern to know the make-up of its audiences, especially in the case of radio. For example:

11/60 Characteristics of the Core Audience to Five Toronto Radio Stations

6/69 Who Listens to CBC Radio? Some Characteristics of Listeners to CBC English-Language Radio Stations and to Competing Stations in Major Markets

71–75 Profiles of Listeners to CBC Radio Stations and Their Competitors in Major Markets (5 reports, title varies)

11/79 Radio Survey Report 1979 – Characteristics of CBC and Non-CBC Radio Listeners

6/82 Maritime Radio Audiences – Characteristics, Attitudes and Interests of CBC Mono Radio Listeners and Potential Listeners

10/82 CBC Often, CBC Occasional and Non-CBC Radio Listeners: Late Afternoon and Evening

5/83 Programming Preferences of CBC Radio, CBC Stereo and Non-CBC Radio Listeners

1/86 The Characteristics of CBC English TV Supporters: Their Demographic Characteristics, Leisure Activities and Media Use, Taste in TV Programming and Their Opinion of the CBC

8/86 A Look at CBC Listeners in Terms of the Amount of Time They Spend with the Service

10/87 Radio Station Formats: The Types of Stations People Listen To

2/89 Another Look at CBC Listeners in Terms of the Amount of Time They Spend with the Service

6/89 Profils médiatiques et culturels des auditeurs des réseaux AM et FM de Radio-Canada

Compared to radio audiences generally, the core audience for CBC radio has tended to be somewhat older, more educated, and better off economically, and to have both an overrepresentation among the professional occupations and a broader range of cultural interests. However, listeners to the CBC's French-language AM service more closely resemble those of the private French-language stations in terms of age, and CBC television does not seem to have as distinctive a core audience. A 1974 study concluded that 'in their attitudes to television and in their perception of various functions for television, CBC viewers are generally no different from those who watch varying amounts of television on competing CTV and TVA stations' and 'there is generally *no* tendency for heavy viewers of CBC to be light viewers of television in general.'[21] Recent studies also indicate that the audience for CBC television is similar to that for television as a whole, although the anglophone audience tends to be slightly older and the francophone audience is somewhat more highly educated.

What most characterizes the approach of the CBC, however, is its interest in qualitative audience reactions. In the years before the panel, qualitative feedback from CBC listeners and viewers was gathered through telephone and personal surveys and was often used to assess new programming formats. Early reports on audience reactions to individual and special broadcasts include:

10/55 Televising a Public Affairs Conference

1/57 'H.M.S. Pinafore' Survey: An 'Experiment' in Collecting Audience Reactions by Telephone

10/57 CBC Coverage of the 1956 Progressive Conservative National Convention: A Survey of the Size and Composition of the Radio and Television Audience and an Analysis of the Audience Reaction to the Way CBC Telecasts Were Produced and Presented

2/58 Farm Forum Reactions to an Agricultural Extension Broadcast

6/59 Réactions du public à une expérience en stéréophonie

Apart from the regular panel reports (under various titles, such as 'Audience Reactions to English TV Network Programs'), the department has produced numerous special reports on qualitative reactions to continuing programs and program series. Some of these are based on panel data; others are based on separate surveys or focus groups. For example:

8/76 CBOT's 'This Day' – Audience Reactions to the Program, to Concurrent Non-CBC Programming and to Its Components and Personalities

5/79 Audience Reactions to Four Locally Produced, Prime Time Vancouver Television Shows – 'Reach for the Top,' 'Trivia,' 'Pacific Report' and 'What's a Nice Show Like You'

10/80 'La fine cuisine d'Henri Bernard' – Commentaires formulés lors de quatre entrevues de groupe

8/82 Enjoyment of 'The Fifth Estate': The Program Overall, the Hosts and Individual Segments (also 3/83)

5/84 Evaluation of Six Television Programs – Vancouver Focus Group Results

6/85 Audience Reaction to CBUT Early Evening News – A Qualitative Study (also for CBMT, 2/86)

8/85 Lawyers – Results of PEAC and Focus Group Testing with Summary of Audience Data from 1984–85 Season Telecasts

1/89 'Charamoule': Réactions d'enfants âgés de 6 à 12 ans à une émission de la série

4/89 Survey of 'Radio Noon' Listeners: CBL, Toronto

The CBC research department has also produced a large number of reports on qualitative reactions to types of programming. For example:

1/56 Some Dimensions of News Listening and News Interest

2/56 Audience Reaction in Canada to Certain BBC Programs

7/59 What Ontario Parents Think of Children's TV Programs: A Study in Cooperation with the Ontario Home and School Association

8/59 Stereophonic Broadcasting: A Survey of Listener Reaction in Toronto

8/63 CBC Radio Newscasts: An Assessment of Performance

4/64 Knowledge, Viewing and Appreciation of TV Serials by French-Speaking Persons 20 Years of Age and Over in the Montreal Area

6/64 Knowledge, Viewing and Appreciation of Some Variety Programs – Telephone Survey

9/65 Fans of Evening TV Movies and Total and Partial Viewing of Feature Films – Summer 1962

4/66 Audiences and Their Reactions to CBC English TV Network Public Affairs Programs, 1965–66 (also for light entertainment programs, 7/66)

8/68 TV English Network Sports Programs – Summary of Available Information on Size of Their Audiences and on Extent to Which Those Who Watched Them Enjoyed Them 1967–68 and 1966–67

5/72 Audience Attitudes and Reactions to the Late Night National Newscasts on CBC English TV Network and CTV Network

5/75 Audience Reactions to Television Hosts

1/76 Drama Programs Produced By or For the CBC and Presented on the CBC English TV Network: 1965–1975 – Size of Audiences/Extent to Which Those Who Watched Them Enjoyed Them

4/76 CBC Television Network Drama – A Historical Review of Audience Size and Enjoyment, 1965 to 1976

6/76 CBC One Occasion Dramas – A Study of Audience Reaction to a Number of Dramas in the Sunday Night Program: Performance 1974-75 and 1975–76

8/77 The Late-Night Newscasts of the CBC, CTV and TVA: Who Watches Them and How They Are Perceived

9/77 Early Evening Television in Toronto – A Study of Audiences and Reactions to News Programs by Viewers in Metro Toronto and Hamilton/Niagara (Mon–Fri, 6–7 pm)

2/78 CBC Radio and Its Noon-time Programs: A Study of Farmers' Reaction in Ontario and the Three Western Provinces

5/78 Audience Reactions to CBC and CTV Early Evening News Programs

5/79 Early Evening Viewing in Vancouver – Study of Audiences and Their Reactions to News Programming in Vancouver Environs (also 9/81 and for Winnipeg, 5/81, and Toronto, 5/82)

4/81 Audiences Reactions to CBC 'Information Radio': CBW Winnipeg

2/85 Reasons for the Popularity of This Season's TV Drama Specials

6/85 Early Evening News (Toronto) – A Report on Six Focus Group Discussions (also for Regina and Saskatoon, 4/86, and Ottawa, 7/87)

3/86 Portrayal of Women – Results from Questions Included in CBC Panel

1/88 Sunday Night Viewing, Family Viewing and the Acceptability of Sex and Violence on Television

3/88 Opinions about Game Shows – Reactions of CBC English Network Panel Members

11/88 Talk Show Hosts – Audience Test: A Report on the Focus Group Results for 'Shirley' (also for 'Vicki Gabereau Show,' 11/88, and overall results 11/88)

1/89 A Report on the Differences between 'Fans' and Other Viewers of Ten News and Current Affairs Programs: Annual Media Results

2/89 Information Radio: Perceptions of Non-listeners – Focus Group Results

There are also a few reports on stations, cities, or areas that involve qualitative reactions. For example:

8/59 Some Reactions to CBC Televison and Radio in Toronto, Montreal, Vancouver, Winnipeg, and Halifax

9/75 Listener Reactions to Various Aspects of Early Morning Radio on CBQ, Thunder Bay

8/80 The CBC in Montreal – Study of Adult Montrealers Concerning Their Television Satisfaction with the Services Provided by English-Language Television

4/86 CBC Radio Saskatchewan – Regina and Estevan, Qualitative Research Results

Finally, there are reports on networks or the CBC as a whole that focus on qualitative reactions. For example:

2/63 What the Canadian Public Thinks of the CBC – An Empirical Study of Public Attitudes to the CBC and to Certain Other Aspects of Broadcasting in Canada

2/74 What the Canadian Public Thinks of Television and of the TV Services Provided by CBC

1/86 How Canadians Feel about the CBC – A National Survey

2/86 Preliminary Findings from the CBC Qualitative Radio Study: The Degree of Satisfaction among CBC-Listeners with CBC-Radio and CBC-Stereo Programming

11/87 Verbatim: Comments from Listeners about the CBC Radio Services from the 1987 Qualitative Radio Study

/90 Canada's Image of the CBC: Annual Media Survey 1987–1990

THE PUBLIC PARTICIPATION MODEL

The public participation model of audience research assumes that the public knows its own needs and desires with respect to programming better than does any select group of program planners. Audience research is thus used to give the public a say in basic programming priorities. This does not consist simply of determining whether particular programs or aspects of programs are liked or disliked; it also involves the general make-up of CBC programming. This encompasses such things as levels of Canadian content and the nature of any foreign programming; the relative emphasis on national, regional, and local Canadian programming; the balance between information and entertainment generally; the priority given to different kinds of information and entertainment programming in the light of what is available from other broadcasters; the formats adopted in particular programming genres; and the need for new types of programming.

Robin Foster, director of communications practice for the British policy research company NERA, has recently suggested that public ser-vice broadcasters should not only 'show a willingness for their per-formance to be measured and evaluated' but also seek 'guidance (through regular surveys of viewers) on the nature of the service view-ers think public service television should provide.'[22] But the CBC's faith in this approach has been partial and sporadic. It developed the television program 'Marketplace' in response to a survey indicating a widespread public interest in common consumer problems and con-sumer complaints. Its decision to get out of commercial radio was partly determined by the results of a survey on listener attitudes to radio commercials on CBC stations. And in recent years, the research department has sought public input concerning specific programming periods, categories, or services. For example:

1/78 Early Morning Listeners to English-Language Radio Stations in the Ottawa-Hull Area – A Survey of What They Want in an Early Morning Program

5/79 Late Afternoon Listeners to English-Language Radio Stations in the Ottawa-Hull Area: Study of Audience Reactions, Preferences and Expec-tations

1/81 Radio Listener Involvement and Tastes in Music (also 12/81)

11/81 TV Programs: Who Wants More of What Type?

1/84 CBC Radio – Finding New Listeners – A Case Study of CBO-Ottawa

3/84 Listeners' Assessment of a Proposal to Change CBC AM Radio Program-ming in Ottawa to the FM Band

/87 What Do Listeners Want to Hear?

/88 Types of Variety Shows Preferred – Opinions of All CBC English Panel Members

2/88 Latenight Weeknight Television Viewing Preferences

10/88 CBC National Survey of Teens: Canadian Teens' Interests, Leisure Activ-ities, Tastes in Television and Music and Preferences for What They Would Like to See on a Teen Program (also for children aged 8 to 11, 9/88)

However, much of the input that has been sought has been either extremely general (e.g. whether to promote Canadian talent or under-standing between anglophones and francophones) or else rather triv-ial. Examples of the latter include:

2/59 Wrestling or Movies? Saturday Night Preferences in Ottawa-Hull Area

1/88 Preferences for Mini-series Length and Scheduling

2/88 Canadian Hockey Team Preferences by Region – Annual Media Survey Results

4/88 Title Preferences and Likelihood of Watching Adrienne Clarkson's Summer Arts Program

2/89 Desirable Qualities in the Hosts of News and Information Programs: Opinions of CBC English Network Panel Members

2/89 The Amount of Interest in Viewing Future and Potential Movies among the General Public and among Age, Sex and Regional Groupings

Using audience research to find out what Canadians want from the CBC would not be an easy or unproblematic task. It would have to be an ongoing process involving a variety of research tools. It would also have to be done in the context of the kind of programming provided by other broadcasters, and the findings would have to be balanced against practical considerations, including the state of CBC finances. In times of declining support for the very concept of public broadcasting, however, it is vital that the CBC use its audience research facility so as to be as responsive as possible to the expressed needs of Canadians. For this is the surest guarantee that it will continue to serve the public interest and thereby retain the public support on which its survival depends.

Notes

BBM Files   Files of the BBM Bureau of Broadcast Measurement, Don Mills
CBCCR   CBC Central Registry, Ottawa
CBCRD   CBC Research (Department), CBC Head Office, Ottawa
DMC Files   Dunton Memorial Collection, Carleton University*
Morrison Papers   Papers of Neil M. Morrison, National Archives of Canada, MG30 E273
NA   National Archives of Canada
Plaunt Papers   Papers of Alan Plaunt, University of British Columbia
Weir Papers   Papers of E. Austin Weir, National Archives of Canada, MG30 D67

PREFACE

1 Majid Tehranian, *Technologies of Power: Information Machines and Democratic Prospects* (Norwood, NJ: Ablex 1990), 238.
2 Leo Bogart, *Strategy in Advertising* (New York: Harcourt, Brace, and World 1967), 220.

A NOTE ON TERMS

1 BBM Bureau of Measurement, *How to Read BBM Radio Reports: A Useful Guide for Buyers, Sellers and Programmers* (1990), 1 [BBM Files]. Emphasis added.
2 See CBC Ratings Review Committee, *Report* (1960), 11–13 [CBCRD].

---

* This collection consists mainly of materials which were in the CBC's head office library before it was closed in 1986. The library was originally created by the CBC Bureau of Audience Research. The collection includes copies of most of the early reports proposed by the research department, as well as miscellaneous materials which it collected over the years.

CHAPTER 1 From Public Service to Public Participation: The Role of Audience Research

1 E.C. Stewart, 'A Report on a Study of Elliott-Haynes Survey Data and Its Usefulness to the Canadian Broadcasting Corporation' (23 February 1948), 3 [DMC Files].

2 Alan Thomas, 'Audience, Market and Public: An Evaluation of Canadian Broadcasting,' *Occasional Papers on Adult Education* (University of British Columbia, Department of University Extension 1960), 8–9, 23 [DMC Files].

3 CBC Research, 'What the Canadian Public Thinks of Television and of the TV Services Provided by CBC' (February 1974), 33 [CBCRD].

4 Liora Salter, 'Reconceptualizing Public Broadcasting,' in Rowland Lorimer and Donald Wilson, eds., *Communication Canada: Issues in Broadcasting and New Technologies* (Toronto: Kagan and Woo 1988).

5 Royal Commission on National Development in the Arts, Letters and Sciences, *Report* (Ottawa: King's Printer 1951), 297. Hereafter cited as Massey commission, *Report.*

6 Ibid., 268.

7 Frank W. Peers, *The Public Eye: Television and the Politics of Canadian Broadcasting 1952–1968* (Toronto: University of Toronto Press 1979), 67.

8 The copy in question is located in DMC Files.

9 Kenneth P. Adler and Eliette Leblanc, 'Three Competing Radio Stations and Their Audiences: An Analysis of the Relation between Media Content and Audience Characteristics,' paper presented to the Association for Education in Journalism, 30 August 1960, p. 21 [DMC Files].

10 As quoted by Leo Bogart in *Strategy in Advertising*, 243, from an article by Rosten in *Television*, July 1965.

11 Bernard Rosenberg, 'Mass Culture Revisited,' in B. Rosenberg and David Manning White, eds., *Mass Culture Revisited* (New York: Van Nostrand Reinhold 1971), 6.

12 Massey commission, *Report*, 41.

13 Royal Commission on Broadcasting, *Report* (Ottawa: Queen's Printer 1957), 80. Hereafter cited as Fowler commission, *Report.*

14 Quoted in Wilfred Altman, 'The Rise and Fall of the BBC Monopoly,' in W. Altman, Denis Thomas, and David Sawers, eds., *TV: From Monopoly to Competition* (London: Institute of Economic Affairs 1962), 13. The quotation is from Reith's *Broadcast over Britain* (London: Hodder and Stoughton 1924), 34.

15 Peter Trueman, 'Don't Blame the Audience for Cotton-Candy Fare That's Offered on TV Menu,' *Starweek*, 6 January 1990, 84.

16 J.C.W. Reith, *Into the Wind* (London: Hodder and Stoughton 1949), 133.

17 C. Stanley to Alan B. Plaunt, 1 March 1932 [Plaunt Papers, box 1, file 15].

18 Richard McKeon, 'Communication, Truth, and Society,' *Ethics*, 67 (January 1957), 99.

19 Martin H. Seiden, *Who Controls the Mass Media? Popular Myths and Economic Realities* (New York: Basic Books 1974), 5.

20 Ibid., 221.

21 See, for example, Steven Globerman, *Cultural Regulation in Canada* (Montreal: Institute for Research on Public Policy 1983).

22 See, for example, Richard Collins, *Culture, Comunication, and National Identity: The Case of Canadian Television* (Toronto: University of Toronto Press 1990).

CHAPTER 2 Public Broadcasting in Name Only: The Origins of Programming Paternalism

1 From a letter quoted in Arthur Wallace, 'On the Air,' *Saturday Night*, 7 February 1931, 12. It is not clear whether Wallace himself was 'Pro Radio Publico,' who, despite the pseudonym, was opposed to public broadcasting.

2 Canada, Department of Communications, *Report of the Task Force on Broadcasting Policy* (Ottawa: Supply and Services Canada 1986), 261–3.

3 John Watson, 'Democracy and the Universities,' *Queen's Quarterly*, 33 (February 1926), 362.

4 'Two Educators Speak,' *Education by Radio*, 2 (14 January 1932), 5.

5 Reith, *Into the Wind*, 135–6.

6 Ibid.

7 Ibid., 133.

8 Ibid., 169–70.

9 Much has been written about the Canadian Radio League, most of it by supporters of public broadcasting, but the most detailed account remains John E. O'Brien, SJ, 'A History of the Canadian Radio League, 1930–1936' (PhD thesis, University of Southern California, Los Angeles, 1964).

10 See Marc Raboy, *Missed Opportunities: The Story of Canada's Broadcasting Policy* (Montreal and Kingston: McGill-Queen's University Press 1990), esp. 17–47.

11 Plaunt Papers, box 11, file 1.

12 'The Canadian Radio League: Objects, Information, National Support' (December 1930), 11.

13 Royal Commission on Radio Broadcasting, *Report* (Ottawa: King's Printer 1929), 6. Hereafter cited as Aird, *Report.*

14 Aird, *Report,* 26–9.

15 Frank W. Peers, *The Politics of Canadian Broadcasting 1920–1951* (Toronto: University of Toronto Press 1969), 21.

16 Aird, *Report,* 7–8.

17 Ibid., 6.

18 Ibid., 7, 10.

19 Graham Spry and R.W. Ashcroft, 'Should Radio Be Nationalized in Canada?' *Saturday Night,* 24 January 1931, 2–3.

20 John Murray Gibbon, 'Radio as a Fine Art,' *Canadian Forum,* 11 (March 1931), 213–14.

21 Ibid., 214.

22 E.A. Weir to W.D. Robb, 4 May 1931 [Weir Papers, vol. 27, file 4].

23 Graham Spry, 'A Case for Nationalized Broadcasting,' *Queen's Quarterly,* 38 (Winter 1931), 156–7.

24 Ibid.

25 Quoted in Erik Barnouw, *A Tower in Babel,* vol. I of *A History of Broadcasting in the United States* (New York: Oxford University Press 1966), 270.

26 Mary Vipond, *Listening In: The First Decade of Canadian Broadcasting, 1922–1932* (Montreal and Kingston: McGill-Queen's University Press 1992), 101.

27 Merrill Denison, 'Thoughts on Radio,' in William Arthur Deacon and Wilfred Reeves, eds., *Open House* (Ottawa: Graphic Publishers 1931), 112–13.

28 Matthew N. Chappell and C.E. Hooper, *Radio Audience Measurement* (New York: Stephen Daye 1944), 3.

29 Spry, 'A Case for Natonalized Broadcasting,' 155, 168.

30 'Proposals of the Canadian Radio League for the Organization of Broadcasting in Canada,' submission to Special Parliamentary Committee on the Canadian Radio Commission, 7 May 1936 [Plaunt Papers, box 13, file 2].

31 Ibid.

32 Ibid., 153, 169.

33 'Constitution of the Canadian Radio League,' article 1(m) [Plaunt Papers, box 11, file 1].

34 E.A. Corbett, 'Education by Radio,' *Education by Radio,* 2 (14 January 1932), 157.

35 'Constitution of the Canadian Radio League,' article 2(i).

36 Ibid., article 2(g).

37 W.H. Dennis to A. Plaunt, 10 December 1930 [Plaunt Papers, box 2, file 4].

38 'Statement by Graham Spry' (nd) [Plaunt Papers, box 13, file 3].

39 E. Austin Weir, *The Struggle for National Broadcasting in Canada* (Toronto: McClelland and Stewart 1965), 138–9.

40 Ibid., 151.

41 Ibid., 152.

42 For the script of one of the broadcasts, see Roger Bird, ed., *Documents of Canadian Broadcasting* (Ottawa: Carleton University Press 1988), 133–42.

43 Peers, *The Politics of Canadian Broadcasting 1920–1951*, 166.

44 Plaunt Papers, box 2, file 4.

45 Quoted in Arthur Wallace, 'On the Air,' *Saturday Night*, 7 February 1931, 12.

46 Quoted from an editorial in the *Farmers' Sun* by Peers, *The Politics of Canadian Broadcasting*, 110.

47 B. Claxton to A. Plaunt, 10 December 1935 [Plaunt Papers, box 1, file 19].

48 W.E. Gladstone Murray, 'National Radio in Canada: A Survey' (25 July 1933), 9 [Plaunt Papers, box 13, file 3].

49 Weir, *Struggle for National Broadcasting in Canada*, 152.

CHAPTER 3 Divergent Approaches to Audience Research in the United States and Britain

1 Robert Silvey, 'What Is Listener Research?' *Ariel*, June 1938, 278.

2 Frank Foster, *Broadcasting Policy Development* (Ottawa: Franfost Communications 1982), 7.

3 *Sessional Papers*, VI, no. 28, p. 141

4 Peers, *The Politics of Public Broadcasting*, 28–9.

5 Graham Spry, 'Memorandum' to Royal Commission on Railways and Transportation, 14 January 1932 [Plaunt Papers, box 11, file 4].

6 Stella Unger, 'Speaking of Radio,' *Printers' Ink*, 183 (9 June 1938), 57.

7 Roland Marchand, *Advertising and the American Dream: Making Way for Modernity, 1920–1940* (Berkeley: University of California Press 1985), 89.

8 Other early studies include R. Likert, 'Measuring the Sales Influence of a Radio Program,' *Journal of Applied Psychology*, April 1936, 175–82.

9 'Sizing Up the Radio Audience,' *Literary Digest*, 19 January 1929, 54–5.

10 'Rural Radio,' *Printers' Ink*, 186 (9 February 1939), 25.

11 The following account is based primarily on Hugh Malcolm Beville, Jr, *Audience Ratings: Radio, Television, and Cable*, rev. ed. (Hillsdale, NJ: Lawrence Erlbaum Associates 1988), 4–11. For Crossley's recollections, see 'Early Days of Public Opinion Research,' *Public Opinion Quarterly*, 21 (no. 1, 1957), 159–64.

12 S.H. Giellerup, 'It's Time We Took the "Blue Sky" out of the Air,' *Advertising and Selling*, 13 (16 October 1929), 19.

13 'To Check-up Radio Listeners: Effort Will Be Made to Form Radio Audit Bureau,' *Printers' Ink*, 150 (20 March 1930), 36.

14 Eileen Meehan, 'Why We Don't Count: The Commodity Audience,' in Patricia Mellencamp, ed., *Logics of Television: Essays in Cultural Criticism* (Bloomington and Indianapolis: Indiana University Press 1990).

15 Canadian Radio League, 'Radio Advertising: A Menace to the Newspaper and a Burden to the Public' (nd), 4.

16 James G. Webster and Lawrence W. Lichty, *Ratings Analysis: Theory and Practice* (Hillsdale, NJ: Lawrence Erlbaum 1991), 69.

17 'New Wings for Words,' *Printers' Ink*, 184 (28 July 1938), 425–6.

18 Canadian Radio League, 'Radio Advertising,' 4.

19 Beville, *Audience Ratings*, 4.

20 Meehan, 'Why We Don't Count,' 123.

21 William S. Paley, *As It Happened: A Memoir* (Garden City, NY: Doubleday 1979), 104.

22 Ibid., 104–5.

23 Henry L. Ewbank and Sherman P. Lawton, *Broadcasting: Radio and Television* (New York: Harper 1952), 471; Lewis J. Paper, *Empire: William S. Paley and the Making of CBS* (New York: St Martin's Press 1987), 45–6.

24 The factual material in this section is drawn mainly from Beville, *Audience Ratings*, 10–13; Meehan, 'Why We Don't Count,' 123–5; and Webster and Lichty, *Ratings Analysis*, 71–3.

25 Webster and Lichty, *Ratings Analysis*, 71.

26 Matthew N. Chappell and C.E. Hooper, *Radio Audience Measurement* (New York: Stephen Daye 1944), vii.

27 A.B. Blankenship, Chuck Chakrapani, and W.H. Poole, *A History of Marketing Research in Canada* (Toronto: Professional Marketing Research Society 1985), 22.

28 Frederick H. Lumley, *Measurement in Radio* (New York: Arno Press 1971), 29. Reprint of 1934 edition (Columbus: Ohio State University Press).

29 Webster and Lichty, *Ratings Analysis*, 72.

30 Meehan, 'Why We Don't Count,' 124.

31 Beville, *Audience Ratings*, 17–21.

32 Eugene S. Foster, *Understanding Broadcasting* (Reading, Mass.: Addison-Wesley 1978), 284.

33 Meehan, 'Why We Don't Count,' 128.

34 Quoted in Asa Briggs, *The Golden Age of Wireless*, vol. II of *The History of Broadcasting in the United Kingdom* (London: Oxford University Press 1965), 259.

35 Ibid., 263.

36 Reith, *Into the Wind*, 244.
37 Altman, 'The Rise and Fall of the BBC Monopoly,' 15–16.
38 Andrew Boyle, *Only the Wind Will Listen: Reith of the BBC* (London: Hutchison 1972), 151.
39 Quoted in Briggs, *The Golden Age of Wireless*, 267–8.
40 Mark Pegg, *Broadcasting and Society 1918–1939* (London and Canberra: Croom Helm 1983), 97.
41 Quoted in Briggs, *The Golden Age of Wireless*, 279.
42 G.J. Goodhardt, A.S.C. Ehrenberg, and M.A. Collins, *The Television Audience: Patterns of Viewing* (Westmead, Farnsborough, Hants., England: Saxon House 1975), 137.
43 Robert J. Silvey, 'Methods of Listener Research Employed by the British Broadcasting Corporation,' *Journal of the Royal Statistical Society*, 107 (1944); and 'Methods of Viewer Research Employed by the British Broadcasting Corporation,' *Public Opinion Quarterly*, 15 (no. 1, 1951), 89–104.
44 Peter Menneer, 'Measuring the Television Viewing Public's Taste,' *Television: The Journal of the Royal Television Society*, 18 (no. 10, 1981), 4–5; Barrie Gunter and Mallory Wober, *The Reactive Viewer: A Review of Research on Audience Reaction Measurement* (London: John Libbey 1992), 8–9.
45 Robert J. Silvey, 'The Intelligibility of Broadcast Talks,' *Public Opinion Quarterly*, 15 (no. 2, 1951), 299–304.
46 Gunter and Wober, *The Reactive Viewer*, 9.
47 Paddy Scannell and David Cardiff, *A Social History of British Broadcasting*, vol. I: *1922–1939* (Oxford: Basil Blackwell 1991), 376.
48 Ibid., 19.
49 Ibid., 380.

CHAPTER 4 Early Audience Measurement Services in Canada: Elliott-Haynes, ISL, and BBM

1 CBC Commercial Division, 'Saskatchewan Survey: As Prepared from a Report by Canadian Facts, Limited' (1948), 2 [Weir Papers, vol. 15, file 6].
2 For a sketch of Elliott's career, see Ray Whalen, 'New Fellows of the Professional Marketing Research Society: Walter Edward Elliott,' *Imprints*, Summer 1989, 15–16.
3 Chris Commins, 'In Memoriam: Paul Haynes 1909–1989,' *Imprints*, Summer 1989, 26.
4 Elliott-Haynes Limited, '"... from Little Acorns Grow"' (nd). Company pamphlet [DMC Files].
5 Ibid.

6 Blankenship, Chakrapani, and Poole, *History of Marketing Research in Canada*, 22–4, 31–2.
7 Ibid., 31–2.
8 Elliott-Haynes, '"... from Little Acorns Grow."'
9 Elliott-Haynes Limited, 'The Radio and Television Services of Elliott-Haynes Limited' (1956), 9. Company brochure [DMC Files].
10 E.C. Stewart, 'Report on a Study of Elliott-Haynes Survey Data and Its Usefulness to the Canadian Broadcasting Corporation' (23 February 1948) [DMC Files].
11 Robert Pike and Vincent Mosco, 'Canadian Consumers and Telephone Pricing: From Luxury to Necessity and Back Again?' *Telecommunications Policy*, March 1986, 17, 19.
12 A.H. Shephard, 'Report to the BBM Research and Development Committee' (1952), 7 [BBM Files].
13 E.A. Weir to N.M. Morrison, 2 December 1953 [Weir Papers, vol. 10, file 2].
14 Shephard, 'Report to the BBM Research and Development Committee,' 8.
15 Ibid.
16 Blankenship, Chakrapani, and Poole, *History of Marketing Research in Canada*, 43–4.
17 International Surveys Limited, 'The Radio Panel of Canada' (1954) [DMC Files].
18 Ibid.
19 Webster and Lichty, *Ratings Analysis*, 77–8.
20 CBC Research, 'International Surveys: How They Get Their Sample' (May 1954) [CBCRD].
21 These were: Forest L. Whan, 'The 1950 Iowa Radio Audience Survey'; and CBC, 'Test of the Radio Panel of Canada's March Ratings in the Province of Ontario' (June 1951) [DMC Files].
22 See, for example, Athol McQuarrie, 'Getting Away from "Guesstimates,"' *Canadian Broadcaster*, July 1943.
23 My source for much of the material that follows is a scrapbook compiled for BBM by David Adams and available at BBM.
24 CAB Joint Committee on Research, 'Coverage Report' (1944) [BBM Files].
25 Minutes of BBM Technical Sub-committee, 24 July 1945 [BBM Files].
26 Minutes of BBM Finance Committee, 30 May 1945 [BBM Files].
27 For a brief account of the origins of the Broadcast Measurement Bureau, see Sydney W. Head, *Broadcasting in America* (Boston: Houghton, Mifflin 1956), 243.
28 'BBM Parallels ABC: Feltis Addresses Admen,' *Canadian Broadcaster*, 5 (8 June 1946).

29 CBC Research, 'Program Ratings in Canada' (1956), 18–19 [CBCRD].
30 L. Phenner to G. Bannerman, 9 April 1945 [BBM Files].
31 G. Bannerman to L. Phenner, 25 April 1945 [BBM Files].
32 Minutes of BBM Finance Committee, 12 March 1946 [BBM Files].
33 'Many Improvements in 2nd BBM Survey,' *Canadian Broadcaster*, 5 (27 March 1946); 'BBM Reports Refinements,' *Canadian Broadcaster*, 5 (8 June 1946).
34 Stewart, 'Report on a Study of Elliott-Haynes Survey Data,' 7–9.
35 H.F. Chevrier to E.A. Weir, 8 January 1951 [NA, RG41, vol. 344, file 16–7].
36 BBM Research and Development Committee, 'Report on Radio Ratings in Canada' (1952), 4, 28–9 [BBM Files].
37 E.A. Weir to D. Manson, 1 November 1952 [Weir Papers, vol. 10, file 2].
38 Minutes of BBM Research and Development Committee, 25 November 1952 [BBM Files].
39 Harry J. Boyle, 'A Year of Experiment,' *CBC Times*, 5–11 December 1948, 2.

CHAPTER 5 The E-H Ratings and the Missing CBC Audience: Origins of the Bureau of Audience Research

 1 Weir Papers, vol. 10, file 2.
 2 Quoted in Peers, *The Politics of Canadian Broadcasting*, 344.
 3 Stewart, 'Report on a Study of Elliott-Haynes Survey Data'
 4 CBC, *Annual Report for 1947–48* (Ottawa: King's Printer 1948), 56.
 5 Massey commission, *Report*, 37.
 6 Stewart, 'Report on a Study of Elliott-Haynes Survey Data.'
 7 Weir Papers, vol. 10, file 2.
 8 CBC Commercial Division, 'Saskatchewan Survey: As Prepared from a Report by Canadian Facts, Limited' (nd) [Weir Papers, vol. 15, file 6].
 9 Weir Papers, vol. 15, file 6.
10 CBC Commercial Division, 'Saskatchewan Survey.'
11 Ibid.
12 Ibid.
13 Minutes of BBM Research and Development Committee, 31 May 1949 [BBM Files].
14 Weir Papers, vol. 15, file 6. Weir's remarks about being sent an incomplete version were deleted in the final version of this letter.
15 Ibid.
16 Elliott-Haynes Limited, 'An Analysis of the Radio Audiences Tuned to Programs Produced by the Canadian Broadcasting Corporation' (nd) [Weir Papers, vol. 11, file 1].

17 H.F. Chevrier, 'Examination of a Report on Canadian Listening to CBC Non-commercial Programs Prepared for Clifford Sifton by Elliott-Haynes Ltd.' (nd) [Weir Papers, vol. 11, file 1].
18 Ibid.
19 Ibid.
20 Ibid.
21 Ibid.
22 Peers, *The Politics of Canadian Broadcasting*, 393.
23 E.A. Weir to A. Ouimet, 4 December 1953 [Weir Papers, vol. 10, file 2]. In *The Struggle for National Broadcasting in Canada*, Weir wrote (p. xiii) that from 1944 onwards he had been 'responsible for the organization of "Audience Research" though I had nothing to do with its subsequent direction.'
24 D. Manson to W. Haley, 9 July 1951 [Weir Papers, vol. 10, file 2].
25 D. Manson to E.A. Weir, 9 July 1951 [Weir Papers, vol. 10, file 2].
26 Gruneau Research, 'A Study of Radio Listenership in the Province of Quebec' (March 1952) [Weir Papers, vol. 16].
27 Massey commission, *Report*, 298.
28 E.A. Weir to D. Manson, 14 March 1952 [Weir Papers, vol. 15, file 5].
30 Gruneau Research, 'Canadian Public Opinion toward Radio and the Canadian Broadcasting Corporation' (March 1952) [Weir Papers, vol. 16].
30 E.A. Weir to D. Manson, 14 March 1952.
31 N.M. Morrison to D. Manson, 15 April 1952 [Weir Papers, vol. 15, file 5].
32 E.A. Weir to D. Manson, 20 March 1952 [Weir Papers, vol. 10, file 2].
33 Ibid.
34 Weir Papers, vol. 10, file 2.
35 Ibid.
36 E.A. Weir to D. Manson, 20 March 1952.
37 E.A. Weir to A. Ouimet, 12 August 1953 [Weir Papers, vol. 10, file 2].
38 Ibid.
39 Ibid.
40 Ibid.
41 A. Ouimet to E.A. Weir, 27 October 1953 [Weir Papers, vol. 10, file 2].

CHAPTER 6 Organization and Development of CBC Research under Morrison, Laird, and Kiefl

1 James S. Ettema and D. Charles Whitney, eds., *Individuals in Mass Media Organizations: Creativity and Constraint* (Beverly Hills: Sage 1982), 7.
2 E.A. Weir to A. Ouimet, 12 August 1953 [Weir Papers, vol. 10, file 2].

3 Neil Morrison, 'The Simple Joys of Talking on the Radio,' *CBC News*, 6 February 1949.

4 CBC submission to Royal Commission on Government Organization [CBCCR, AR2-2-1].

5 Interview of Ronald Kealey with Nancy Gnaedinger in January 1983 [NA C3798, CBC Oral History Collection].

6 N. Morrison to E. Beach, 1 August 1961 [CBCCR, AR2-2-1].

7 Part of the thesis was published in Kurt Lang and Gladys Engel Lang, 'The Unique Perspective of Television and Its Effect: A Pilot Study,' *American Sociological Review*, 18 (1953), 3–12. In *The Image: A Guide to Pseudo-events in America* (New York: Atheneum 1982), Daniel J. Boorstin described it (p. 270) as 'a study of great subtlety and originality.' See also pp. 26–8 of Boorstin.

8 N. Morrison to R. Lewis, 19 October 1956 [CBCCR, AR2-2-1].

9 N. Morrison, 'Progress Report' (1957) [DMC Files].

10 N. Morrison to A. Ouimet, 17 September 1954, and N. Morrison to director of personnel and administration, 22 September 1954 [CBCCR, AR2-2-4].

11 M. Perron to N. Morrison, 22 May 1957, and M. Perron to N. Morrison, 7 June 1957 [CBCCR, AR2-2-4].

12 R. Lewis to N. Morrison, 4 December 1956 [CBCCR, AR2-2-1].

13 Circular letter containing text of announcement by Marcel Carter, director of personnel and administrative services, 3 December 1953 [Weir Papers, vol. 10, file 2].

14 A. Laird to director of sales policy and planning, 19 December 1960 [CBCCR, AR2-2-3].

15 R. Joynt to N. Morrison, 22 February 1960 [Morrison Papers, vol. 17].

16 J. Twomey to N. Morrison, 3 March 1960 [Morrison Papers, vol. 17].

17 A. Laird to director of sales policy and planning, 19 December 1960 [CBCCR, AR2-2-3].

18 A. Laird to E. Hallman, 26 September 1960 [CBCCR, AR2-2-1].

19 E.A. Weir to D. Manson, 20 March 1952 [Weir Papers, vol. 10, file 2].

20 N. Morrison, 'Progress Report' (1957).

21 See 'Conclusions and Recommendations of the Audience Research Study of the 1956 P.C. Convention Broadcasts' (October 1957) [CBCRD].

22 Interview of Neil Morrison with author in December 1991. Material on Morrison was also drawn from an interview with Nancy Gnaedinger in January 1983 [NA, C3806–3807, CBC Oral History Collection].

23 N. Morrison to E. Hallman, 5 August 1961 [CBCCR, AR2-2-1].

24 A.J. Laird, 'Report on an Enquiry into the Effects of Broadcasting' (January 1951) [DMC Files].

25 A. Laird to K. Adler, 5 May 1959 [CBCCR, AR5-4].

26 A. Laird to M. Ouimet, 24 February 1970 [CBCCR, AR2-2-1].
27 Arthur Laird, 'The CBC Research Department: What It Does and Why It Does It' (23 April 1981). Talk to CBC Head Office staff [DMC Files].
28 A. Laird to I. Shulman, 26 February 1962 [CBCCR, AR1-5-1].
29 A. Laird to J.-P. Kirouac, 28 May 1965 [CBCCR, AR2-2-1].
30 A. Laird to assistant vice-president, programming, 8 March 1965 [CBCCR, AR2-2-1].
31 A. Laird to director of personnel, 14 June 1968 [CBCCR, AR2-2-3].
32 A. Laird to M. Ouimet, 24 February 1970 [CBCCR AR2-2-1].

CHAPTER 7 The CBC and the Ratings Maze, 1954–1970: The Growth and Decline of Industry Competition

1 CBC Research, 'An Experimental Study of the Format of the CBC Audience Panel Diary' (June 1967), 5 [CBCRD].
2 A. Laird to K. Buhr, 2 February 1965 [CBCCR, AR1-39].
3 CBC Research, 'International Surveys: How They Get Their Sample' (May 1954) [CBCRD].
4 M. Leckie to H.F. Chevrier, 13 April 1954; appended to H.F. Chevrier, 'Some Notes on the Application of Elliott-Haynes Ratings' (June 1954) [DMC Files].
5 Ibid., 11.
6 Morrison, 'Progress Report' (1954), 3–4 [DMC Files].
7 CBC Research, 'Program Ratings in Canada' (1956) [CBCRD].
8 M. Munro to N. Morrison, 18 March 1959 [CBCCR, AR2-2-1].
9 CBC Research, 'Radio Listening Patterns in a Canadian Community ... "Before" Television' (December 1955), 10 [CBCRD].
10 CBC, 'Position of the Canadian Broadcasting Corporation in Respect to the Bureau of Broadcast Measurement' (January 1956), 3 [NA, Morrison Papers, vol. 17].
11 C.R. Vint to J.A. Ouimet, 18 January 1956 [NA, RG41, vol. 344, file 16–7].
12 Bureau of Broadcast Measurement, 'A Report to the Membership on the CBC's Statement with Respect to BBM' (1 February 1956) [NA, RG41, vol. 344, file 16–7].
13 C.R. Vint to J.A. Ouimet, 1 February 1956 [NA, RG41, vol. 344, file 16–7].
14 C.R. Vint to J.A. Ouimet, 1 February 1956; J.A. Ouimet to C.R. Vint, 7 February 1956 [NA, RG41, vol. 344, file 16–7].
15 CBC, 'Position ... in Respect to the Bureau of Broadcast Measurement,' 6.
16 Television Audience Measurement Limited, 'Proposal for the Study of the Measurement of Audiences to Radio and Television in Canada' (September 1956) [DMC Files].
17 A.C. Nielsen of Canada, 'NBI' (1956 brochure), 7 [DMC Files].

18 Broadcast Audience Measurement Committee, 'A Report on Broadcast Audience Information in Canada' (nd) [Morrison Papers, vol. 17].

19 CBC Ratings Review Committee, 'Report' (July 1960), 3–4 [CBCRD].

20 Minutes of BBM Research and Development Committee, 29 May 1959 [BBM Files].

21 N.M. Morrison to J.A. Ouimet, 24 February 1960 [Morrison Papers, vol. 17].

22 N.M. Morrison to Vice-President, Programming, 23 March 1960, Morrison Papers, vol. 17].

23 'Some Considerations Concerning a CBC Subscription to the Bureau of Broadcast Measurement' (23 March 1960) [Morrison Papers, vol. 17].

24 K. Purdye to N. Morrison, 27 July 1960; N. Morrison to K. Purdye, 28 July 1960; N. Morrison to B.K. Byram, 29 July 1960; N. Morrison to J.-P. Kirouac, 4 August 1960; N. Morrison to R. Lewis, 4 August 1960; and N. Morrison to B. Byram, 4 August 1960 [CBCCR, AR1-9-4].

25 CBC Research, 'A Technical Evaluation of the Radio-TV Audience Measurement Services Available in Canada' (June 1962) [CBCRD]. This appears to be largely an update of the technical sections in the unauthorized report of the ratings review committee.

26 CBC Ratings Review Committee, 'Report,' 4, 44.

27 Ibid., 32.

28 Ibid., 34–8.

29 Ibid., 50.

30 Senate Committee on Interstate and Foreign Commerce, US Congress, *Television Inquiry, Part 7: The Television Ratings Services*, 85th Congress, 2nd session, June 1958 (Washington: GPO 1959).

31 House Committee on Interstate and Foreign Commerce, US Congress, *Evaluation of Statistical Methods Used in Obtaining Broadcast Ratings*, House Report 193, 87th Congress, 1st session, 1961 (Washington: GPO 1961). The quotation is taken from 'Just How Is It Done?' *Business Week*, 16 March 1963, 34.

32 Peter D. Fox, 'Noncooperation Bias in Television Ratings,' *Public Opinion Quarterly*, 27 (Summer 1963), 314.

33 'Overrated?' *Newsweek*, 14 January 1963, 66.

34 House Committee on Interstate and Foreign Commerce, US Congress, *Broadcast Ratings*, Hearings before the Special Subcommittee on Investigations, 88th Congress, 1st and 2nd sessions, 1963–1964 (Washington: GPO 1964–5).

35 CBC Research, 'Syndicated Ratings Services 1964' (12 February 1964) [CBCRD].

36 Quoted in 'Puzzle: Who Knows Who Looks at TV?' *U.S. News & World Report*, 8 April 1963, 45.

37 'Broadcast Ratings Lose Spell,' *Business Week*, 13 April 1963, 30.

38 *U.S. News & World Report*, 8 April 1963, 47.

39 Ralph Schoenstein, '60,000,000 Projections Can't Be Wrong,' *Saturday Review*, 8 June 1963, 56.

40 Minutes of CBC Research & Statistics meeting, 1 November 1961 [DMC Files].

41 CBC Research, 'A Technical Evaluation of the Radio-TV Audience Measurement Services Available in Canada' (June 1962), 123–4 [CBCRD].

42 Quoted in 'BBM Teams Research Expansion,' *Canadian Sponsor*, 18 September 1961.

43 Minutes of BBM Research and Development Committee, 19 April 1960 [BBM Files].

44 Minutes of BBM Research and Development Committee, 24 November 1961 [BBM Files].

45 Minutes of BBM Research and Development Committee, 5 February 1953 [BBM Files].

46 BBM scrapbook prepared by David Adams [BBM Files].

47 'J.N. Milne's Speech,' 24th annual general meeting of BBM Bureau of Measurement, 9 May 1968 [BBM Files].

48 B.K. Byram, 'President's Report,' 24th annual general meeting of BBM Bureau of Measurement, 9 May 1968 [BBM Files].

49 CBC Research, 'Ratings and Circulation Services: Recommendations for Purchase 1964–65' [CBCCR, AR1-39].

50 A. Laird to vice-president, programming et al., 29 March 1968 [CBCCR, AR1-39].

51 K. Purdye to G. Ralph, 20 June 1969 [CBCCR, AR1-11-4-1].

52 A. Laird to J. Malloy et al., 24 February 1970 [CBCCR, AR1-39].

53 Ibid.

54 CBC Research, 'A Review of the Corporation's Current Contracts for the Purchase of Syndicated Audience Measurement (Ratings) Services and a Recommendation for a Substantial Savings in Costs' (24 February 1970) [CBCCR, AR1-39].

55 A. Laird to J. Malloy et al., 24 February 1970.

56 Interview of Stan Staple with author in June 1993.

CHAPTER 8 The CBC and the Ratings Maze, 1971–1993: From Personal Diaries to People Meters

1 Quoted in BBM Bureau of Measurement press release, 2 August 1989 [BBM Files]. Newell was vice-president of Harrison, Young, Pesonen and Newell Inc. and a member of BBM's subcommittee on meters.

2   B.K. Byram, 'President's Report,' minutes of 29th annual general meeting of BBM Bureau of Measurement, 27 April 1973 [BBM Files].

3   Minutes of 29th annual general meeting of BBM Bureau of Measurement, 27 April 1973 [BBM Files]

4   Ibid.

5   For example, Audits and Surveys (New York), 'All Radio Methodology Study' (September 1966) and studies by the Committee on Nationwide Television Audience Measurement (CONTAM) in 1969 and 1970.

6   BBM, 'The BBM Quality Control Test' (April 1973) [BBM Files].

7   BBM, 'The BBM Tests of Revised and Single Media Diaries' (15 February 1974) [BBM Files].

8   BBM, 'The "Radio Only" TC Validation' (January 1974) [BBM Files].

9   A.E. Paull, 'A Critical Appraisal' (25 March 1974), 2, 7 [BBM Files].

10   Minutes of 30th annual general meeting of BBM Bureau of Measurement, 28 March 1974 [BBM Files].

11   Peter Jones, 'Separate Diaries,' minutes of 30th annual general meeting of BBM Bureau of Measurement, 28 March 1974 [BBM Files].

12   Minutes of 31st annual general meeting of BBM Bureau of Measurement, 26 June 1975 [BBM Files].

13   Minutes of Executive Committee of BBM Bureau of Measurement, 30 July 1975 [BBM Files].

14   Minutes of 34th annual general meeting of BBM, 19 April 1978 [BBM Files].

15   'President's Report,' minutes of 31st annual general meeting of BBM Bureau of Measurement, 26 June 1975 [BBM Files]. The BBM scrapbook says the loss was $135,000.

16   Minutes of BBM annual general meeting, 19 April 1978 [BBM Files].

17   Minutes of 35th annual general meeting of BBM Bureau of Measurement, 25 April 1979 [BBM Files].

18   Minutes of BBM Executive Committee, 18 February 1976 and 23 June 1977 [BBM Files].

19   Minutes of 34th annual general meeting of BBM Bureau of Measurement, 19 April 1978; minutes of 36th annual general meeting of BBM Bureau of Measurement, 23 January 1980 [BBM Files].

20   Minutes of 40th annual general meeting of BBM Bureau of Measurement, 6 December 1983 [BBM Files].

21   Interview of Barry Kiefl with author in October 1992.

22   BBM Bureau of Measurement, 'Reliability in BBM Radio Surveys or the Battle of the Bounce' (4 June 1984) [CBCRD].

23   P. Sisam to D. Fitzgerald, vice-president and general manager of City-TV Much Music, 18 June 1986 [CBCCR, AR3-1-64].

24 William S. Rubens, 'High-Tech Audience Measurement for New High-Tech Audiences,' *Critical Studies in Mass Communication*, 1 (1984), 196.

25 Kathryn Baker, 'Networks Balk at Signing for Nielsen People Meters,' *Globe and Mail*, 9 June 1987; 'Nielsen's People-Meter Prompts CBS to Tune Out,' *Toronto Star*, 7 July 1987.

26 Ken Auletta, *Three Blind Mice: How the TV Networks Lost Their Way* (New York: Random House 1991), 374.

27 B. Kiefl to G. Gauthier and D. McKie, 29 January 1985 [CBCCR, AR3-1-64].

28 B. Kiefl to P. DesRoches et al., 4 March 1985 [CBCCR, AR3-1-64].

29 J. Foss to P. Swain, 24 July 1985 [CBCCR, AR3-1-64].

30 Interview of Barry Kiefl with author in October 1992.

31 Minutes of 42nd annual general meeting of BBM Bureau of Measurement, 10 December 1985 [BBM Files].

32 M. Chercover to B. Kiefl, 13 June 1986 [CBCCR, AR3-1-64].

33 E.J. Delaney to D. Tattle, 19 June 1986 [CBCCR, AR3-1-64].

34 B. Kiefl to S. Whittaker, 11 December 1986 [CBCCR, AR3-1-64].

35 Kenneth Kidd, 'Rating the TV Ratings,' *Toronto Star*, 29 May 1988, F1–F2.

36 John Partridge, 'Firms Cancel Bid to Gauge TV Viewing,' *Globe and Mail*, 3 May 1988.

37 *Halifax Daily News*, 15 October 1989.

38 Barry Kiefl, 'People Meters vs. Diaries' (27 March 1991), presentation to Broadcast Research Council [CBCRD]. See also Anne Mathieu, 'Comparison of Viewing Levels: Nielsen People Meter and BBM Diary (Oct 1–Nov 25, 1990)' (1991) [BBM Files].

39 Ken Purdye and Gerard Malo, 'Who Killed the BBM Meter Project? or the Buttons Did It' (1992) [BBM Files].

40 John Partridge, 'Ratings Services Reunite: BBM, Nielsen Resume Talks,' *Globe and Mail*, 1 February 1991.

41 BBM Bureau of Measurement, 'BBM's TAM Television Audience Meter' (April 1990) [BBM Files].

42 Ken Purdye and Gerard Malo, 'Don't Count Out the Paper Diary Yet!' *Worldwide Broadcast Audience Research Symposium* (Advertising Research Foundation/European Society for Opinion and Marketing Research), 387.

43 Ibid., 403.

44 Committee on National Television Audience Measurement, *Nielsen People Meter Review, Conducted by Statistical Research Inc.*, 6 vols. (New York: CONTAM 1989).

45 Quoted in Erik Larson, 'Watching Americans Watch TV,' *The Atlantic*, 269 (March 1992), 77.

46 'Who Is Listening?' *Audience Research Bulletin* (March 1959), 9.

47 William S. Rubens, 'High-Tech Audience Measurement for New High-Tech Audiences,' 204.

CHAPTER 9 Audience Power versus Public Needs: Five Arguments against Ratings

1 Meehan, 'Why We Don't Count: The Commodity Audience,' 127.
2 Quotation (unidentified) in Jeffrey B. Abramson, 'Four Criticisms of Press Ethics,' in Judith Lichtenberg, ed., *Democracy and the Mass Media* (Cambridge: Cambridge University Press 1990), 262.
3 Arthur Laird, 'Broadcasting Research in the CBC,' presented at the annual meeting of the Canadian Association of Broadcasters in Quebec City, 6 April 1964 [CBCRD].
4 I. Shulman to A. Laird, 16 March 1964 [CBCCR, AR1-39].
5 A. Laird to E. Hallman, 29 October 1963 [CBCCR, AR2-2-7].
6 Eileen Meehan, 'Ratings and the Institutional Approach: A Third Answer to the Commodity Question,' *Critical Studies in Mass Communication,* 1 (1984), 221.
7 Donald Hurwitz, 'Broadcast Ratings: The Missing Dimension,' *Critical Studies in Mass Communication,* 1 (1984), 205.
8 Gleason L. Archer, *Big Business and Radio* (New York: American Historical Company 1939), 414.
9 Matthew N. Chappell and C.E. Hooper, *Radio Audience Measurement* (New York: Stephen Daye 1944), 1–2.
10 Ibid., ix–xi.
11 Frank Stanton, 'Parallel Paths,' in Norman Jacobs, ed., *Culture for the Millions? Mass Media in Modern Society* (Princeton, NJ: D. Van Nostrand 1959), 89.
12 Martin Mayer, 'The Nielsens versus Quality,' *American Film* (March 1979), 12.
13 Beville, *Audience Ratings,* 240.
14 David Paul Nord, 'An Economic Perspective on Formula in Popular Culture,' in Ellen Wartella and D. Charles Whitney, eds., *Mass Communication Review Yearbook,* vol. 4 (Beverly Hills: Sage 1983), 294–5.
15 Meehan, 'Why We Don't Count: The Commodity Audience,' 127.
16 G.J. Goodhardt, A.S.C. Ehrenberg, and M.A. Collins, *The Television Audience: Patterns of Viewing* (Westmead, Farnsborough, Hants., England: Saxon House 1975), 75.
17 Goodhardt et al., *The Television Audience,* 76.
18 Ibid, 77.
19 Ibid., 78–9.

20 A.S.C. Ehrenberg, *Advertisers or Viewers Paying?* (1986), 8. See also Patrick Barwise and Andrew Ehrenberg, *Television and Its Audience* (London: Sage 1988).

21 Michael Svennevig and David E. Morrison, 'The Problem of Quality' (1991), 44.

22 Ibid., 53.

23 CBC Research, 'How Canadians Feel about the CBC' (January 1986), 68–9 [CBCRD].

24 CBC Research, 'What the Canadian Public Thinks of Television and of the TV Services Provided by CBC' (February 1974), 8 [CBCRD].

25 Ibid., 12–15.

26 Jacques Ellul, *The Technological Society*, trans. John Wilkinson (New York: Random House 1964), 168. First published in 1954.

27 C.E. Hooper, 'What *Is* a Radio Program Rating Anyway? Here Are Leading Factors in Its Make-up,' *Printers' Ink*, 187 (no. 6, 11 May 1939), 25.

28 John Gould, 'The Curse of Ratings,' *New York Times*, 17 February 1946.

29 CBC Research, 'Audiences for CBC Television Theatre' (1957) [CBCRD].

30 Blaik Kirby, 'CBC Ratings Winner, but There's Nothing for Mind in Top 20 Shows,' *Globe and Mail*, 22 December 1970.

31 CBC Research, 'Religious Programs' (July 1956), 2 [CBCRD].

32 CBC Research, 'An Appraisal of Three CBC Country Music Shows' (June 1965) [CBCRD]. Although the questionnaire also included two CTV programs – 'Jack Paar' and 'Let's Sing Out' – for the purposes of 'camouflage,' the results for these programs were not included in the analysis.

33 Ibid., 9–12.

34 Peter Menneer, 'Audience Appreciation – A Different Story from Audience Numbers,' *Annual Review of BBC Broadcasting Research Findings*, no. 13 (1987), 25.

35 CBC Research, 'Program Ratings in Canada' (1956), 1–3 [CBCRD].

CHAPTER 10 Towards More Meaningful Public Input: From the Schwerin Technique to Image Studies

1 Quoted in *Toronto Daily Star*, 25 August 1959.

2 E.A. Weir to D. Manson, 20 March 1952 [Weir Papers, vol. 10, file 2].

3 Morrison, 'Progress Report' (1957), 14 [DMC Files].

4 Soucy Gagné, 'The CBC Image' (26 February 1959) [CCBCR, AR5-4].

5 R.C. Gunthern, '"Diagnostic Research" Shapes TV Programs,' *Toronto Star*, 5 March 1984.

6 Miles Beller, 'How Networks Test for Audience Impact,' *New York Times*, 3 June 1979, 1, 29.

7 Gilbert Seldes, *The Great Audience* (New York: Viking Press 1951), 222–3.

8 E.A. Weir to D. Manson, 20 March 1952 [Weir Papers, vol. 10, file 2].

9 V.C. Gruneau to E.A. Weir, 25 January 1952 [Weir Papers, vol. 10, file 2].

10 D. Manson to E.A. Weir, 28 March 1952 [Weir Papers, vol. 10, file 2].

11 E.A. Weir to D. Manson, 1 November 1952 [Weir Papers, vol. 10, file 2].

12 Morrison, 'Progress Report' (1957), vi.

13 CBC Research, 'Report on the Viewing of the "Plouffe Family" in Regina'
(July 1956), 9 [CBCRD].

14 Laurence Bergreen, 'Witch Doctors, Mind Readers and Seers,' *TV Guide*, 17
November 1979, 19.

15 CBC Research, 'The National: Findings from Focus Group Tests on the Use
and Viewing of National Television Newscasts' (February 1990) [CBCRD].

16 B. Kiefl to J. Shewbridge, 13 February 1991 [CBCRD].

17 CBC Research, 'Report on the Viewing of the "Plouffe Family" in Regina,' 1
[CBCRD].

18 CBC Research, 'Nursery School Time Study' (1958), 1 [CBCRD].

19 CBC Research, 'How CBC Television Is Perceived in Vancouver' (January
1959), 2 [CBCRD].

20 CBC Research, 'The National Radio-TV Study' (7 April 1960), 4 [CBCRD].

21 Andrew MacFarlane, 'Irate Pros Charge Mrs. A "Cooking" Her TV Survey,'
Toronto Telegram, 26 August 1959, 3.

22 Aitken, 'Report on National Radio-Television Study,' 3 [DMC Files].

23 Patrick Nicholson, 'Ottawa Report: Welfare for Freedom,' *Charlottetown
Guardian*, 18 August 1959.

24 Quoted in 'CBC Overhaul by Mrs. A.,' *Toronto Daily Star*, 25 August 1959, 2.

25 Aitken, 'Report on National Radio-Television Study,' 3.

26 Quoted in MacFarlane, 'Irate Pros Charge Mrs. A "Cooking" Her TV Sur-
vey,' 3. Other critical reactions included Gordon Sinclair, 'Dear Kate: Who
Gives You the Right ... to Undermine Programs?' *Toronto Daily Star*, 27
August 1959; John Manning, 'Please Call It Off, CBC,' *Detroit Times*, 28
August 1959; Arthur Blakely, 'The Aitken Plan,' *Montreal Gazette*, 31 August
1959; and 'Spare the CBC This,' *Ottawa Journal*, 31 August 1959.

27 'The Well-Meant Folly of a Lady's Aid for the CBC,' *Maclean's*, 26 September 1959, 4.

28 'Let 2,500 Run the CBC?' *Toronto Daily Star*, 24 October 1959.

29 These letters, dated 26 and 25 August respectively, are filed in CBCCR, AR3-
1-20.

30 Letter dated 1 September 1959 [CBCCR, AR3-1-20].

31 '2,000 Armchair Critics across Canada Will Decide CBC Programs,' *Toronto
Daily Star*, 26 August 1959.

32 For example, 'Mrs. Aitken's Armchair Critics,' *Ottawa Citizen*, 26 October

1959, and Arthur Blakely, 'Talent Scouts,' *Montreal Gazette*, 28 October 1959.

33 CBC Research, 'The National Radio-TV Study' (1960), 160, 174, 177.

34 'CBC Armchair Critics "Love Those Horses,"' *Montreal Gazette*, 28 January 1960.

35 Minutes of 9th meeting of Board of Directors, 26–28 January 1960, p. 216 [NA, RG41, vol. 669 (microfilm T-3044)].

36 'CBC Armchair Criticism Secret,' *Ottawa Citizen*, 30 April 1960.

37 CBC Research, 'National Radio-TV Study,' 159–60.

38 Ibid., 161–70.

39 Ibid., 167.

40 Ibid., 172. The underlining in the original text has been deleted.

41 A. Laird to B. Kiefl, 27 June 1991 [CBCRD]. Written in response to draft chapter.

42 CBC Research, 'An Analysis of Letters Written to New Liberty Magazine about Canadian Television' (December 1956) [CBCRD].

43 R. Fraser to N. Morrison, 10 June 1958 [CBCCR, AR5-4].

44 Ibid.

45 J.A. Ouimet to N.M. Morrison, 5 November 1958 [CBCCR, AR5-4].

46 J.A. Ouimet to controller of broadcasting et al., 5 November 1958 [CBCCR, AR5-4].

47 N.M. Morrison to D.C. McArthur, 25 September 1959 [CBCCR, AR5-4].

48 CBC Research, 'CBC Image Study (Toronto)' (August 1960) [DMC Files].

49 CBC Research, 'What the Canadian Public Thinks of the CBC: An Empirical Study of Public Attitudes to the Canadian Broadcasting Corporation and to Certain Other Aspects of Broadcasting in Canada' (June 1963), 3 [CBCRD].

50 Ibid., 16.

51 CBC Research, 'What the Canadian Public Thinks of Television and of the TV Services Provided by CBC' (February 1974) [CBCRD].

52 CBC Research, 'How Canadians Feel about the CBC' (January 1986) [CBCRD].

CHAPTER 11 Beyond the Ratings Mentality? The CBC Network Television Panels

1 A. Laird to E. Hallman, 29 January 1965 [CBCCR, AR3-1-39].

2 CBC Research, 'The National Radio-TV Study' (1960), 170 [CBCRD].

3 House of Commons, *Debates*, 7 May 1959, p. 3412.

4 House of Commons Special Committee on Broadcasting, Minutes of Proceedings and Evidence, no. 12, 16 June 1959, pp. 419–20.

5 Massey commission, *Report*, 296–9.

6 Fowler commission, *Report*, 43.

7 Special Committee on Broadcasting, 16 June 1959, pp. 419–20.

8 Ibid., 420.

9 Minutes of 4th meeting of CBC Board of Directors, 22–24 June 1959, pp. 79–80 [NA, RG41, vol. 669 (microfilm T-3044)].

10 Ibid.

11 S. Yasin to E. Kliman et al., 14 July 1959 [CBCCR, AR3-1-19].

12 E. Kliman to J.J. Trainor et al., 17 July 1959 [CBCCR, AR3-1-19].

13 R. Lewis to R. Silvey, 16 July 1959 [CBCCR, AR3-1-9].

14 E. Kliman to N. Morrison, 19 October 1959 [CBCCR, AR3-1-19].

15 CBC Research, 'The National Radio-TV Study' (1960), 171.

16 E. Hallman to A. Laird, 21 February 1962 [CBCCR, AR3-1-19].

17 A. Laird to C. McFarlane, 23 April 1963 [CBCCR, AR3-1-19].

18 C. McDonald to A. Laird, 20 October 1964 [CBCCR, AR3-1-39].

19 CBC Research, 'An Appraisal of Three Country Music Shows' (June 1965), 2 [CBCRD].

20 E. Hallman to A. Laird, 12 April 1967 [CBCCR, AR3-1-42].

21 A. Laird to E. Hallman, 29 January 1965 [CBCCR, AR3-1-39].

22 Ibid.

23 Ibid.

24 CBC Research, 'Estimates of Cumulative Audiences to CBC English TV Network Programs Derived from CBC Audience Panel: An Experimental Study' (January 1967) [CBCRD].

25 Ibid.

26 Ibid.

27 A. Laird to L. Rampen et al., 20 October 1966 [CBCCR, AR3-1-42].

28 CBC Research, 'An Experimental Study of the Format of the CBC Audience Panel Diary' (June 1967), 3 [CBCRD].

29 For example, Roy Shields, 'The CBC's Secret Army in the TV Ratings War,' *Toronto Daily Star*, 5 March 1966, and 'TV,' *Toronto Telegram*, 4 March 1969.

30 E. Kliman to A. Laird, 2 December 1967 [CBCCR, AR3-1-43].

31 CBC Research, 'Experimental Study of the Format of the CBC Audience Panel Diary,' 10.

32 McDonald Research, 'Telephone Cross-Checks on the Weekly Television Panel' (May 1965) [DMC Files].

33 CBC Research, 'Experimental Study of the Format of the CBC Audience Panel Diary,' 11.

34 K. Purdye to A. Laird, 23 February 1967 [CBCCR, AR3-1-42].

35 CBC Research, 'Experimental Study of the Format of the CBC Audience Panel Diary,' 27–8.
36 CBC Research, 'An Appraisal of Three CBC Country Music Shows,' 10.
37 Erin Research, 'Please Indicate Your Opinion of This Index ...' (April 1987), 5 [CBCRD].
38 K. Purdye to A. Laird et al., nd, circa 1967 [CBCCR, AR3-1-42].
39 Telex to L. Starmer et al., 7 November 1966 [CBCCR, AR3-1-42].
40 Telex to L. Starmer, 14 November 1966 [CBCCR, AR3-1-42].
41 CBC Research, 'CBC-Television Audience Panel Weekly Report: Week of Friday, November 12 through Thursday, November 18, 1976,' 1, 4 [CBCRD].
42 CBC Research, 'Street Legal: CBC English Network Panel Results – "Complex Offer"' (July 1990), 1 [CBCRD].
43 C. McDonald to A. Laird, 13 June 1966 [CBCCR, AR3-1-42].
44 C. McFarlane to C. McDonald, 28 June 1966 [CBCCR, AR3-1-42].
45 A. Laird(?) to D. Macdonald, 6 October 1966 [CBCCR, AR3-1-42].
46 CBC Research, 'Experimental Study of the Format of the CBC Audience Panel Diary,' 14.
47 CBC Research, 'Dimensions of Audience Response to Television Programs' (June 1973) [CBCRD].
48 Ibid., 37. Edited slightly.
49 G. O'Connor to A. Laird, 19 November 1968 [CBCCR, AR3-1-43].
50 I. Shulman to A. Laird et al., 12 March 1976 [CBCCR, AR3-1-19].
51 CBC Research, 'Report of the Committee to Assess Methods of Measuring Audience Reaction' (June 1986) [CBCRD].
52 R. Cain to P. Charbonneau, 23 August 1977 [CBCCR, AR3-1-19]. Emphasis added.

CHAPTER 12 Three Models of Audience Research and the Case of the CBC

1 Barry Kiefl, 'What Is Public Television: Mass or Maximum Audiences?' talk prepared for the Pacific Mountain Network's television consortium in Monterey, California, 11–13 April 1990.
2 Ien Ang, *Desperately Seeking the Audience* (London: Routledge 1991), 31–2.
3 Ibid., 30.
4 Ibid., 1–2.
5 Ibid., 22.
6 Ibid., 10.
7 Ibid., 2.
8 A. Laird to L. Sinclair, 26 June 1974 [CBCCR, AR2-2-1].
9 N.M. Morrison, 'Progress Report' (1957), 2 [DMC Files].

10 I. Shulman to L. Dexter, 13 November 1962 [CBCCR, AR1-5-1].

11 Dallas W. Smythe, *Dependency Road: Communications, Capitalism, Consciousness, and Canada* (Norwood, NJ: Ablex 1981). See especially chapter 2.

12 BBM Bureau of Measurement, 'Reliability in BBM Radio Surveys or the Battle of the Bounce' (4 June 1984), 21 [BBM Files].

13 Ang, *Desperately Seeking the Audience*, 21.

14 E.A. Weir to N. Morrison, 10 February 1954 [Weir Papers, vol. 10, file 2].

15 Dennis Braithwaite, 'CBC Should Ignore Audience and Program to Suit Itself,' *Toronto Daily Star*, 10 March 1976.

16 Quoted from *Report of the Committee on the Future of Broadcasting* (London: HMSO 1977) in Peter Meneer, 'Measuring the Television Viewing Public's Taste,' *Television*, July/August 1981.

17 N.M. Morrison, 'Progress Report' (1957), iv.

18 Arthur Laird, 'Broadcasting Research in the CBC,' paper presented at the annual meeting of the Canadian Association of Broadcasters in Quebec City on 6 April 1964.

19 Quoted in CBC Research, 'Program Ratings in Canada' (c. 1956), 15 [DMC Files].

20 Quoted in Dean Walker, 'Canadian TV – The Wasteland and the Pasture,' *Television Quarterly*, 1 (no. 1, August 1962), 31.

21 CBC Research, 'What the Canadian Public Thinks of Television and of the TV Services Provided by CBC' (February 1974), 53–5 [CBCRD].

22 National Economic Research Associates, 'Public Service Television: Accountability and Finance,' discussion paper, September 1991, p. 2 [CBCRD].

Select Bibliography

Allor, Martin. 1988. 'Relocating the Site of the Audience: Reconstructive Theory and the Social Subject,' *Critical Studies in Mass Communication*, 5: 217–33

Ang, Ien. 1985. 'The Battle between Television and Its Audiences: The Politics of Watching Television,' in Phillip Drummond and Richard Paterson, eds., *Television in Transition*. London: British Film Institute

– 1991. *Desperately Seeking the Audience*. London: Routledge

Atkin, D., and B. Litman. 1986. 'Network TV Programming: Economics, Audiences and the Ratings Game 1971–1986,' *Journal of Communication*, 36 (3): 32–50

Auletta, Ken. 1991. *Three Blind Mice: How the TV Networks Lost Their Way*. New York: Random House

Ball-Rokeach, Sandra, and Muriel G. Cantor. 1986. *Media, Audience, and Social Structure*. Newbury Park, Calif.: Sage

Banks, Mark James. 1981. 'A History of Broadcast Audience Research in the United States, 1920–1980, with an Emphasis on the Ratings Services.' PhD thesis, University of Tennessee

Barwise, Patrick, and Andrew Ehrenberg. 1988. *Television and Its Audience*. London: Sage

Bauer, R.A. 1964. 'The Obstinate Audience,' *American Psychologist*, 19 (May): 319–28

– 1973. 'The Audience,' in Ithiel de Sola Pool, Wilbur Schramm, et al., eds., *Handbook of Communication*. Chicago: Rand McNally

Berman, Ronald. 1987. *How Television Sees Its Audience: A Look at the Looking Glass*. Newbury Park, Calif.: Sage

Beville, Hugh Malcolm, Jr. 1988. *Audience Ratings: Radio, Television, and Cable*, rev. ed. Hillsdale, NJ: Lawrence Erlbaum Associates

Biocca, F.A. 1988. 'Opposing Conceptions of the Audience: The Active and Passive Hemispheres of Mass Communication Theory,' in *Communication Yearbook*, 11. Newbury Park: Sage

Blankenship, A.B. 1977. *Professional Telephone Surveys*. New York: McGraw-Hill

Blankenship, A.B., Chuck Chakrapani, and W.H. Poole. 1985. *A History of Marketing Research in Canada*. Toronto: Professional Marketing Research Society

Blau, Herbert. 1990. *The Audience*. Baltimore and London: Johns Hopkins University Press

Blumer, Herbert. 1966. 'The Mass, the Public and Public Opinion,' in Bernard Berelson and Morris Janowitz, eds., *Reader in Public Opinion and Communication*, 2nd ed. New York: Free Press. First published in 1946

Bogart, Leo. 1956. *The Age of Television: A Study of Viewing Habits and the Impact of Television on American Life*. New York: Ungar

Bower, Robert T. 1973. *Television and the Public*. New York: Holt, Rinehart and Winston

– 1985. *The Changing Television Audience in America*. New York: Columbia University Press

Branston, Gill. 1991. 'Audience,' in David Lusted, ed., *The Media Studies Book: A Guide for Teachers*. London and New York: Routledge

Caplan, G., and F. Sauvageau (Chairmen). 1986. *Report of the Task Force on Broadcasting Policy*. Ottawa: Supply and Services Canada. See chapter 5, 'Programs and Audiences,' pp. 81–130

Chang, Briankle G. 1987. 'Deconstructing the Audience: Who Are They and What Do We Know about Them?' in *Communication Yearbook*, 10. Beverly Hills: Sage

Collins, Richard. 1990. *Culture, Communication, and National Identity: The Case of Canadian Television*. Toronto, Buffalo, London: University of Toronto Press. See chapter 8, 'The Television Audience,' pp. 228–49.

Crowley, David, Liss Jeffrey, and Fraser McAninch. 1988. *Trends in Television Viewing: Documentaries and the Audience for Information Programming*. Montreal: National Film Board of Canada

Drummond, Phillip, and Richard Paterson, eds. 1988. *Television and Its Audience*. London: British Film Institute

Frank, Ronald E., and Marshall G. Greenberg. 1980. *The Public's Use of Television: Who Watches and Why*. Beverly Hills and London: Sage

– 1982. *Audiences for Public Television*. Beverly Hills and London: Sage

Gans, Herbert J. 1974. *Popular Culture and High Culture: An Analysis and Evaluation of Taste*. New York: Basic Books

Goodhardt, G.J., A.S.C. Ehrenberg, and M.A. Collins. 1975. *The Television Audi-*

ence: Patterns of Viewing. Westmead, Farnsborough, Hants., England: Saxon House

Gunter, B. 1988. 'The Perceptive Audience,' in *Communication Yearbook,* 11. Beverly Hills: Sage

Gunter, Barrie, and Mallory Wober. 1992. *The Reactive Viewer: A Review of Research on Audience Reaction Measurement.* London: John Libbey

Hackett, Robert, Richard Pinet, and Myles Ruggles. 1992. 'From Audience-Commodity to Audience-Community: Mass Media in B.C.,' in Helen Holmes and David Taras, eds., *Seeing Ourselves: Media Power and Policy in Canada.* Toronto: Harcourt, Brace, Jovanovich

Hooper, C.E., and Matthew N. Chappell. 1944. *Radio Audience Measurement.* New York: Stephen Daye

House Committee on Interstate and Foreign Commerce, US Congress. 1961. *Evaluation of Statistical Methods Used in Obtaining Broadcast Ratings,* House Report 193, 87th Congress, 1st session, 1961. Washington: GPO

– 1964–5. *Broadcast Ratings,* Hearings before the Special Subcommittee on Investigations, 88th Congress, 1st and 2nd sessions, 1963–1964. Washington: GPO

Hurwitz, Donald Lee. 1983. 'Broadcast Ratings: The Rise and Development of Commercial Audience Research and Measurement in American Broadcasting.' PhD thesis, University of Illinois

– 1984. 'Broadcast Ratings: The Missing Dimension,' *Critical Studies in Mass Communication,* 1: 205–15

Jeffrey, Liss. 1993. 'Audiences for Cultural Industries: A Review of Recent Research, Models and Sources.' Unpublished paper

Jensen, Klaus Bruhn, and Karl Eric Rosengren. 1990. 'Five Traditions in Search of the Audience,' *European Journal of Communication,* 5: 207–38

Kiefl, Barry, Ken Leclair, and David M. Tattle. 1992. 'Problems of Non-response and Non-cooperation in a People Meter Panel,' pp. 265–82 of *Worldwide Broadcast Audience Research Symposium* (1–3 June 1992, Toronto). Advertising Research Foundation/European Society for Opinion and Marketing Research

Lindlof, Thomas R., ed. 1987. *Natural Audiences: Qualitative Research of Media Uses and Effects.* Norwood, NJ: Ablex

– 1988. 'Media Audiences as Interpretative Communities,' in *Communication Yearbook,* 11. Beverly Hills: Sage

Lumley, Frederick H. 1971. *Measurement in Radio: History of Broadcasting, Radio to Television.* New York: Arno Press. Reprint of 1934 edition (Columbus: Ohio State University)

Mattelart, Armand. 1991. 'Audience Measurement: Towards a Bar-Coded

World?' Chapter 8, pp. 144–59 of *Advertising International: The Privatisation of Public Space*. London and New York: Routledge

Meehan, Eileen R. 1983. 'Neither Heroes nor Villains: Towards a Political Economy of the Ratings Industry.' PhD thesis, University of Illinois

– 1984. 'Ratings and the Institutional Approach: A Third Answer to the Commodity Question,' *Critical Studies in Mass Communication*, 1: 216–25

– 1990. 'Why We Don't Count: The Commodity Audience,' in Patricia Mellencamp, ed., *Logics of Television: Essays in Cultural Criticism*. Bloomington and Indianapolis: Indiana University Press

Morrison, Neil M. 1958. 'CBC Audience Research Division,' *Food for Thought*, January, 162–70

Neuman, Russell W. 1991. *The Future of the Mass Audience*. Cambridge: Cambridge University Press

Pegg, Mark. 1983. *Broadcasting and Society 1918–1939*. London and Canberra: Croom Helm

Rubens, William S. 1984. 'High-Tech Audience Measurement for New-Tech Audiences,' *Critical Studies in Mass Communication*, 1: 195–205

Salter, Liora. 1981. '"Public" and Mass Media in Canada: Dialectics in Innis' Communication Analysis,' in William H. Melody, Liora Salter, and Paul Heyer, eds., *Culture, Communication and Dependency: The Tradition of H.A. Innis*. Norwood, NJ: Ablex

– 1988. 'Reconceptualizing Public Broadcasting,' in Rowland Lorimer and Donald Wilson, eds., *Communication Canada: Issues in Broadcasting and New Technologies*. Toronto: Kagan and Woo

Scannell, Paddy. 1990. 'Public Service Broadcasting: The History of a Concept,' in Andrew Goodwin and Garry Whannel, eds., *Understanding Television*. London and New York: Routledge

Seiter, Ellen, Hans Borchers, Gabrielle Kreutzner, and Eva-Maria Warth, eds. 1989. *Remote Control: Television, Audiences, and Cultural Power*. London and New York: Routledge

Seldes, Gilbert. 1951. *The Great Audience*. New York: Viking Press

Silverstone, Roger. 1990. 'Television and Everyday Life: Towards an Anthropology of the Television Audience,' in Marjorie Ferguson, ed., *Public Communication*. London: Sage

Silvey, Robert. 1974. *Who's Listening? The Story of BBC Audience Research*. London: Allen and Unwin

Smith, Anthony. 1973. *The Shadow in the Cave: A Study of the Relationship between the Broadcaster, His Audience and the State*. London: Allen and Unwin

Steiner, Gary. 1963. *The People Look at Television: A Study of Audience Attitudes*. New York: Alfred A. Knopf

Wartella, Ellen, et al., eds. 1993. *Towards a Comprehensive Theory of Audience*. Boulder, Colo.: Westview Press

Webster, James G., and Lawrence W. Lichty. 1986. 'Audience Behavior in the New Media Environment,' *Journal of Communication*, 36 (3): 77–91

– 1989. 'Television Audience Behavior: Patterns of Exposure in the New Media Environment,' in J.L. Salvaggio and J. Bryant, eds., *Media Use in the Information Age: Emerging Patterns of Adoption and Consumer Use*. Hillsdale, NJ: LEA Publishers

– 1991. *Ratings Analysis: Theory and Practice*. Hillsdale, NJ: L. Erlbaum Associates

Willis, Janet, and Tana Wollen, eds. 1990. *The Neglected Audience*. London: British Film Institute

Withers, Edward, and Robert S. Brown. 1991. 'The Broadcast Audience: A Sociological Perspective,' in Benjamin D. Singer, ed., *Communications in Canadian Society*, 3rd ed. Scarborough: Nelson

Index